BORN IN THE GHETTO

BORN IN THE GHETTO

MY TRIUMPH OVER ADVERSITY

ARIELA ABRAMOVICH SEF

Translated by Kathrine Judelson and S. Abramovich

English edition edited by S. Abramovich

GAINSBOROUGH HOUSE PRESS

LONDON • PORTLAND, OR

First published in 2014 by Gainsborough House Press

Middlesex House	920 NE 58th Avenue, Suite 300
29/45 High Street	Portland, Oregon
Edgware, Middlesex, HA8 7UU	97213-3786
UK	USA

British Library Cataloguing in Publication Data
A catalogue record for this book is available from the British Library

ISBN 978-1-909719-00-2 (Hardback)
ISBN 978-1-909719-01-9 (Paperback)
ISBN 978-1-909719-03-3 (Ebook)

Printed by TJ International, Padstow, Cornwall

CONTENTS

List of Figures   vii
Who's Who   xi
Introduction by Solomon Abramovich   1

PART I: Ariela's Life
Born in the Ghetto   9
To the Orphanage   21
Mama Julia   23
Liberation   31
Our Scattered Family   36
Rescuing Lost Children   40
Restaurants   44
Uncle Naum, Aunt Lily and Anya   46
Madames Kupritz and Tsitses   51
School   54
A Funeral   58
Our New Nanny Onute   60
The Fur Coat   62
Yadviga Vikentievna and Nina Rachkovskaya   64
Our Yard   69
The Black Staircase   73
Summer Holidays   77
Aunt Lily and Uncle Naum Return   84
Special Occasions   89
Mother, Father and Leaving Home   91
Discharged and Expelled   96
The Bakulev Heart Institute   98
Paris   99
Hammersmith Hospital   103
Disasters Strike   106

The Novi Cabaret   108
Do I Stay or Go?   114
Back in the USSR   117
Kaunas and Moscow   119
Kitty   126
Returning to Paris   135
The Loeb Twins   140
Andrei   145
Adventures with Andrei   152
Returning to Palanga   159
A Sitting Tenant   162
Birthdays and Goodbye   165

Part II: Memories of Ariela
Kama Ginkas: I Too was Born in the Ghetto   169
Solomon Abramovich: Sister Ariela   172
Alla Demidova: I'm Still Expecting her Phone Call   178
Alexander and Lilia Mitta: Ariela as We Remember Her   187
Yulii Gusman: Ariela – A Name that means Lioness   195
Makvala Kasrashvili: A Kind Heart is a Gift from God   197
Nelly Belskaya: The 'Blue Disease'   199
Sergei Nikolaevich: A Present from Ariela   204
Olga Yakovleva: Our Distant Youth   208
Andrei Yakhontov: They were an Impressive Couple   213
Karen Shakhnazarov: Recalling Ariela Sef   214
Ksenia Muratova: Ariela, Dear Heart   215
Svetlana and Vitalii Ignatenko: We Remember Her   224

Appendix 1: Letter of Dr Jacob Abramovich to
his brother Arno in England, 1945   227

FIGURES

1. Yakov's brother Beno, who was shot in August 1941 in Kaunas Fort VII.
2. Ariela's Birth Certificate Nr 122 (in Lithuanian); born in the Ghetto at 12 Raguchio Street in Kaunas. Issued by the Ghetto police, 1941.
3. Ariela aged 2, next to the house where the family lived in the Kaunas Ghetto, 1943. Her grandfather used to say, 'She's not just a baby, she's a picture'.
4. Certificate of employment (in German). 'Herewith is certified that Dr Jacob Abramovich of Raguchio 12 is employed as first aider at the Airforce Building section. His family consists of 6 persons. Works Department, 30 November 1941.'
5. Ariela's father (centre) as a doctor during his military service in the Lithuanian Army, 1938.
6. Yakov's brother Ruvim was amongst 3,000 Jews from Kaunas Ghetto deported to Estonia in September 1943 and perished.
7. Yakov's brother Max was removed from the Kaunas Ghetto in December 1943. He died in Auschwitz concentration camp in 1944.
8. Ariela's mother as a student in London, 1937.
9. Testament dated 26 February 1944 written by Ariela's parents (father) both in English and in Russian in which they provide information about Ariela having been adopted by the Dautartas family.
10. Ariela's grandmother, Sira Abramovich, with an empty food bowl and a piece of bread in her other hand in the queue for food in Kaunas Ghetto, winter 1944.
11. Ariela's grandparents Sira and Solomon-Itzik Abramovich with cousins Borya (first left) and Boris who perished in the Ghetto

and concentration camps. Ariela's cousins Rivochka, Miriam and Josef (standing) survived in the concentration camps. Photo taken before the War, Kaunas 1936.

12. Yakov's sister Rebecca who perished in Stutthof concentration camp on 21 January 1945.

13. Ariela's father (seated on the right) with his brothers Leon and Aron before parting, Plombières-les-Bains, France, 1935.

14. Ariela with her foster mother Julia Dautartas who took her from Dr Baublys children's home during the War, 1945.

15. Ariela after the liberation, 1944.

16. Ariela's first birthday at home after the Ghetto. From left to right: Naomi Gurvich, Mika Karnovskaya, Ariela Abramovich (holding a doll), Esya Elin, Dalia Judilevich. At the back from left to right: Moisei Rosenblum, Yakov Taft, Kama Ginkas.

17. Ariela with her doll, 1944.

18. Ariela's parents Jacob and Bracha Abramovich with Ariela's grandmother Berta Maizel in Kaunas just before the War, 1939.

19. Ariela's father with the children from the orphanage who he helped, Kaunas, 1945.

20. Ariela with her mother, 1946

21. Ariela's parents with Ariela, Solomon and adopted Anya, Kaunas, 1949.

22. The Abramovich family after the liberation in the garden of the War Museum, Kaunas. Ariela's dress is made from white parachute silk given by pilots, 1945.

23. Ariela's father on the Baltic beach in Palanga, 1949.

24. Ariela with her family in Palanga, 1953.

25. Ariela with her brothers and cousin on the beach in Palanga, 1954

26. Ariela in the park of the stately home of Count Tishkevich, Palanga 1953.

27. Ariela with her cousin Anya and her brothers next to the statue of a lion in the stately home of Count Tishkevich, Palanga 1953.

28. Ariela as a student at the Institute of Foreign Languages in Moscow, 1959.

29. Just before setting off to Paris, December 1960.

30. First summer in France.

31. Ariela in Paris in the 1960s

32. Ariela and her husband Roman Sef at the Louvre, 1991.

33. Ariela's mother with their dog Kitty, Kaunas, 1973.

34. Ariela in Paris. The photo taken by her friend photographer Denise Colomb, 1961.

35. Andrei Schimkewitsch just before leaving Moscow for Paris, 1957.

36. Ariela and Roman Sef in her favorite Brasserie Lipp, Paris, 2006.

37. Solomon, Ariela and Ben in England, 1978.

38. Ariela with her nephew Alexander, London, 1994.

39. New Year's Eve celebrated in Ben's house in London, 2000.

40. Ariela with actress Alla Demidova at a theatre festival in Riga.

41. Ariela at a business seminar in Vilnius, 1989.

42. Ariela and the artist Rustam Khamdamov, Villon, Vilnius 1994.

43. Ariela and Ben in the Hotel Villon outside Vilnius, 2006.

44. Ariela and Margaret Thatcher at the British exhibition in Moscow, 1993.

45. Singer Elena Obraztsova, Ariela and Alla Demidova at the Bolshoi Theatre, Moscow, 2002.

46. At Ben and Lena's wedding in London, 1990. From left to right: Lena, Ben, Ariela and Solomon.

47. At a dog show in Moscow, 1989. The Afghan hound, Jardin, won three medals.

48. Ariela with her husband Roman Sef and her brother Solomon after the film presentation at the International Film Festival, Cannes 1991.

49. Ariela in Villon, 2006.

50. Ariela and Roman Sef in Villon, Vilnius 2006.

51. Outside the house of Count Tishkevich, Palanga 2006.

52. Ariela and Maria, daughter of the writer Vladas Dautartas and granddaughter of Ariela's foster mother Julia Dautartiene, Vilnius, October 2008 (last photo of Ariela).

WHO'S WHO

Solomon Abramovich – Senior ENT Surgeon at Imperial College London.

Nelya Belskaya – writer (France).

Alla Demidova – actress and People's Artist of the RSFSR (Russian Soviet Federation Socialist Republic).

Kama Ginkas – theatre director and Merited Artist of the Russian Federation.

Yulii Gusman – film director, Merited Artist of the Russian Federation.

Svetlana Ignatenko – wife of Vitalii Ignatenko

Vitalii Ignatenko – Director of the ITAR-TASS news agency.

Makvala Kasrashvili – singer, People's Artist of the USSR, soloist of the Bolshoi Theatre, director of the opera troupe of the Bolshoi Theatre.

Alexander Mitta – film director, People's Artist of the Russian Federation.

Lilya Mitta – designer.

Kseniya Muratova – Professor at the Sorbonne (France)

Sergei Nikolaevich – editor-in-chief of the journal *Citizen* K (Russia).

Karen Shakhnazarov – film director, director of the 'Mosfilm' Studios, People's Artist of the Russian Federation

Andrei Yakhontov – writer.

Olga Yakovleva – actress and People's Artist of the Russian Federation.

INTRODUCTION

This book about Ariela Abramovich Sef is a personal testimony and memoir played out against a background of some of the most momentous historical events of the twentieth century, and brings these events to life. It spans from the pre-Second World War period to the year 2000. If a writer of fiction had decided to invent the life-story of a heroine for a novel or film, they would have been unlikely to come up with a more dramatic and gripping plot than the life story of this real woman shaped both by circumstances and her determination to overcome them.

The author of the book is unique by virtue not only of her very birth but also of the time and, most of all, the place of her birth. There are only a few people who had similar experiences because Ariela was born in the Kaunas Ghetto in Lithuania in 1941, just a few days prior to the Great Action when small children, the elderly and infirm were selected to the left side to die and others to the right side to prolong their life to work. Everything seemed to conspire against her being born at all and even more so, surviving. Smuggled from the ghetto by her parents in a potato sack and abandoned on the doorstep of a Christian orphanage, her survival there is nothing short of a miracle. Ariela was taken in by a fisherman's family and Ariela believed for a long time that the woman who had taken her in was her mother. She was finally reunited with her parents who had miraculously succeeded in escaping from the ghetto and hiding from the Nazi manhunt under the floor of a shed for livestock. This is a unique and a powerful account of a 'hidden child'. To those in these pages who saved the lives of children, a debt of homage and admiration is due for the grave risks they took to show that in the midst of evil there were human faces and humane individuals

The book contains Ariela's memories in the form of short stories, in which her reminiscences about the ghetto form only part of her seemingly endless odyssey. Most of her writing was done lying in bed because, due to her severe congenital heart trouble, Eisenmenger syndrome, she would get tired working at a table. She used to read her stories to her younger brothers and close friends in Paris, London and Moscow. I encouraged her to write for future generations of our family, reassuring her that a lot of interesting writing was done by authors lying in bed, such as Marcel Proust in Paris. However, Ariela did not manage to complete her reminiscences, and her book *Rozdennaya v Getto* [Born in the Ghetto] was published posthumously in Russian in Moscow in 2009.

Ariela's family lived for generations in Lithuania, which after the Russian Revolution for a short period (1918–40) until the beginning of the Second World War became a small independent Baltic state. As in Kafka's stories the family sensed the turmoil to come in Europe. They were worldly, speaking many languages and the young people were full of aspirations. Ariela's father spoke perfect German as his birthplace was on the border with what used to be East Prussia. He also went to Berlin where his two eldest brothers had settled, but in 1928 living conditions were harsh and food was in short supply so he went to France to study medicine. Ariela's mother also had left home to study in London and having settled in Hampstead had not intended to return. Yet they came to visit their families and her father to complete his military service in Lithuania as a doctor. Ariela's parents married in 1939 in Kaunas and did not manage to leave Lithuania before the outbreak of the Second World War.

A treaty of Non-Aggression between the USSR and Germany, the so-called Molotov-Ribbentrop Pact, was signed in August 1939 by the foreign ministers of the two countries. The treaty included a secret protocol concerning the division of Eastern Europe into spheres of influence and territorial control. The invasion of Poland by Nazi Germany began on 1 September 1939, only a week after the signing the pact. It marked the outbreak of the Second World War. Soon the Soviets forced Lithuania to sign the Pact of Mutual Soviet-Lithuanian assistance and on 15 June 1940 annexed Lithuania. Immediately a rapid programme of 'Sovietisation' was enforced. All the land was nationalized, all religious and political organizations with the exception of the Communist Party were banned, and an estimated 12,000 'anti Soviet' elements, mostly former military officers, political figures, intelligentsia and perceived capitalists, were deported to Siberia.

Without formally declaring war, Germany broke the Molotov-Ribbentrop Pact, and on 21 June 1941 attacked the Soviet Union. Within a few days the Germans occupied Lithuania's territory. Many Lithuanians were German sympathizers and against what they saw as Soviet encroachment, others who were aware of the brutal Nazi ideology and anti-Semitism willingly collaborating with German Nazis in barbarities and atrocities against the Jewish population. By the end of the Second World War around 200,000 Lithuanian Jews – 94 per cent – were killed, which was proportionally one of the highest rates of loss in Hitler's Holocaust.

Ariela' adored her father, Jacob Abramovich, who comes across as an amazing individual in the book. There was never anything forced or over-dramatic about him, despite the fact that he was involved in extremely hazardous activities in rescuing and finding homes for many orphaned children after the end of the War.

Soon after the war Ariela's parents adopted the daughter of one of their relatives who had been considered politically undesirable, was arrested during the Stalinist regime and persecution and banished to the labour camps of the Soviet Union in Mordovia soon after their daughter was born. As a child Ariela kept this secret for nearly ten years until the parents of the girl returned after Stalin's death.

The world in which Ariela was brought up was not normal. Her father was determined that Ariela should learn French: an impossible dreamer, he could not get Paris out of his mind and even told the protesting schoolgirl, 'But what language are you going to speak when you go to Paris'. On hearing this Mother hissed as this kind of 'cosmopolitism' was not tolerated in those days: there was even a law against it.

At the beginning of the 1960s Ariela left for Moscow to take up her studies in the University of Foreign Languages. She married a postgraduate French student and left the Soviet Union for Paris in the years of what became known as the 'thaw' under Khrushchev. The repercussions for marrying a westerner during the time of the Iron Curtain and lingering Cold War were that she was expelled from Moscow University, and it is likely that marrying a woman from the Soviet Union robbed her husband of the chance to become a French diplomat.

Ariela describes with a gentle sense of humor how she first arrived in Paris and embarked upon her far from easy early life in France, studying at the Sorbonne, teaching and singing in cabaret. In passing, and with no more than a fleeting sentence, Ariela writes calmly and without drama that her husband left her for another woman and her flat almost burnt down.

Few people knew that Ariela had a severe congenital heart condition called Eisenmenger syndrome with severe pulmonary hypertension, and that doctors in both London and Paris predicted that she had only a few years to live. They did not know the hardship and pain she had been through and with what truly amazing courage she coped with her illness.

Her circle of friends included many extremely interesting and talented people from different countries and her own varied and rich biography is reflected in her stories. Against the background of Paris cafes, of encounters and friendships with interesting people and international celebrities, sculptors, artists, writers and theatre directors, Ariela tells us about some of her setbacks first in France and then back in Soviet Russia. She remarried, this time to Roman Sef, a Russian children's writer, and spent her time between Paris, London and Moscow, involved in and helping with various creative projects.

Of particular interest are the pages devoted to Andre Schimkewitsch (stepson of sculptor Jacques Lipchitz), who lived in Paris in a house designed by their family friend, Le Corbusier. As a teenager, while visiting his father in Moscow, he was arrested and spent twenty-five years in the Stalinist labour camps in Russia. There he met Ariela's second husband and they all eventually met in Paris. Ariela encouraged Andre to testify in Sweden that he had encountered the legendary diplomat Raoul Wallenberg while in Soviet captivity. This created a sensation as Wallenberg had mysteriously disappeared without trace and was thought to be dead. Wallenberg saved thousands Jewish people in Budapest during the Second World War by issuing them with Swedish passports which protected them from deportation to extermination camps.

The stories describe how a young beautiful woman could survive the ghetto, the Cold War and the 'thaw' period in the Soviet Union, migration to the West and with amazing courage also cope with a serious illness. Ariela shares with her readers not only her interesting life in Paris, Moscow and London, but also her pain, loss, endurance and nobility of spirit, gentle sense of humour and episodes of happiness. It is impossible to doubt the importance of helping others after reading Ariela's story. It is impossible to have doubts about the importance of living life to the full after hearing of Ariela's life. It becomes clear after learning of Ariela's passions that art, fashion, theatre and music are not merely a past time in life, but are like the very oxygen she breathed. But what matters most of all for Ariela? The humanity and flow of life. Despite the enormous number of setbacks, injustices and cruelty that Ariela experienced it is difficult to convey how gripping the stories are, in spite of her low-key writing style.

Solomon Abramovich
London, 2013

PART I
ARIELA'S LIFE

BORN IN THE GHETTO

I begin my memoir today, 9th May 2007 – the day that Victory Day is celebrated in the former Soviet Union where I grew up (not on 8th May as in Western Europe) – and for me the most important holiday of all, more important than New Year or Passover. My father, a doctor, had been on duty in an army hospital when the Second World War began. When he heard that the Germans were marching into Kaunas, he telephoned the medical director of the hospital and said: 'The Germans are coming and we need to do something with the patients.' The reply? 'Don't stir up panic, things will get sorted out without you.' Father never saw that doctor again, yet he himself was unable to escape. My parents were marooned in occupied Lithuania. Father, his brother Beno and my mother were arrested as communist sympathisers a few days after the German invasion. They released my pregnant mother, but Father did not think that he would get out alive. Mother had given him some gold jewellery to take with him, in case he could escape, but he gave it to his brother Beno for the same reason. However, Beno was led off and shot in the Seventh Fort, and Father, thanks to Mother, who had run round to all the Lithuanian army doctors who her husband had worked for before the war, was released.

While Father was in prison, Germans broke into our flat accompanied by Lithuanians. They came in two lorries armed with a very precise list (a caretaker or servant must have tipped them off). They took everything she had inherited from her mother: pictures, silver and diamond necklaces purchased at various auctions when she was travelling in Western Europe. Some German – or was it a Lithuanian? – had pushed his pistol up against mother's belly, pregnant with me, and demanded she bring out all the items on the list. She did not resist, and

Figure 1. Yakov's brother Beno, who was shot in August 1941 in
Kaunas Fort VII.

they took everything, including the furniture. The lorries drove off
crammed to the top and when father was released, the two of them
were sent to the Ghetto. They were some of the last to be sent, and
without belongings, so a small room in a communal flat was ample.

I was born prematurely at the end of October 1941 during the round
up in the Kaunas Ghetto, as the Germans were approaching Moscow.
Bad timing, but there was nothing to be done. At just five days old, I was
wrapped up against my mother's breast, and sent to the *Great Action*,
when everybody in the Ghetto was sent into Democrats Square, which
was cordoned off. The ill, elderly, disabled and new-born babies were
selected and sent off to die or, to use the German term, do 'lighter labour'
while the young and healthy were sent off to work 'for the good of Germany'. Early that morning the Lithuanian volunteer policemen, who
called themselves partisans, had started searching all the flats, cellars and
attics, emptying the whole Ghetto. The SS commander Rauca, standing
on raised ground, so as to get a better view of the crowd, was in charge
of the operation. People were walking along in groups, families and
households. And so the Selection began; Rauca pointing with his trun-
cheon to indicate who should go to the right and who to the left,
separating families. Relatives were pushing and straining towards each
other. People did not yet realise that right meant death and left life. They
were anxious and agitated. It was also one of the coldest winters on

record. Our relatives clustered tightly around me and my mother, and we managed to get to the 'good' side with the whole of our family except our old, wise grandmother. In order not to upset her family, she'd hidden in the crowd with those selected for death. Suddenly, my father took three leaps over to the 'bad' side, hunted out and dragged Grandmother out of the crowd. Then he ran back with his mother, who had no idea what was happening. When they tried to stop him, amidst heart-rending noise, weeping, barking dogs, the curses and lashings meted out by the Lithuanian Polizei, father ran up to an officer and explained to him in fluent German that he had been given permission to go and fetch his mother.

'Who gave you permission? Why did they give you permission? What error was made?'

Before they had time to realise what was happening, father had brought my grandmother back. Later my father was asked: 'How come you weren't afraid. You could have been shot. You're a hero!' 'Hero? I was simply frightened, more than everyone else. That's why I ran.'

Father was often plagued by doubts, but in serious situations I don't know anyone who could be more decisive. He once saved our mother too. She had pulled up a carrot in the garden plot next to the house where they lived. It was dark so she thought that nobody would see her, but a high-ranking German officer caught her in the act. He stopped her, but because he was hurrying somewhere at the time, merely instructed her to report to the commandant's office the next morning, where she was bound to given a harsh punishment for thieving. When our father came home at the end of his work shift he found mother sobbing. It was clear that she might well be shot or, at best, sent to the nearby camp. She kept asking, 'What shall I do? Who will look after the baby?' Father replied in a tired, calm voice, 'Don't do anything, just don't go.' So Mother didn't.

All the members of our family on Father's side, with the exception of Uncle Beno, were somehow granted a little longer to live. When it became known that there was going to be another raid my father said firmly, 'Ariela's not going to be rounded up.' He gradually came round to the idea of hiding me. We were a warm and close-knit family, and all thought he was out of his mind, but he persisted, 'I'm going to get her out of here.' Sometimes children were thrown outside the Ghetto fence or gates and would be picked up by friends or acquaintances, or complete strangers. But his sister, brothers and parents begged him not

Figure 2. Ariela's Birth Certificate Nr 122 (in Lithuanian); born in the Ghetto at 12 Raguchio Street in Kaunas. Issued by the Ghetto police, 1941.

to do that: 'Such a lovely child! We've all been feeding her … Just look how pretty she is, how beautiful.' Grandfather kept saying, 'She's not just a baby, but a work of art. What will happen to us? If something happens, perhaps God will help.' Father replied that he could not take the risk and nor did he intend to start negotiating with God.

I spent two years in the Ghetto. Our relatives and the other tenants of our communal flat used to feed and clothe me. They knitted me little dresses and socks out of old jumpers. At that time hardly any children were being born in the Ghetto. In 1942 the Germans forbade pregnancies and births in the Ghetto. If the Polizei came across any newborn babies, they were killed straightaway. By the time I was 18

Figure 3. Ariela aged 2, next to the house where the family lived in the Kaunas Ghetto, 1943. Her grandfather used to say, 'She's not just a baby, she's a picture'.

months old, I knew which of the neighbours would be eating their dinner, and I would make sure to be at the right door at the right time. I was nicknamed the 'little white gypsy'. Although we had nothing I was given a wickerwork cot when I was born, the only ornament in the tiny room into which we had moved within the Ghetto.

The Ghetto was shrinking in size as people were sent to the concentration camps, and the Nazis were gradually eliminating the Ghetto. My father, being a doctor, could have worked in the Ghetto, but he worked with a special work brigade out at the aerodrome, to which he and his fellow workers (initially his brothers Ruvim and Max and his beautiful daughter, Rivochka) would be sent under escort to work on the construction of the air base and to break up the remains of shot-down Soviet aircraft and lorries known as *Stalintsy*. The work was physically much harder, but there were perks in the form of extra rations and the opportunity to get food from the local people. The work was in fact a passport to survival, preventing deportation to the camps.

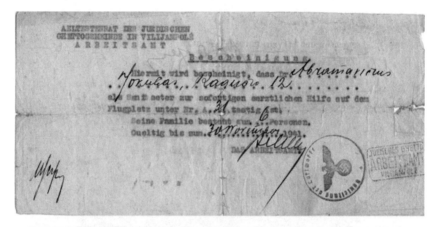

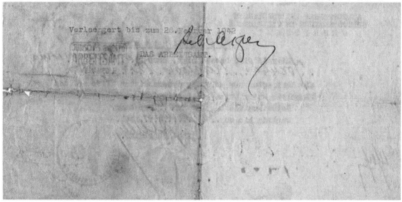

Figure 4. Certificate of employment (in German). 'Herewith
is certified that Dr Jacob Abramovich of Raguchio 12 is
employed as first aider at the Airforce Building section.
His family consists of 6 persons. Works Department,
30 November 1941.'

Before the war, Father, despite the fact that he was descended from
a family of merchants, had never sold or bartered anything. My grandfather and two uncles had traded in fabrics, while my father – the
youngest of seven children – had studied medicine in Paris before starting work as a junior hospital doctor in Hospital Saint Louis in Paris.
He had come back on a temporary visit to Lithuania for a short period
of military service and had also worked as a doctor in the army. He
had been planning to go back to France after his military service and
then to French Canada for two years for French citizenship and the
right to permanent work.

Figure 5. Ariela's father (centre) as a doctor during his military service in the Lithuanian Army, 1938.

My uncles, initially, proved less adaptable in the Ghetto, less healthy, older than their years. My grandfather of course was very old. The only member of the family to find his bearings was my father. But then he was the only one with a baby. The local inhabitants used to go over to the Jewish prisoners and were only too happy to barter with them. The Jews risked being shot, but as they had no choice, took risks. At first the Germans used to look the other way. Most of the guards were old soldiers, who had been through the First World War, serving in the rear, almost too old to still be in the army. They were not malicious, and it was possible to come to an understanding with them, especially for those prisoners who spoke good German, like my father. They knew that he was the doctor in his work-team, that he had studied in Paris and were prepared to accommodate him. One officer even said to him, 'I'm ashamed to be a German now.' On one occasion, my father managed to come to the rescue of an unlucky barterer, a clumsy man in glasses who became so carried away with his dealing that he would have been shot, had father had not stepped in with some far-fetched explanation. The man in question, Jacob Rabinovitch, became the editor of the German *Allgemeiner Journal* in America and sent us a letter from Canada, saying how grateful he had been to our father, who had helped him and other prisoners. It would not have been possible for Father to accomplish as much as he did, if he'd been up against Lithuanian policemen instead of old German soldiers.

Our neighbours were mostly educated people. My main friends were the neighbours' two boys, 11-year-old Beba and 9-year-old Veva Mintz. Before the war their father had been a professor, but in the Ghetto was in acute pain because his stomach ulcer had flared up. He was completely incapable of heavy physical labour. At work, Father used to exchange their valuables for food. Other people not employed in his work-team, who were unable or unwilling to take risks, used to give him their belongings as well. Father used to barter honestly and quite successfully. Admittedly there was one disgraceful occasion when he was given a whole can of oil, which turned out to be motor, not cooking oil.

Beba and Veva completed their school syllabus at home, working long and hard as if they had been preparing for the entrance exams for a place in a gymnasium or university, rather than the crematorium or firing squad. I used to repeat the names from their lessons; Napoleon Bonaparte, Napoleon III, Marshal Foch, Cardinal Richelieu. When I was finally taken out of the Ghetto, they wanted to come too. But two boys of obvious Jewish appearance would not have found anyone to take them in. They perished along with the rest.

In 1943 people started to dig a tunnel, a hideout, where it would be possible to shelter during bombing raids. The Russians were already advancing westwards. People hoped it would be possible to hide there when prisoners were being rounded up. But because of me – the small child who might cry at the wrong moment – our family was not allowed in. Numbers in the ghetto kept dropping as more and more Jews were shot or sent off to concentration camps.

In September 1943, the Germans took the whole of Uncle Ruvim's family out of the Ghetto along with three thousand other Jews. They were sent to Estonia. Uncle Ruvim was already ill by then and his son, 12-year-old Borya, went with him to the same camp. They say that he was a remarkable boy with a real talent for poetry and mathematics, always inventing devices for everyone in the Ghetto. One of them was for stealing electricity. Borya used to spend all his time with his father, although he realised that his father was hardly likely to be selected for work and that his days were numbered. No-one saw them again. Uncle Ruvim's wife, Basia, and daughter Miriam survived – some of the few who did – and at the time of the Liberation found themselves in the American Zone of Germany. Later they left for Canada. Basia's sister, Marusya, and her husband used to come over from Switzerland or Israel, and much later to Paris in the 60s where they would make a point of finding me. They bought me clothes, and took me to restaurants and exhibitions. They always talked about my father in very warm terms, clearly recalling what Basia used to say.

Figure 6. Yakov's brother Ruvim was amongst 3,000 Jews from Kaunas Ghetto deported to Estonia in September 1943 and perished.

In December 1943 Uncle Max was taken off with his family: his son, beautiful daughter Rivochka and his wife. They were all sent to the Šančiai camp. From there on Uncle Max and the family was sent to Auschwitz quite soon afterwards, where he and his son perished. His wife and daughter, however, survived. My aunt, his wife, settled in Israel and married a second time. Her daughter settled in America.

Figure 7. Yakov's brother Max was removed from the Kaunas Ghetto in December 1943. He died in Auschwitz concentration camp in 1944.

Later on Mother used to tell me about the kinds of people to be found in the Ghetto. There was a famous professor, Dr Elkes, whom the Germans had initially been prepared to release. He was a well-known doctor who had been living in Germany before Hitler came to power. He and his wife had decided not to leave and remained behind with their fellow Jews. A young nurse had been working with him in the Ghetto and he had assisted at the birth of her child in March 1942. It had been in the basement so that no-one would hear the cries of either mother or child. The nurse's husband, Marcus Kamber, had been conscripted into the 16th Lithuanian Division at the very beginning of the war and then set off for the front. He had had no idea that his wife was pregnant and that he would be the father of a baby daughter. It was Dr Elkes who protected the little girl and helped her reach safety. He later perished in a concentration camp.

Then there was the surgeon, Dr Zakharin, who had been universally respected before the War. He had said to my terrified mother about me, when I was ill, 'Well, if she dies, she dies. What difference does it make? What would become of her, after all, if she did survive? There would just be one more whore.' I survived, but he later received summary justice. People in the Underground were very keen to take him off with them to their partisan detachments. He refused to go without his senior nurse, although his other two nurses had been sent to join the partisans earlier. They had promised to take her on later. When numbers in the Ghetto were declining dramatically, he too was taken to Auschwitz where he was appointed doctor in charge of the prisoners. They say that he did not treat people well, especially fellow Jews from the Kaunas Ghetto. After the war he was tried by the Russians and given a harsh sentence.

Another of Father's friends at that time was young Dr Abraham Zilberg. Before the German occupation he had fought for a time in Spain in the International Brigade against Franco. In the Ghetto he joined the Underground and was fearless in his efforts to remain in contact with the partisans and the world outside. He undertook highly complicated assignments, and never returned from the last of them. His son, however, did survive. He had been born in the Ghetto and later became a doctor like his father.

Haim Elin, uncle of my childhood friend, 'wunderkind' Esther (who went on to be a pianist and take part in international music competitions) was one of the most prominent members of the Underground. He used to warn people before round-ups. Thanks to him many Jewish children were saved, far more than in other Ghettos. The Germans used to trust him, but when they found out the truth, they killed him brutally. Esther was rescued by the widow of the composer and artist, Mikalojus Čiurlionis. Her father, who had graduated as a construction engineer in Berlin, became a writer and journalist and wrote a book about the Jewish Underground in Kaunas.

A young doctor by the name of Miron Ginkas (who had worked in a team alongside my father) had been sent to the small border town of Taurage a few months before the German invasion. During the days following the occupation, Lithuanian fascists had murdered most Jews in that town. A few hours before, Miron had left the place on foot to join his wife and five-week-old son back in Kaunas. He walked for two whole days to get there. Soon afterwards all three of them were in the Ghetto. Miron was also one of those who survived. After the war he was put in charge of the health service in Kaunas and was later the head doctor of the ambulance service in Vilnius. His baby son was initially taken in by the family of the Lithuanian poet, Kazys Binkis, then passed from one family to another until the very end of the war. He became the theatre director, Kama Ginkas.

There were large numbers of non-professional people too: craftsmen, cab drivers and shop assistants. They were the majority, and were tougher and quicker. Life seemed more complicated for the educated people. Almost all of them spoke excellent German and had been brought up to love German poetry and culture. In Lithuania there were many Jewish households where only German was spoken – and many went to German universities, but my parents had not been Germanophiles to that extent. My father had studied in France and Mother in England, but most of the intelligentsia or young people from affluent families used to spend a good deal of time in Germany. Their parents used to spend holidays and take the waters in German spas. Their splendid libraries consisted mainly of German books, which the occupying forces eventually took with them back to Germany. My English-speaking mother could recite Heine in German. In Kaunas most educated young Jews spoke German or Russian. Almost all of them knew Hebrew as well (in educated circles usually only the elderly spoke Yiddish). They would all have been brought up on German literature and science, and felt so disorientated; they were incapable of understanding what was going on in the beginning.

Figure 8. Ariela's mother as a student in London, 1937.

TO THE ORPHANAGE

Through young members of the underground my parents learnt it would be possible for a small, pretty, blonde girl to be given shelter in an orphanage, where a certain Dr Baublys was the director. Father had known him before the War, as a colleague. My parents would have to clamber through a hole in the wire fence, make their way out of the Ghetto with me, carry me a fair distance and then leave me outside the orphanage door. But the rest of the family was in tears. 'How could you abandon a pretty little girl loved by everyone, virtually on the street, in the freezing cold?' It was −25°C. On 14 December 1943 Father gave me an injection to send me to sleep, and after my parents had dressed as peasants, they took me out of the Ghetto. My father carried me to the orphanage and left me by the door in the porch in a sack with a label on it which read: *I am an unmarried mother and unable to care for my child and ask for my daughter Bronya Mažilyte to be taken into your care.* (Mother's maiden name had been Maizelyte.) Apparently, when I woke up, I began to scream from fright, and was taken into the building. Through those same members of the underground, Father managed to let Dr Baublys know what my real name was. Thanks to him more than twenty Jewish children were kept safe in that orphanage. My parents were back in the Ghetto the next morning. There was nowhere for them to hide. For a time they did not receive any news about me. Father was still going under armed escort to work at the aerodrome, while Mother remained inside. Meanwhile Jews were being deported en masse to concentration camps or simply being killed.

It turned out that I had retained word-perfect everything our neighbours' sons had taught me. Well aware that this attracted attention, I started reciting the names I had learnt: Napoleon, Marshal Foch and so on. 'That can't possibly be an abandoned bastard child!' was the response. To make matters worse, when I cut my finger I asked for streptocide! It had only just come out at that time. Soon, it was all too clear. A little Yid! Despite my blonde hair, a pronounced blue vein on my forehead, and my not very Jewish features (my eyes were brown, not a common combination with blonde hair among Lithuanians). That was what really worried the woman looking after me, the only Jew-hater in that orphanage, who was of the opinion that all Jews should be wiped out. The rest of the staff were loyal to Dr Baublys. She stopped putting my shoes on in the orphanage and I was made to patter about barefoot on the tiled floors. She often didn't bother to dress me properly. 'We're having to look after little Yids as well! As if there weren't enough of our own kind.' There was nobody to protect me. Dr Baublys could not give himself away. If he had, all the other Jewish children would have perished too, along with him. The only thing that kept my tormentor from informing on me was her certainty that I would die anyway. One day Dr Baublys sent word that I was very ill, and that my parents needed to come and fetch me. Yet taking me back into the Ghetto was not an option.

MAMA JULIA

My father, who was still in the forced labour brigade, as well as a medical officer (giving him a little more liberty than most others), began searching desperately for someone else who would take me in. A fisherman, who used to sell fish to people nearby in their summer cottages before the war, turned up one day where father was working outside the Ghetto. He recognised him as a member of the family that he used to sell fish to, and Father began talking him round to the idea of fostering me. The fisherman said he would have to talk to his wife and sons. My father gave him the only photograph that had been secretly taken of me in the Ghetto (photography was strictly forbidden). I looked pretty enough, and, most importantly, was blonde. On the night of 3 January 1944, Father and Mother, after saying goodbye to his sister Rebecca and his elderly parents, left the Ghetto for good and set off to persuade the fisherman's family to take me in. Mother was always very persuasive and in this case more so than ever, since she truly believed in the unique beauty and brilliance of her child. She described to them how clever I was, and all about the small blue vein on my forehead through which the blue blood flowed. In short, there was no better decision they could possibly take, even though the last thing the family needed was an extra member. Yet those people were deeply religious and their own daughter had died not long before. My parents succeeded in convincing them that it would be the right thing for the God-fearing to do. The idea appealed to them.

After that Mama Julia set off with her son Zigmas, an officer from the Lithuanian Army, to the orphanage to fetch their wondrous little 'granddaughter'. Mama Julia had two grown-up sons at home. When the Soviet regime had been imposed in Lithuania, they deserted from the Lithuanian Army and had not joined the Soviet one. They had simply stayed at home, helping out. Mama Julia Dovtort (Dautartiene) could not read or write and her son filled out all the documents. I was duly handed over to them. The woman who thought the 'Aryan' child in her care was a 'little Yid' was made to feel very sheepish.

Mama Julia was told that the little girl was clever and blonde, but what was handed to them was a blood-stained mess. They could not very well just abandon their 'indisposed granddaughter', and brought me back to their home in a state of panic. They felt deceived. I was a squealing creature, who seemed as if she was about to die. Their faith got the better of them and they started praying for me to recover. My parents meanwhile had decided to find out if everything had worked out all right. They came back to my new home, walking through the woods for several days in the bitter cold. A horrific sight greeted them! Mother's first reaction was that there must have been a mistake. Then at last, when she recognized a mole somewhere, she accepted that it was me and managed to persuade the family to try and save me. Zigmas kept quiet and so it was up to Mama Julia to decide. My father promised that he would come over at night-time to help and that he would get hold of medicines and treat me. Homeless now, Father disguised himself as a peasant and went into town. He started doing the rounds of the pharmacists whom he had known before the war. Some of them shut the door in his face, but others gave him medicines and even let him and Mother shelter in their warm homes for a few days. But no-one could let them take refuge for long. With the medicines he needed, Father worked his magic. The walk was twenty kilometres to the village of Shilialis, and he did it night after night. Mama Julia's husband also knew a good deal about folk remedies, with a reputation in the village as a healer. He made herbal infusions and cleaned my wounds with them. They brought me back from the brink faster than they would have thought possible. I regained consciousness and began to get better. My hair started growing back. I started talking again, although only in Polish, like Mama Julia and her husband. My Russian did not reappear after my illness – so much the better in the circumstances.

On his last visit Father brought my mother with him. It was cold and Mother was very tired. On the way they had seen a peasant with a cart. They waved him down, but after a mere two or three words the peasant whipped his horse and galloped off. My parents realised that he had guessed they were Jews. After that they forgot their tiredness and made their way to their destination as fast as they could. Zigmas and the second son Juozas, hurried my parents into the shed and covered them with logs. The Germans came rushing over soon afterwards: they searched the whole house, jumped about on the logs in the shed, but when they failed to find anyone, asked the family if they had seen two run-away Jews. Zigmas said that some had run past and he pointed out the direction they had taken. When the Germans set off in pursuit, the brothers pulled my parents out from under the firewood. Then my parents left the following instructions with a member of the family:

We, Jacob Abramovitch and Bronia (Bracha) Maisel-Abramovitch, residing before the war at Maironio Street No. 14, beg to inform our relatives that wanting to rescue the life of our only child we are compelled on the 26th February 1944 to give away our little daughter Ariela Abramovitch under the name of Bronia Mažilyte born on the 24th September 1941 to the family Dovtort (Dautortas). The family Dovtort has been so kind and obliging as to adopt the child and look after her till the end of the war. We ask our relatives at the first possibility to take our child to themselves and to bring her up. The family Dovtort after having returned the child to you, should be compensated.

Dr Jacob Abramovitch (Signature also in Hebrew and official stamp of Dr Abramovitch) 26 February 1944

The letter was written both in Russian and in English and was dated as 26 February 1944. The English version of the letter was intended most likely for the relatives who had escaped into USA and UK before the War. The letter was kept enclosed in the envelope. On top of the envelope was written 'Testament 1943'.

They did not come to visit me again until the Liberation. Nor did I really need them. Mama Julia and 'Grandad' Dovtort (Dautartas) were very fond of me. People believed that I was their family's child and they used to tell the neighbours a fairy-tale to the effect that they had taken me in, after their daughter had had a child by a German, dying soon afterwards. They had me christened at the nearby church and used to take me to services there every Sunday. I used to pray

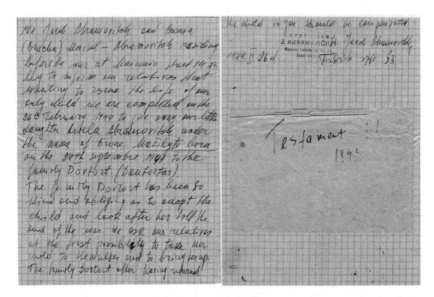

Figure 9. Testament dated 26 February 1944 written by Ariela's parents (father) both in English and in Russian in which they provide information about Ariela having been adopted by the Dautartas family.

very earnestly. I would learn my prayers faster than the other children of my age in the village. Everything was splendid. I even used to go with the other village children to the local SS headquarters where the Germans gave us chocolate. I used to come away with more chocolate than anyone else, making a deeper impression on the Germans than the other village children because my hair was so fair. Yet when the Germans used to come by, Vladik, the youngest son in the family (who later became the writer Vladas Dautartas) tried to take me away on a boat. He was fourteen then and had no confidence in me. He thought I might give myself away. He used to lay me on the bottom of his boat, cover me up with this jacket and gave me strict orders not to peep out until we had got over to the opposite bank. Later, he recalled, how, like an obedient, clever little dog I would lie there quietly sensing the danger, staying there till the boat-ride was over.

Mama Julia's third son Leonas (also known as Lyonka) was serving in the police. He was married with children of his own. He had a terrible weakness for the bottle and used to get out of control. He used to try and wheedle money out of his parents and threatened to give me away. Mama Julia used to cry and gave him money, while the brothers did not react at all. When the Germans withdrew, he left with them, leaving his wife and three children behind. Many years later he wrote his parents a letter, with gratitude for the help given his children and invited his family to join him in Canada – and for us to pay him a visit too. My parents did not write to him but via Vladik, who relayed to him that they knew about his threats. In response Lyonka later wrote back: 'Yes, I did make threats, but I did not betray her.' That had indeed been the case. He could have betrayed me and was duty bound to do so, particularly since he was in the local Polizei, but God moves in mysterious ways. My family, on the other hand, helped his relatives – Mama Julia's grandchildren.

Eventually, my parents made their way to the Lukšakaimis farm near the village of Kulautuva, where Father's family had rented a *dacha* (summer holiday house) before the War. Every summer all the children of the extended family would meet up again at the dacha to enjoy the hospitality of the elders. The head of the household, Jurgis Kumpaitis, who was German by descent, had driven them to their rented cottage from the town. By then the Russians were already advancing West. Father promised him a reward after the war and the Kumpaitis family let my parents live under the floor of a shed housing cows and pigs. They spent seven months there, only coming out for fresh air at night. The animals were at ground level and my parents in the cellar. They were given food at the same time as the animals. They survived. If things had turned out badly, the lives of the Kumpaitis family would have been at risk, but they were convinced that my father would be able to help them after the war, for they had known his whole family. They were right. They had been prosperous peasants and they could easily have been sent to Siberia. The first shipment of 'bourgeois' elements had been dispatched east to the camps before the war by the Soviets entering Lithuania following the notorious Molotov-Ribbentrop Pact of 1939. After the war there was a second round of deportations. Immediately after the Liberation of Lithuania, however, helping Jews stood people in good stead, yet a little later on it was better forgotten. During the 1950s, my parents rented a summer cottage nearby and showed me that cowshed.

As they retreated, the Germans blew up and burnt the Ghetto. The people who took shelter in the underground tunnels, to which they had refused our family access because of me, were all burnt alive. My grandparents were led out of the Ghetto in March 1944, together with two thousand other old people and children. They died as they were being driven along. Or maybe they were shot!

Figure 10. Ariela's grandmother, Sira Abramovich, with an empty food bowl and a piece of bread in her other hand in the queue for food in Kaunas Ghetto, winter 1944.

Our other relatives were taken to the Kunda camp in Estonia or Auschwitz in Poland. My uncles Beno, Ruvim and Max and their sons perished, while their wives and daughters survived. My aunt Rebecca also perished in the camp at Stutthof, but both her son (who suffered from poliomyelitis) and husband, survived, managing to get to the USA.

Figure 11. Ariela's grandparents Sira and Solomon-Itzik Abramovich with cousins Borya (first left) and Boris who perished in the Ghetto and concentration camps. Ariela's cousins Rivochka, Miriam and Josef (standing) survived in the concentration camps. Photo taken before the War, Kaunas 1936.

Figure 12. Yakov's sister Rebecca who perished in Stutthof concentration camp on 21 January 1945.

Immediately after the war, Father wrote a letter to his brothers, Aaron in England and Leon in the USA, who both left Berlin in the 1930s when the Nazis came to power [see Appendix 1].

Figure 13. Ariela's father (seated on the right) with his brothers Leon and Aron before parting, Plombières-les-Bains, France, 1935.

LIBERATION

When the occupation was over, there was utter euphoria. My parents came to see me the day after Liberation. I was in the garden, stained with juice, stuffing berries into my mouth. They were delighted. Yet as soon as it was explained to me that I had other parents, I started sobbing, clinging on to Mama Julia's skirt. It was only after my parents had visited me several times that Mama Julia was able to pull me away from her. I did not recognise my father, saying 'Good day Pan, good day Pan, (or Good day Sir)'. I sailed into Kaunas in a boat with Mama Julia's husband, Dedunya and Vladik. I would only agree to leave home by boat. I had been duly delivered, but now, somehow, I had to be helped to adjust to a new life.

Figure 14. Ariela with her foster mother Julia Dautartas who took her from Dr Baublys children's home during the War, 1945.

Even though the war was not yet over in the rest of Europe, my parents started LIVING again, desperately keen to make up for all the time they had lost. They moved into the same house in Laisves (Freedom) Avenue as before the war, but this time in the flat opposite the original one, which was now inhabited by the old and very devout sister of the woman who had owned the whole house before. The owners themselves had left to live in the country, to lie low rather than be sent into internal exile in Siberia, as they had been wealthy before the war. In the flat there were two mattresses in one of the rooms, bare parquet floors in the other two, and three pictures by Remeris on the wall. My parents used to go to restaurants instead of cooking, taking me with them. They would dance and dance, while I sat on my little couch. However, dining room furniture soon appeared in our flat, which still stands in my brother's house in London.

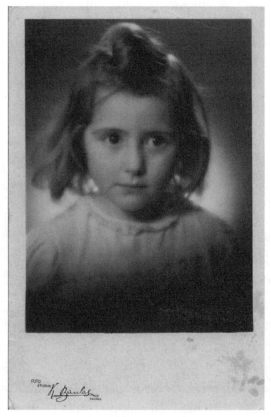

Figure 15. Ariela after the liberation, 1944.

People started coming back to Kaunas from wherever they had been evacuated. Families of the old Jewish intelligentsia began reappearing, the Per, Grodzenskii, Yudelevich and Gink families. The survivors. They had been the élite of the Lithuanian Jewish intelligentsia in the old days. People from the forces would start appearing, air-force officers, army surgeons. They would fly in and have supper with us and sometimes even spend the night. They all loved playing cards. Father used to like playing belote. They would go on playing all night. My father used to smoke heavily. They all did. It was all very friendly, although there were many heated arguments. The pilots used to give me chocolate, but sweet things did not appeal. Sausages were all I wanted; they were hard to come by and very expensive. Sometimes as a special treat I would be given two skinny sausages.

Figure 16. Ariela's first birthday at home after the Ghetto. From left to right: Naomi Gurvich, Mika Karnovskaya, Ariela Abramovich (holding a doll), Esya Elin, Dalia Judilevich. At the back from left to right: Moisei Rosenblum, Yakov Taft, Kama Ginkas.

I remember the army doctor Rebelski. A good deal has been written about him. I remember him clearly. He brought me a talking doll back from Germany. The doll could shut its eyes and even walk, and you could wind it up with a key. For all that, she came to a sorry end. Aza, the dog of one of our friends, bit off her head.

Figure 17. Ariela with her doll, 1944.

Private patients used to come to see Father from the countryside and they would bring food: eggs, smoked meats, butter and even bread, which was in short supply. Sometimes pick-pockets would pull ration cards out of people's bags as they stood waiting in the queue, so that only when someone had reached the cash-register would they notice that their ration cards had vanished. Often those people in the queue would beg for some more ration cards so as not to die from hunger. On one occasion my octogenarian nanny Mariona went out to exchange her ration cards for food and later came back with nothing. She had given her food to a German refugee with a babe-in-arms from Königsberg. Those refugees had no ration cards and were at their wits' end, and were just following their noses. Mariona had been very worried that someone would start making a fuss, asking why she had given the ration cards to Germans, but no-one reprimanded her. She was a nun living in the outside world and loved everyone, regardless of where they came from. My nanny Mariona used to live in our flat in Kaunas when we moved in. Papa used to say that she was over 80, because she had already reached that age before the war. During the occupation she had withdrawn to a convent, but it was no longer really safe out there: believers were being persecuted by Soviet authorities and so she had moved in with us. Whenever I disobeyed her, Mariona would start crying and complain: 'I'm a poor wretched orphan and you have parents, who love you so much.' Then I would start crying too and we would sit there together comforting each other. I felt very sorry for her. She wore a black skirt that came down to the floor and she was all hunched. She spent all her time praying and crying. When Mariona was in better spirits, she would start polishing the floor in the empty room without straightening up, despite the fact that it was already shining like a mirror. Spending time with Mariona was boring for me. She did not tell me any fairy stories or read me books. All she did was frighten me with tales of the witch Nevralka.

After the war my mother became completely indifferent to material belongings. She no longer bought expensive furniture, clothes or jewellery, although opportunities were there, as beautiful pieces could be had for almost nothing. All she had, as far as I can remember were two or three dresses from pre-war days, a blouse, cardigan and an Astrakhan coat bought in a commission store, full of darns and patches – the only winter coat she had right up until the time she left for Israel.

OUR SCATTERED FAMILY

I had always wanted grandparents. Many non-Jewish children in Kaunas still had them. The role of Lithuanians in the war was complex, some were German sympathisers, and against what they saw as Soviet encroachment, others were only too aware of the brutal nature of Nazi ideology. There was no Lithuanian army or general public resistance to the German occupation, so many fathers and grand fathers were spared. It was the Jewish community that was decimated by the Nazis and their Lithuanian collaborators. My grandfather on my mother's side, Isaac Maizel, had died in 1937, and his wife – my maternal grandmother – had left for Palestine in 1940. Although from a more modest family, she was an educated woman, interested in art and music and gave her children a wonderful education. They all spoke Russian in her very hospitable home, but also knew Hebrew, Latin and German. Grandmother's life was secular and she used to travel to Europe. Grandfather however, was always ready to cover her expenses. She'd bring everything she could from those European travels: china, pictures, vases and silver. Only the best was ever good enough. Their house was prosperous and she put off their departure to the very last minute, when Soviet troops had already entered Lithuania.

Grandfather was highly educated and had travelled extensively in Europe on business. He had religious sensibilities, proud of the fact that he was from a family in which there had been rabbis for nine generations, and showed an interest in Palestine. He had made several trips there, and bought a house in Haifa. Like Kafka, it was as if he sensed the turmoil to come in Europe, sensing also that his family would eventually move there. My aunts, his eldest two daughters, fled

Figure 18. Ariela's parents Jacob and Bracha Abramovich with Ariela's grandmother Berta Maizel in Kaunas just before the War, 1939.

to Palestine at the outbreak of war. His eldest daughter Lisa, who had graduated from two conservatoires (Berlin and Paris), married an engineer at the end of the 1930s, and Nadya, who'd qualified as a doctor in Kaunas, married after the war. She also acted in an amateur company and later appeared in Berlin with the second troupe of the Moscow Arts Theatre. Grandmother bore him four children: three daughters and a beloved son, my Uncle Naum. Naum, too, turned out to be gifted, becoming a lawyer and embarking on a brilliant career before the War. Our mother was the youngest of the four. She had left home to study in London and had not been planning to come back. Yet she had to, for her father's funeral.

Our father's family was more modest, their world was quite unlike Mother's of snobbish hospitality, where people talked both Russian and Hebrew and had an impressive knowledge of Latin and Greek. Our paternal grandfather had been one of twelve children in a poor family from the little Lithuanian market town of Tauroge near the border of what used to be East Prussia (Germany). As a small boy he had left on a *Schiffskarte* (green card) for America. On the way over he had worked as a ship's boy, later as an acrobat in a travelling circus, and in the theatre. He also had a remarkable singing voice and sang in a synagogue choir. Soon he started out as a small trader and made money fairly rapidly. He was a very energetic man. After acquiring considerable wealth, he decided to leave for South Africa where he continued to prosper. Soon he invited two of his sisters over and found them husbands. Yet for some reason he grew restless, eventually returning to Lithuania, where he found a very beautiful young woman to marry – our paternal Grandmother Sira Propp. They had many children but only seven survived. The youngest was my father.

Grandfather had a complex character. He was a non-believer, and blessed with a wonderful singing voice. Grandmother only managed to drag him to the synagogue for Yom Kippur, saying, 'What will people think … you must come and pray on the Day of Atonement'. When the children used to meet up at their parent's summer dacha, Grandfather used to ask questions, and the children would answer patronisingly with whatever came into their heads. Grandfather – a clever and witty man – would say, 'We all know that you are very clever, it has been proved countless times, but why do you think that other people are stupid.' He gave his sons and daughter the chance to obtain higher education. His eldest son Leon had left for Germany back in the 1930s and had qualified as a doctor there, marrying Kisyuta, a professor's daughter from St Petersburg, whose family had fled after the Russian revolution. He too had had musical talent, leading a choir of Berlin doctors, and his wife was a custodian in one of the Berlin museums. They stayed in Germany until the Nazis came to power. My father's sister, Rebecca, had also received a university education in Kaunas, where she qualified as a dentist.

Our father left home as well. He spoke perfect German as Taurage, his birthplace and where he spent his childhood, was on the German (East Prussian) border. First he went to Berlin where his two elder brothers had settled, but in 1928 living conditions were harsh and food was in short supply. He then went to France, to Montpellier, where he enrolled at the university and then later to Paris where he completed his medical studies. Father's family – except Leon the physician, and Aaron the businessman – stayed on in Lithuania. When the War began they all ended up in the Kaunus Ghetto, with the exception of Beno, shot dead by the Nazis in the first few days of the war. The only members of Father's family who survived were the brothers who'd left Lithuania long before the war and who had fled Berlin for England (Aaron) and the USA (Leo). Ruvim, Max and their sons, Beno and his sister Rebecca and his parents perished either in the Ghetto or concentration camps. The only ones who remained alive were the brothers' wives, their daughters and the husband and son of Aunt Rebecca. The Americans and British had liberated their camps and they ended up in the USA and Canada. So fate scattered them all over the globe. We however remained in (by then) Soviet Lithuania. After the international Reunification of Families agreement in 1973 my parents left for Israel.

RESCUING LOST CHILDREN

They say that there are two types of people, givers and takers. My father was a giver. His work to find homes for Jewish children seemed for a time to be his whole living. He was a very well-known and highly regarded ear, nose and throat surgeon. Father had earnest discussions with Dr Rebelski and another officer behind closed doors. They were organising networks to rescue Jewish children who were still hidden in villages scattered throughout Lithuania. Some of the men in uniform were also doctors as there was a huge military base and hospital nearby. Some of them rescued Jewish children after the war, and went out looking for them in the villages. Sometimes children would be brought back to our house although a Jewish orphanage of which my father was one of the trustees had been set up. Almost every day Father had an urge to adopt another child: one day it would be Tedik and the next a boy with the surname Gold, who went on to become a motorcycle racer – and an alcoholic. Most of the children were ill and frightened – all having complex and painful stories of loss and suffering. Although now in a place of safety, their damage was internal.

One day one-eyed Tedik (he had lost an eye in a fight) turned up with his little sister. Their parents had died, and they had managed to get home all the way from Tashkent on foot. Tedik was around 12 or 13 and his sister no more than 7. Tedik was an accomplished thief by this time – making sure his sister had everything she needed. Father was very fond of him. He was unable to settle into the orphanage, so he came to live with us. Naturally he did not steal anything from the flat. He was even trusted to take me for walks and was the last person who would have lost me. He was an adult already, kind and sensible.

Figure 19. Ariela's father with the children from the orphanage who he helped, Kaunas, 1945.

My father was very keen to adopt him, but Mother was completely opposed to the idea, as she would soon be having another child of her own. While they were discussing where they could find a home for him, Tedik disappeared. We never saw him again. For a long time Father used to reminisce about him.

Other children appeared in our house as well. They would be settled into the orphanage, adopted, sent to Poland – or further. Doctor Rebelski saw to the travel arrangements (unfortunately he is no longer around). Many young Jewish officers were travelling from village to village, bringing children back, risking their lives at a time when it was still far from safe. There were nationalist 'Green Brothers' at large in the forests, Lithuanians who would not show Soviet officers any mercy. That was how one of them, Samuel Peipert, fell by the wayside. Some people would give children back happily and voluntarily. Others were loath to lose additional work-hands and the officers would have to pay them for the children – of whom some became extremely fond. In each case it was vital to get to the bottom of what had actually happened to each individual child.

The children were brought to Kaunas, some of them to the Jewish orphanage, while others were adopted straightaway. Orphaned children sometimes found parents among childless couples. Tamara Kadishaite, for example, was adopted by remarkable people who were no longer young, but nevertheless able to give Tamara a wonderful life. But many were adopted by people who were of a nervous disposition and could not cope with distressed children struggling to come to terms with their past. Sometimes people left the country with these children. Some of the children were unable to adapt to their new parents.

After the war it was possible to send some of those orphans abroad. The pilots, with a good deal of help from my father, would personally take the children or make arrangements with army trains or convoys to transport them to Poland. At that time there was naturally a constant stream of military planes and trains moving through Poland and Germany, and they managed to get some of the children to the West. Once they were there, the Red Cross, Jewish organisations and other charitable organisations took over.

All of these arrangements were illegal in by-now Soviet Lithuania and everyone involved could have been sent to prison. As a result of their efforts, many of the children reached America, Palestine or Western Europe. My father was extremely happy when he successfully completed such operations. He devoted a great deal of energy and time to that orphanage. He treated countless children and many passed through our home, complete with their snuffles and squints. Somehow he found refuge for them all. He carried out this work with Dr F. Gurvichiene, who was reputed to be one of the best children's doctors in Lithuania. She was also a cousin and close friend of the popular Russian childrens' writer, Samuil Marshak, and would bring me his books as presents.

Father probably did not realise how dangerous that work had been, but was obsessed with the Jewish cause. After the Ghetto, his sense of Jewish identity became very strong. Almost every day Father had the urge to adopt another child, but Mother put her foot down, otherwise I would have had a whole crowd of brothers. Soon, she gave birth to one of my own, Solomon. The Jewish orphanage in Kaunas was closed in 1950.

My father once gave medical treatment to a little girl called Yolanta – although he did not operate on her cleft palate. She was adopted by a Jewish couple, but the husband died young and the woman was left on her own and, being emotionally unstable, was unable to cope. Her adoptive mother took Yolanta to Palestine where an aunt and uncle from America (who owned a chain of mail-order stores and were millionaires) found her. She had become so attached to the child, they almost had to *buy* the child from her. Yolanta (or Ilana), suddenly found herself a millionaires. She underwent facial surgery three times and was a real beauty by the end. She later married and used to throw her money about. I came to know her in Paris in the house of the Diner family, who had been my parents' neighbours in the Ghetto.

The Diner family had shared the same ground-floor flat and had known me from the first days of my existence. The father of the family had been a well-known lawyer before the war and had brought his wife to Kaunas from Hungary. They had ended up in the Ghetto and from there had been taken to the camps. After Liberation they had been in the French occupation zone of Germany and made their way to France. They lived near Paris in Montrouge, in a typical small suburban house, bought with German compensation money. A son of their own was born to them when they were far from young. There could be no question of the father resuming his career as a lawyer in Paris. They set up a small work-room in their house where the parents used to make plush dolls from morning till night. The dust from the plush made Mr Diner cough. Once a week they would take the toys round the shops.

It turned out that Yolanta's uncle and aunt had been distant relatives of the Diner family. Before I left for Paris in 1961, my parents had given me their address. During my first year in Paris they had taken me under their wing. Yolanta used to go out to Montrouge to visit them as well – always smartly dressed, bearing presents. She and I became friends and I helped her enrol at the Sorbonne. She told me about what she remembered of my father, about how he had treated her and taken her into his care. A few years after that she was killed in a car accident.

RESTAURANTS

At the age of 4, in 1945, I was taken to a restaurant almost every evening, the 'Metropole' or the 'Versailles'. At first it was all very frightening: loud music and people running around in bow ties and white dinner jackets carrying trays above their heads with plates of food and bottles. What stops it all tumbling down? I thought, they're magicians. I've seen people like that at the circus. My parents go dancing. While they dance, I sit on a small couch and watch. What I like most of all is when my Papa dances the tango. He moves beautifully and I can't take my eyes off him. Other people are watching him too. Between dances my parents eat. They try to feed me as well but I say, 'I don't like eating'. The second restaurant they used to frequent was the 'Versailles', which used to impress me far more. It was an Art Nouveau building and it had a revolving dance floor. At any rate my parents used to dance there and, as it seemed to me, almost forgot their little girl sitting on the couch. Restaurants are something I loved from an early age and still love.

That life does not appear to have lasted for long. My parents would arrange things carefully. They would choose a table in the corner to make sure there was a little couch for me to fall asleep on when I became tired. In the 'Versailles' they even had their favourite table and there was a wonderful round dance floor. This wonderful life only filled the evenings, for by day the town was a very sad place. I had only recently been brought back there from my life in the country in Mama Julia's house. When I first used to go to restaurants with my parents, I used to pull all the china off the table with the tablecloth when I grew tired of sitting there by myself. I used to cry and make a fuss. Soon though I got used to it and would behave well. Even the waiters got used to me: they would recognise me, show me every kindness and even bring me presents. Sometimes I would start wondering to myself whether life was better in the restaurant or the countryside. There is music in the restaurant and Mama and Papa are there. How lucky I am to have parents. How lucky I have been to have Mama Julia and 'Dedunya'. Before long we start going less often to the restaurant. Friends start coming to our house in the evenings after work. They are nearly all in uniform. Mainly officers ... They fly in and fly out again and talk things over with my father.

Figure 20. Ariela with her mother, 1946

UNCLE NAUM, AUNT LILY AND ANYA

A few months after Solomon was born, our little cousin Anya was brought to us. Anya was the daughter of Uncle Naum, my mother's brother, and had been born in prison, from where she had had to be rescued. Her appearance had been totally unexpected for me. After that there was no more talk of adopting anybody else's children. My Uncle Naum, of whom I had been very fond, used to come from Vilnius to visit us, bringing presents and telling me fairy-stories. One day he turned up with a woman and said that she was his wife, Lily. He had met her after returning from Russia, where he had been evacuated. Uncle Naum had encountered by chance this girl from Germany, who had survived in Vilnius and was the daughter of a rich Leipzig furrier who had fled with his family in 1933 back to his home country, Poland. When the Germans entered Poland, Lily's parents had been killed and in 1940 she found herself in Vilnius, which by then had already been annexed by the Soviet Union. That was how Lily survived during the Nazi occupation, and, moreover, she could easily pass for an Aryan. She spoke both her native German and Polish very well, even managing to keep back some of her 'movable property'. After the war, Lily was able to go back to Poland or Germany, and from there to join the family in Palestine which she decided to do with our Uncle Naum.

My parents were also keen to leave Lithuania, where everything reminded them of the recent genocide, with 94 per cent of the Lithuanian Jewish population murdered. Getting hold of the necessary 'Polish' documents was not difficult and soon we managed to get our hands on some. Perhaps that was why we did not have adequate furniture for very long in our flat. Lily still had her diamonds and she and my uncle found a more comfortable way of leaving the country, unlike the hoards of refugees moving west. Lily was pregnant by this time and so was our mother. In the end there were only nine days between the births of my brother Solomon and Anya.

Lily and Naum found an airman called Volodya or Seryozha – or rather the airman found them, agreeing to take them out by air. My parents then also decided that was how they would like to travel, but Lily and Naum persuaded them not to leave at the same time. 'We shall fly first, because you've got a small child and not a very hardy one: flying might spoil everything. We'll let you know when we get there and then you'll be able to arrange things with the same airman.' There was no news from them for a long time and Father, feeling hurt by their behaviour, went to look for the airman himself. He was, however, not at the address where my father had expected to find him. My parents then decided to make the journey the same way as everyone else. Then news came from Lily and Naum – who were in Vilnius prison. As soon as they had been airborne, the airman came back down again. 'Airman Volodya' had been working for the NKVD (People's Commissariat for Internal Affairs, the Soviet police and secret police from 1934 to 1943 and the police from 1943 to 1946), fulfilling his quota of arrests. All their diamonds and money were taken. As the NKVD people pocketed them, they kept saying: 'To the Devil with it.' For a long time after that Lily used to think that the Russian word for devil was pocket! They were put in Vilnius prison as spies and traitors to the homeland. It was a strange thought – what relationship could Aunt Lily possibly have had to the Soviet homeland? She was sentenced to eight years and my uncle to the full ten. Sometimes God seems to be punishing us, but then grants our desires. We should be grateful for the fact that our relatives had refused to take us with them.

It was while Aunt Lily was in prison that Anya was born. As a child of 'Enemies of the People' she should have been sent to a special orphanage. My parents got to know either the governor of the prison or someone from the NKVD. I was unaware of the nuances at that age, but I remember very clearly that the man in question had a shaven head and a moustache, and my parents invited him to a restaurant. My father then took him on as a patient and treated him. Father explained that our relatives were in prison near Vilnius. Mother asked him to help us. In response to that the man said: 'Do you realise what all this involves? They have been convicted under Article 58 Point 1a. Do you realise what that means?' Mother answered: 'Not really. Before the War '1a' meant top quality, the very best…'. Eventually the man warned them: 'Listen, stop trying to help them or you'll end up inside yourselves.' There seemed to be nothing more to be said. Yet the governors of the Vilnius men's and women's prisons were husband and wife. Papa operated very successfully on their son too. The governors did not send our relatives further afield and for a whole two years, while they were in charge of the prisons, Uncle Naum and Lily were able to stay where they were, rather than being dispatched further east. Anya was released to live with us.

Figure 21. Ariela's parents with Ariela, Solomon and adopted Anya, Kaunas, 1949.

The governors' appetites, meanwhile, were growing. Our magnificent, gradually acquired twenty-four piece dinner service and the money Father was earning were not enough. By this time almost everything Father was earning went to the prisons. Our grandmother in Palestine began sending us parcels, mainly lengths of material. My father possessed a suit which, as I remember, a neighbour from the house opposite had re-modelled and reversed several times and when he asked the tailor to 'renovate' it yet again, the latter protested indignantly. 'Doctor, don't you realize that any piece of cloth only has two sides and you can't reverse it ten times over?' All the material in Grandmothers parcels went to the 'bosses'.

Anya, of course, had the same surname and was our sister. Yet her initial appearance on the scene was a fright, a horrible, squealing creature, covered in spots and eczema. I was told she was my little sister. This time though I drew the line (I had not really needed a brother either). Previously all attention had been centred on me, and nobody else. Mother often used to go to Vilnius with parcels for Lily and Naum. She would stand in the queue, first at the men's prison and then at the women's. One day, when she was in Vilnius, she went into labour prematurely. That was when my brother Solomon was born. Mother was taken into hospital and, asked who needed to be informed of the birth, gave them the address of a kind distant relative, a psychiatrist, Dr Gutman, who at the time was still a bachelor. He naturally came running to the hospital and they brought out the baby, showering him with congratulations. The hospital staff did not let him get a word in edgeways. It took about two or three days before Father found out and was able to make the journey. I was left behind with a friend of the family, Grandad Malkin. I was very scared of him. He wanted me to like him and he used to tell me stories, which made me cry my heart out. At last, my parents re-appeared with my little brother. Lord, what an unpleasant surprise! But there was Anya too. If she was not happy about something, she would throw herself on the ground and work herself into a frenzy. She began talking very late, when she was four, and coming out with curious incomprehensible words. It was clear that her birth in prison could not have gone very smoothly.

When Anya started talking, Mother left the rest of us at home one day and took Anya off to show her to her real mother in the camp at Rybinsk on the White Sea Canal. That was where Aunt Lily saw her pretty little daughter for the first time. Mother had dressed Anya in clothes that had been sent from abroad. A year later Mother took Anya to see Lily again, but this time she only had to go as far as the Arkhangelsk Region, to which Lily had been transferred. Uncle Naum was in a camp in Kemerovo in Siberia at that time, but Mother felt daunted at the prospect of a trip so far with a small child.

In the course of all those years my parents used to send the 10-kilo parcels every single month to all corners of the Soviet Union. Mother would sometimes get dates muddled up, but Father never did. If Mother failed to have one of the parcels ready in time, there would be fireworks at home. Father would grow indignant. 'They're hungry out there and we aren't ready in time! We're just sitting here, eating ourselves silly.' I never remember my father getting as indignant about anything as he did about those parcels. He would be beside himself. And they were not even his relatives but Mother's.

At the age of 6 I learnt the truth, that Anya was not my real sister, but Uncle Naum's daughter. I was given strict instructions not to tell anyone about it. I duly promised. Indeed, I did not say a word to anyone, even when provoked. By 11 or 12 I had acquired a bluish complexion because of my heart condition, later to be diagnosed as Eisenmenger syndrome – a congenital heart condition with pulmonary artery stenosis with defects in the heart, a condition so complex it was inoperable. Someone had heard something somewhere, rumours travel fast and people said: 'The older sister is probably not their child'. I endured it all. I never let myself say that it was not true and that I *was* my parents' daughter, even though I knew the whole story. It was a real achievement. Anya lived with us till the age of 9, when her parents re-appeared from the Soviet labour camps. Father had helped them, through his connections and contacts as a well-known doctor. Having family in the West, as well as in a labour camp, made him an unlikely appointment as head of his department. They recognised his brilliance as a surgeon.

I shall never forget, when I was ill and not allowed out, father stood me on the window-sill and said, 'There goes an NKVD officer'. We children had come to feel terrified at the mere thought of them. We were told that if were naughty, the Witch Nevralka or captain from the NKVD notorious for their interrogations and severe repressions would come and catch us.

My father, like his father before him, used not to go to the synagogue before the War. Straight afterwards though, Father had acquired a very strong sense of his Jewish identity which acquired a whole new meaning for him. He used to listen to the BBC and the 'Voice of America' which was not forbidden and was not jammed in those early post-war years. When Israel was established, he began listening to 'Kol Zion la Gola' ('Voice of Zion aimed at the Diaspora') and used to get up at six in the morning. He preferred to listen in the foreign languages he remembered so well, rather than in Russian. The radio, a cup of strong coffee and feeding Hexe the Siberian cat – those were his favourites moments in the morning and this routine lasted for the rest of his life, even when Soviet regime started jamming the programmes from the West.

MADAMES KUPRITZ AND TSITSES

Sometimes on Sundays I was taken to the house of my friend Anita Kupritz, so as not get under the feet of my baby brother and cousin Anya. Anita will soon be 6, a year older than me. I love going to visit that family. It's very interesting to watch Anita's Mama. Madame Kupritz is quite different from my mother. Dressed in a silk kimono, she spends all day having her women friends round to see her, sitting in an armchair, drinking coffee out of a dainty little cup and smoking cigarettes in a very long holder. Her red nails are long too, and she has red lips and skin as white as snow. Her hair is dark and curly and she always wears amazing perfume called Oubigan. Its fragrance fills the whole flat and even the stairs leading up to it. Anita and I sit on the great big carpet and play with our dolls. Anita has lots and lots of dolls: dolls that can talk, shut their eyes and some even walk! They are all 'trophies of war' like most of the other things in the house, bought from officers coming home from Germany. Madame Kupritz plays cards with her women friends. When they are not there, she just plays Patience or combs Anita's hair. She says that Anita is like Natalia Goncharova, Pushkin's wife, and she puts curlers in her hair to make her look like Natalia in the old-fashioned engraving hanging on the wall of their sitting room.

Madame Kupritz had lived like that before the war. Her husband had been the sickly, only son of a prosperous factory owner, who also owned a whole chain of shops. They had even had their own car, complete with chauffeur and many salesmen working for them. When Soviet troops had entered Lithuania, almost all the wealthy had had their property expropriated and their belongings confiscated, but the Kupritzes had not been dispatched to Siberia. But then young Mr Kupritz died from illness and shock at the beginning of the occupation. Not long afterwards a suitor had appeared at Madame Kupritz's side – a slim young salesman with a pencil-line moustache and sleeked hair, like that of Mr Morales, our Argentinian hairdresser. He was ten years younger than his former employer's wife and probably did not realise at first how luck was smiling on him. Madame Kupritz became his wife and he took great pride in her, just as he might have done in a new house. Naturally he tried hard to justify the trust she'd placed in him and quickly found employment in retail. He also started working on the side to please his languid wife of substantial means.

Soon Anita announced that Uncle Kaplan was now her daddy. It was all so delightful. Madame Kupritz, now Kaplan, gave birth to a brother for Anita, but she herself fell ill and died. Anita, however, left the country for Poland with her new Papa and little brother. Kaplan had originally come from Poland and when Gomulka, General Secretary of communist Poland, drove all the Jews out of his country, he moved to Paris.

In addition to the fortunate Madame Kupritz, beautiful Madame Tsitses embarked on the same path. After the war she was on her own with a small daughter Larissa, who suffered from tuberculosis. She proceeded to marry a butcher by the name of Tsitses and bear him a child. The butcher helped Larissa recover. She grew to be a healthy and happy little girl. Madame Tsitses meanwhile, was now the wife of a rich butcher, who had some business on the side. She used to walk proudly down the street in her diamonds and emeralds, setting her green eyes off to perfection.

Another small girl I knew in those days was Rina. She also had a beautiful mother and suffered from tuberculosis. Her mother also married a 'businessman' but things did not turn out so well. His appetite was far greater than those of the two gentlemen mentioned above and he ended up in front of a firing squad for trading in hard currency and valuables on an unusually grand scale. He ensured that Rina and her mother and the small son of her 'business-like' husband were well provided for before he was brought to trial at the same time as Rokotov and Faibishenko, two Soviet citizens sentenced to death for so-called 'economic crimes' in 1961 after a case which attracted considerable attention both inside and outside the USSR.

Not long afterwards I was placed in the care of Yadviga Viken-tievna, a highly intelligent woman who considered that children should be taken to the park for fresh air or to ballet classes, rather than go and visit Anita. She and I lived very different lives, and afterwards our paths never crossed again. Yet I always remembered languid Madame Kupritz and her little daughter who resembled the young Natalia Gon-charova. They say that Anita's stepfather and brother lived in France, while she herself settled in America.

SCHOOL

I was sent to school before my seventh birthday. It involved a good deal of string-pulling as sending children to school before the age of 7 was forbidden. But my father was determined. There were now three children at home: two younger than I was and a fourth about to appear. School at least meant that one was taken care of. The school was only two hundred metres from the house, and it was a Jewish one. That was the most important thing for my father. What other school could I possibly have gone to in 1948 after the Ghetto? The school and orphanage shared the same building. It was a primary school with four classes. The teacher of Class 3 was Mr London, who was an expert on the Bible and who had been a professional teacher in a Jewish orphanage before the war. The Class 4 teacher was Elena Hatskelis, the director of the school, a highly educated woman, born to be a teacher. She devoted her whole life to teaching.

In the first and second classes the teachers were not qualified: a Mr Gertner and his wife who had completed external courses at a teacher's training institute as mature students. They had survived by fleeing their own small town at the beginning of the war and had decided to become teachers. We were the first pupils they were let loose on. Their one advantage was that they spoke Yiddish. There were forty of us in the first class. We spoke all sorts of languages: Russian, Yiddish or Lithuanian. We did not always understand each other and some of the pupils did not want to understand anyway. All the children were lice-ridden, some of them from the Jewish orphanage, but they were usually among the cleaner ones. What proved hardest for Mr Gertner, was keeping everyone quiet. Some of the small boys were simply under-age hooligans. In order to weld all these mischief makers into one group, we were taught a common language – Yiddish. First of all we had to learn to copy parallel lines and the letters of the Yiddish alphabet from left to right. We were taught to trace out sloping lines, and then letters as finely as possible, avoiding any blots or grease marks on the page.

During morning break the children from the more affluent families would bring out their second breakfast provided by home, which usually consisted of bread spread with chicken fat and crisp chicken skin, which in the warmth of the school heat used to drip on to our exercise books, seeping through the pages. I had always hated the smell of fat. There were pleasant moments during those break-times as well. The orphanage children were given cocoa and biscuits, but it was hard for the women handing them out to know who was and was not from the orphanage. In the end they decided to give everyone cocoa. Those were the best moments in my school life. Hot sweet cocoa. On the other hand, I did not like eating – so much so that I was always late for the first lesson. I was led to the breakfast table and not allowed to leave it until I had finished what was put before me. I would sit there with the food rolled up in a ball in my cheek till the time for the end of the first lesson had come round. I would then be dispatched to school in time for the beginning of the second lesson. On the way I would spit out what I still had in my mouth and run happily to school looking forward to the cocoa. The teachers would not have had time to eat anything during break. There was hardly any space to play in. The building consisted of just four classrooms, a small staff-room and a locked hall that was only used for special occasions before festivals.

The rascals from Mr Gertner's class and that of his wife could well have knocked the living daylights out of each other, so he used to eat his second breakfast during class time. He would unwrap it on his desk and the enticing smell would spread round the room. His bread would probably be spread with chicken fat as well and he would lay it out on a napkin with a newspaper underneath, which he would read at the same time as his pupils were dutifully copying something out. The hungry children would sit there with their eyes glued to his sandwich, incapable of tracing out lines or letters. It was most important to avoid breaches of discipline at those moments. If noise did erupt, Mr Gertner would swell with anger, turn red in the face, take hold of the offender by the ear and drag him to the back of the class. Those who failed to write neatly would have their knuckles rapped with a ruler. Nobody ever struck me. I was a very quiet pupil, frightened of both the teachers and my fellow pupils.

After a mere three months of that first school year, I fell ill with scarlet fever and had to spend a long time in the hospital for infectious diseases. After that I had to stay in a neighbour's flat in order to be isolated from my cousin Anya, brother Solomon and the newly born Ben. Much to my parents' surprise I was put up into the second class and even invited to a party for the school's best pupils. To mark the occasion Mother quickly had a dress made for me out of white parachute silk that had been given to us by pilot friends. I am wearing that dress in all the family photographs of the next few years.

Figure 22. The Abramovich family after the liberation in the garden of the War Museum, Kaunas. Ariela's dress is made from white parachute silk given by pilots, 1945.

At one of the school concerts in 1949 the teachers and pupils danced and sang Yiddish songs. Some singers and musicians were in the audience, but what made the biggest impression on all the parents was the performance of one of the little boys from the orphanage. He recited a poem he had made up himself:

I am an orphan, I am happy.
I have no Mummy, I have no Daddy,
But I have Comrade Stalin:
He is my Daddy and so I am the happiest of all.

I completed my year in Class 2 without any major upsets. In the end we conquered the Yiddish alphabet. We learnt to add and subtract and even do a little multiplying. We shed our lice, our teacher grew more skilled and somehow we mastered the basics. When it came to Class 3 however, we had to move to a different school. Our Jewish school went on running until 1950. Only one set of children completed all four classes there. Accusations of Jewish 'cosmopolitanism' started appearing in the press and the school was closed down. The accusations were used during Stalin's campaign of 1948–53 mainly against intellectuals as charges of lack of full allegiance to the Soviet Union and for their international connection with the West and their ideology. All those who had the chance to study in the classes of Mr London and Elena Hatskelis received quite a good grounding in Yiddish language and literature, and an introduction to Jewish culture in general. My year did not enjoy that privilege. Later on however, our Mr Gertner became quite a good English teacher in a Lithuanian school.

For Class 3 I was sent to a Russian school. That was when we had to start solving problems like 'If a train leaves Station A for Station B...', and variations on that theme. I do not remember where those trains were going and why and what I had to work out. Other children were not very different from me and almost all of them had to stay back a year. My new teacher there advised my mother to let me repeat the year as well, particularly as I seemed under-developed. My mother, in her usual diplomatic fashion, replied that her daughter would not stay down a year and that it was more likely that her teacher was the under-developed one. Mother insisted that her daughter was talented and could speak and even write French (which was true) and went to dancing lessons at the opera house (no longer true as I had to abandon the lessons after my bout of scarlet fever). With the help of Yadviga, my invaluable governess, I made progress in vital subjects and became a star pupil again, but this time for real. On many occasions after that Mother would remind me that I was 'under-developed', quoting my Class 3 teacher.

A FUNERAL

The spring holidays are just starting and all the children are playing out in the yard. Our courtyard is one you can walk right through and out the other side, just like the neighbours'. Ours is much more fun though. Immediately behind the house is a row of little lean-to sheds, one for each household. That is where people keep potatoes, pickles and all sorts of odds and ends. The first two sheds have been joined together making one big one to hold all the rubbish. Everyone empties their rubbish there and then they lock the door tightly after them. The yard-sweeper Maria keeps a careful check on it, because her door is right next to it and the rubbish dump is always seething with rats. The small boys sometimes manage to prise open this door and frightened rats start running all over the yard – making the small girls squeal.

There was one rat though, which wasn't frightened of anyone. Even the girls talked to it. The rat would stay still and listen, but it wouldn't let anybody touch it. I'm only allowed out into the yard as a rare treat, but I have managed to see that special rat a few times. It isn't terrible at all, it's clever and pricks up its little ears. I like it, but one day I notice from our balcony that the children are standing in a tightly packed circle, all talking about something. That day I was kept inside because there were too many children out in the yard. My parents were worried I might catch something, so I was allowed no further than the balcony. I leaned over the railings as far as I could to see what was going on, to find out why they were all clustering round. Our rat was lying there, dead.

We decided that the rat must be buried with due honours, the funeral organised without delay. Virtually all the children from our yard assembled. They drew up in two lines – four children in each: the rat laid out on an old tie in a shoe-box. The neighbour's son, who went to music-school, brought his trumpet along and another boy his father's accordion. The rat was solemnly taken off to be buried with full musical accompaniment. Young Vova, an active member of the Young Pioneers, delivered a speech, and ginger-haired Buska dug the grave with his brother. I watched all of this from the balcony. The rat was duly covered over with earth but now something had to be written on the wooden board to mark the spot. Nobody knew what we should call the rat. All of a sudden I called down from the balcony: 'Pat the Rat'. They went along with my idea and the children wrote: 'Here lies Pat the Rat'.

Recently I went back to our house and its courtyard. The lean-tos were no longer there. Rather sickly little trees had been planted instead. The two yards still merged into each other but there were no children playing there, no pale little girl sitting out on the balcony. All you could see were the offices of air travel agencies.

OUR NEW NANNY ONUTE

Then our nanny left us. It was unimaginable ... Four children: I was 8, Solomon and Anya were 4 and Ben only a year old. Father was out at work, Mother was out at work and there was nobody to look after us. Where could they start looking for another nanny? Who would cope with four children? Father decided that he would have to look for someone amongst his patients. There were plenty of them and they were always grateful. He was always a most attentive doctor, even for very ordinary patients and always managed to find a common language with them, well aware that patients from the poorest rural families had limited opportunities for medical care. Many of them came to the house. Early in the morning people would start queuing on the staircase leading up to our flat. Father used to receive his patients at home as people from the country were not entitled to go to the municipal city hospital or health-centre.

It was vital to find someone straightaway. Father was offering the post of house-keeper for our wonderful family to anyone that was suitable. There was the tempting offer of a flat with only one family in it and a separate little room (more like a box) next to the kitchen for the lucky candidate. And then there was the promise of eventual registration (permission to move to the city) so they could live in Kaunas. How could anyone possibly resist such an enticing offer? In the villages and collective farms people were not being paid wages in money, only in kind, and if you had no Kaunas registration it was virtually impossible to find a job in any of the town's factories. Using every drop of eloquence he could master, Father would assure any possible candidate, 'Don't worry about there being four of them, at least none of them are babies'.

A few girls agreed to the terms and in the end Onute came to join us. She had brought her younger sister along for treatment and dreamt herself of moving into the town. She was brought into our home and given little Ben to hold. Onute almost collapsed with the shock. Here she was a total stranger, with children yelling at every turn, our mother not yet come home from work. Then all of a sudden Ben stopped crying. I, being the eldest, was not crying anyway and Solomon had always been a sensible little boy. Thankfully Anya, although she could not yet talk, always used to follow Solomon's lead. Onute spent three years with us and afterwards our father helped her find the factory job that he had promised.

After that whenever a new home-help was taken on, my parents would reassure them saying: 'At least none of them are babies!' Eventually that would be true!

THE FUR COAT

As a child I was never dressed properly. My parents were working, there were four children to be looked after and my clothes were not a major concern. Bearing in mind that I was not particularly pretty as a young schoolgirl, my general appearance was rather down-at-heel. Up to the age of 12 I had never had a warm winter coat, let alone a real fur one. I only had a light red coat with worn sleeves, which came down to just beneath my elbows. My baggy trousers on the other hand trailed along the ground, getting wet and dirty on the asphalt roads. They often had holes and had sagging bulges at the knees. My parents probably had guilty consciences about that, but they had no time or energy for standing in endless queues. But many children had much less than I, and I was not particularly bothered.

My father had carried out an operation and received a length of beaver lamb for a fur coat for Mother from the grateful patient, who was the director of an experimental factory for fur garments. That was an extremely rare gift in those days. When Mother came home from work and saw the beaver lamb, it made her angry and she started shouting: 'Who do you think I am, just a maid, to start wandering around in a beaver lamb coat or jacket. Before the war only maids walked around in things like that!' The present was put away out of sight. It could not possibly be sent back where it came from. Winter would soon be upon us and my practical 8-year-old cousin Anya came up with the bright idea. 'Have a coat made for Ariela, she's a grown-up now.'

The problem had been solved and a furrier invited round to the house to measure me up: it took four sessions, each lasting one and a half hours. On one occasion I nearly fainted. There was too much material. The coat was made to 'allow for growth'. As a result I ended up with an extremely heavy garment coming down to my heels. That was how I had to make my way to school. If I tried to climb into a bus wearing it, I would stumble over the long hem. So instead I used to trudge all the way to school in it on foot. It was too loose for me and that made it draughty. I ended up far colder than I would ever have been in my little lightweight autumn coat. Hanging this coat up in a cloakroom was impossible. It was enormous and kept falling off the hooks. Then it would get trodden on. I was given a folding coat hanger to take about with me so I could hang it up more easily. There was no hope of using that coat hanger inconspicuously, so I would just push it right down to the bottom of my school bag, so that nobody would see it.

In addition to the coat they made me a tall hat out of the leftovers, which made me look like a Cossack. The tall hat made up roughly a third of my total height, so that my frozen Jewish nose looked twice as long as usual. The whole outfit made me a perfect target for snowballs. They used to land in my eyes, on my head, in my stomach, on my nose. Life was impossible. I had simply become a winter scarecrow. Yet I wore that coat till the end of my schooldays. My parents forced me to take it with me to Moscow where I continued my studies at university. I married a Frenchman in it but refused point-blank to take it to France. Only then did I manage to escape that winter coat, which in fact was heavier than I was, my husband pointing out that the French climate was milder. The matching hat still served a purpose for breeding moths and for cleaning shoes.

YADVIGA VIKENTIEVNA AND NINA RACHKOVSKAYA

By the age of 5 I was quite out of control. Mother was back to work by then and her days were very busy. She was teaching final-year pupils in the town's best *gymnasium* for boys, which had been renamed Komsomol School No.1. It was the best school of its kind in the whole of Lithuania, and before the war its pupils had included sons of members of the Lithuanian government and the high-ranking military, i.e. the élite. After the war many of its pupils were fatherless. Some of the fathers had left the country with the Germans, others had been shot by the Soviets or banished to Siberia. The pupils left behind were mature, clever boys who were well educated and already had tragic experiences behind them. The teachers were very fond of them and felt sorry for them. They tried to help those boys and were well aware that they could well turn out to be the future Lithuanian intelligentsia. Mother often had to stay on late at meetings to hear new directives and discussions. Father, meanwhile, worked very long hours at the hospital. In the evenings his time was often taken up by the orphans. There was poverty and devastation all around us. People who were considered politically undesirable by Stalin's regime were being taken off to Siberia by the trainload. Bread was rationed and the streets seemed full of beggars, pick-pockets and men crippled by the war. There was no normal world to be brought up in.

Meanwhile Father was determined that I should learn French. That was, of course, a necessity of the first order! Father had always been an impossible dreamer and could not get Paris out of his mind. All of a sudden the dream seemed attainable. One of Father's patients, Yadviga

Vikentievna, came to see us. She was a little old lady with a grey bun at the back of her neck. There was something about her appearance that was reminiscent of the women in the 'People's Will' movement, a Russian revolutionary organization in the nineteenth century best known for its assassination of the Tsar Alexander II in 1881. She lived with her sister or a woman friend in a small wooden house in the centre of town. Her house was just like that belonging to the family of Nikolsky, the director of the Russian *gymnasium*, the same painted floorboards, the oak sideboard with panes of stained glass in it, a round table and several Vienna chairs. In the corner there was a large writing desk. Years later it reminded me of Chekhov's house in Yalta. Before the Revolution Yadviga Vikentievna had completed the Bestuzhev courses for young ladies in St Petersburg. She travelled first to Poland and from there into Western Europe. She had worked for a Russian newspaper in Berlin and for a short time as Gorky's secretary. But why she happened to be in Lithuania just before the war started I do not know. All we did know was that one of her relatives had left her the small house in Kaunas. She and her sister lived there quietly and modestly. They cut themselves off from other people almost entirely and always seemed to be fearful.

Yadviga Vikentievna had a wonderful knowledge of French. For the sake of our father, with whom she always used to converse in French, she agreed to take me on. That was how I acquired a friend, governess and teacher. I enjoyed learning all the names for animals, birds and plants in French as we walked through the municipal gardens, or while she was accompanying me to ballet lessons. No more than a year later I wrote a letter to my Uncle Aaron in England – in French. It was the first letter I had ever written. We used to read together the stories of Madame de Ségur in leather-bound volumes, which had been a present from Yadviga Vikentievna. They were full of little cats and little dogs, little girls and little boys of the nineteenth century. All very engrossing. Yadviga Vikentievna also used to bring me pre-revolutionary picture books in Russian.

No wonder it was hard to get over the shock when I went to a real school. Admittedly my first year there was not a very long one. I fell ill with a serious form of scarlet fever. My mother had just given birth to my younger brother but at the same time it was impossible to leave me on my own in the hospital. Yadviga Vikentievna accompanied me and we remained there for the whole of the quarantine period, more than two months in total. For Yadviga Vikentievna it was almost like being under house arrest. After that she stopped coming to look after me, she herself was in need of help. She had almost lost her wits after all that and only came back to help out in an extreme situation, when I needed a grounding in basic subjects before going to my new school. From being one of the dunces, I moved to the top of the class in Russian language, with the best marks in literature.

Soon after that Yadviga Vikentievna died and I was left without my friend and mentor. In the new school my class teacher was an officer's wife from the nearby army base. She was from outside Lithuania and when she used foreign borrowings in Russian she always put the stress on the wrong syllable. Half the children in our class were also from the army families stationed nearby, children of junior officers. The books we read were about partisans and Zoya Kosmodemyanskaya, books like *Young Guard* and *General Dovator.* I used to get teased for the way I spoke French. The other children would tie themselves up in knots laughing at me.

After that I refused to have anything to do with foreign languages. All the beautiful books in their fine leather bindings were pushed to the back of the bookcase. I began to forget my French. A few years later my parents did, after all, find someone else to fill the gap – Nina Rachkovskaya. She seemed to float along in another world, yet at the age of 30 all decisions about her life were still being taken by her mother. The family had escaped to Lithuania after the Revolution; her father had been shot by the Bolsheviks. Nina's brother, a talented young doctor, had drowned and after that Nina's mother had joined her in Paris. Nina was as pretty as a picture and keen to become an actress, but her stupidity and lack of talent would appear to have stood in her way. In Paris she was famed for her beauty, as well as throughout Russian and Lithuanian artistic circles. At the beginning of the war in Europe Nina and her mother had had to return to Lithuania. After the German invasion they found themselves destitute. Yet, thanks to her beauty, Nina did find herself a protector in the shape of the former Lithuanian ambassador to America – the writer Vairas Rachkauskas, who was thirty-five years her senior. After the War the Soviet government didn't lay a finger on Rachkauskas. On the contrary, strenuous efforts were made to bring the well-known representative of the

Lithuanian intelligentsia into its camp. Nina's husband was a relative of the poet Petras Cvirka and a friend of Paleckis and Ilya Ehrenburg. He viewed the new regime as unavoidable. They had a large flat opposite that of the First Secretary of the Kaunas Party Committee. In the huge study, all the walls were lined with books and there was a large carved writing desk at which Rachkauskas sometimes used to fall asleep.

They had no children and I introduced a little vitality into their ordinary routine. Nina was a great lover of little Pincher dogs. Her Betsy, Mitsy and Pootsy used to remind me of the rats in our yard. The old man sometimes tried to talk to me, but unfortunately we did not have many common subjects of interest. I used to laugh to myself about Nina and her little dogs fitted out with tiny hand-knitted jackets jumping all over the armchairs and settees. Out of politeness I used to look at the Paris photographs, take tea or lunch with them and occasionally read some Alphonse Daudet or Victor Hugo in French with Nina. Sometimes I encountered Snechkus (the First Secretary of the Central Committee of Lithuana) and Paleckis (Prime Minister of Lithuania and member of the Presidium of the Soviet Union) in their house. There would also occasionally be ladies from the pre-war world, the wives or widows of former generals who had fled Lithuania with the Germans, or been shot or exiled to Siberia.

For me it was far more interesting to go and see Alla Varchenko, whose father had been transferred from the military camp into Kaunas. He worked as some kind of security officer attached to the local military. That family, naturally enough, lived in a communal flat. They kept their onions and potatoes in their room so as to make sure the neighbours did not steal them. The flat always smelt of cabbage soup and washing. I used to threaten my parents saying I refused to go to the idle Rachkauskas household, that I did not want their stupid French or little dogs with crooked paws. I insisted that those pre-historic people were of no interest to me. One day my father asked me: 'But what language are you going to speak when you go to Paris?' On hearing this my mother hissed at my father so fiercely that he stopped in mid sentence. This kind of 'cosmopolitism' was not tolerated in those times. There was even a law against it.

At school I was a reluctant student of German and deliberately mispronounced it. I was perfectly capable of reproducing what I heard from our teacher, a real live German, but I was loath to let anyone hear my correct pronunciation. As a result of all that, my French was better at the time I was due to leave school, and so French was the language I chose to take for my school-leaving certificate. After studying for a year at the Kaunas medical institute in keeping with my father's wishes I eventually gained a place at the Maurice Thorez Institute of Foreign Languages in Moscow with a little help from outside. Getting in was a real problem as I was Jewish. Many popular higher-education establishments only took in a minimum quota of Jewish students, those who were categorised as being of Jewish ethnicity in their Soviet internal passport. Two years later, after marrying a Frenchman, I did indeed set off for Paris.

Eventually Nina Rachkovskaya's elderly husband died. Before his death the couple had adopted a little girl but the experiment was not a success. They would appear to have grown used to having a child in the house after all my visits. Nina still had her head in the clouds and went on living in the past, but her circumstances obliged her to go out to work and she began to teach French at the Polytechnic. The students there, most of whom were from the country or from small provincial towns, used to make fun of her, but could nevertheless sense her superior cultural background. She used to write to me and ask which balls or exhibitions I had been to and what was now fashionable in Paris. What could I write by way of reply? I used to concentrate on exhibitions. Balls, as she understood them, were not something I would often go to and neither was I qualified to comment on fashion. Nina made me a present of her pre-war photographs. She had decided that I would look after them better than her adopted daughter. Nina really was a beauty – on a par with Greta Garbo. Those were my true Teachers: beautiful Nina Rachkovskaya and Yadviga Vikentievna.

OUR YARD

Flour and sugar were distributed in our yard once a month. A long queue formed and why our yard was used as the distribution point I did not know. On the side facing the street there was a sausage shop and then a little further down a grocery: in our yard though there was room for lots of people and not even the end of the queue stretched as far as the street, so nothing spoiled the appearance of Stalin Avenue (the original Freedom Avenue now renamed). There was nothing for us to complain about. From our balcony you could see how things were moving and rush down to take your place in the queue at a moment's notice. We always went down together because each person, even a child, was entitled to a kilo of flour, and there were four of us children. Why should we need so much flour and sugar? When we were really young, some of the flour would be used for milk puddings, but the only baking that was ever done was when Mama started preparing for high days and holidays although she did sometimes make homemade macaroni on Sundays.

On distribution days we children felt very important. After receiving what was due to us, I went home straightaway, but the others went on playing in the yard. People waiting for their turn in the queue often 'borrowed' them. Little cousin Anya managed to be issued with three or even four kilograms. She knew quite well that it was important not to appear in the same outfit each time she turned up in the queue and she often put an extra hat or jacket on so as to look different. Anya sometimes disguised Solomon as well. Ben, who was still only very small, used to play the part without needing any disguise. Adults always picked him up or hoisted him on to their shoulders. It was hard to work out who all the children really belonged to. Sometimes a child was recognised and then people started quarrelling and pushing. 'He's already had his share!' At moments like that Anya sensibly took the other children upstairs to the flat. All the children, not only those in our family, liked to join in this sport. Then they started working out who had got the most.

In the winter I grew cold very quickly and Anya would shout out loudly at the whole queue: 'Ariela, what are you standing around for? You're in the Young Pioneers!' Anya already understood what party privileges are. She was the leader when it came to standing up for children's rights. My brother Solomon was a quiet, clever and honest little boy, but at moments of crisis he was often quicker off the mark than any hardened adult burglar. When our parents were away, if an inspector or some other person from the tax office came round, the home-help tried not to let them in and just said: 'The grown-ups are out.' The tax men would try to push their way in anyway, keen to check the place, to see if they could find any signs of private practice which was restricted by then. While everyone was arguing at the door, Solomon would quickly collect up all the medical instruments lying around, and throw them into the linen drawer inside the divan. How could a 6-year-old react so quickly and find the strength to hide all the equipment? The top of the divan he had to lift was very heavy and he only ever had a few brief moments to clear everything away. My little brother would then come out to speak to the tax men, and like a real grown-up would say to the home-help: 'You'd better let them in, so that they can have a look around wherever they want to. They need to show their documents first though.' 'All right now, you're a clever boy. Well done. Does your father receive any patients at home?' 'What patients? The patients are at the hospital.' By this time all traces of medical activity had disappeared.

Solomon and Anya complemented each other. There were only nine days between them and everyone regarded them as twins. Naturally Solomon assumed the role of elder brother. Anya still did not know that she was our cousin rather than our sister, and that her real parents were in a prison camp. Anya used to take charge of everything, while Solomon used to follow in her footsteps like a poodle. They were very fond of each other. When they were 6, Anya had only just learned to speak properly. Before that she produced tongue twisters of incoherent words full of lisping. 'Anya wants wed bewwies.' The only person who could understand what she was saying was Solomon, who would translate for other people and diplomatically calm down his sister when she got cross.

At the age of 5 she would often pretend she was planning to leave the household. She would pack her things – both her own and Solomon's – in a large suitcase, would summon her brother – and they'd set off. He was prepared to carry the suitcase but tried to stop Anya and make her change her mind. He always succeeded in the end. Anya used to bite other children very hard. At the slightest provocation she was ready to bite another child's finger or hand if they treated her badly. Father often had to patch up the bleeding hands of other people's children. Once she almost bit right through a little boy's tendon. It caused a real scandal. People were threatening to call out the militia or an ambulance. In the end our father sorted everything out himself. To look at though, Anya was a very sweet little girl, like a china doll. She was dressed like one as well, thanks to all the clothes sent to her from her real mother's sister who lived in England.

Mother would take her dressed up in her pretty clothes all the way to Rybinsk on the canal linking the White Sea and the Baltic, to Potma and Archangelsk to show her off to Aunt Lily, but admittedly only once a year. Anya would cry as she set off, because she did not like going anywhere without Solomon. Nothing was really interesting to her without him.

They started school together and at first they sat next to each other, but after a few days they had to be moved to opposite ends of the class. The teacher would ask the pupils questions and Solomon would answer. Anya would not say anything, just blush and wriggle as if none of it had anything to do with her. There would be a long silence and then the teacher would ask the question again. This time Anya would burst out: 'Can't you hear properly Solomon? She's asking you a question.' That was how Anya tried to get used to school. Going there at 6 would appear to have been too early for her. The whole atmosphere and the tension had such a negative effect on her that she started wetting and dirtying her knickers. Solomon felt horribly embarrassed and would take her off home to change. His friends would tease him, saying: 'Your sister smells of poo!' By this time my brother was wishing the earth would swallow him up. It was decided to cut Anya's school career short for the time being and send her back when she was 7, the official starting age. It was the first time in their lives that she and Solomon had been apart even for a few hours each day.

The two small boys from the neighbour's flat – Buska and Emka – were also fond of Anya, but even more so of Solomon. Somehow they got hold of a whole supply of fly-papers, rat poison and other insecticides which they then proceeded to share out with Anya, Solomon and Ben. Anya as the most enterprising of the group decided that all these commodities could be sold. So the children of well-known Dr Abramovich set off to try their hand as street-vendors. They even managed to clinch a few deals. At any rate they involved 2-year-old Ben and naturally the sons of the next-door neighbours who had come by the 'goods' in the first place.

Buska was an enormous red-haired hulk and little Emka all fair hair and blue eyes. Their mother was 'Aunty Olka', a well-endowed woman from Odessa, whom 'Uncle Kasimov' had married and brought back to Kaunas. She had come as part of a package complete with her old mother, her 'rogue' brother – always out of work – and a second brother with one leg and a chest-full of medals, who found a job making gloves in some private workshop or other. Olka used to terrify the wits out of her husband, a quiet little local Jew. It seemed to me that he was frightened of Olka's brother but got on well with the war-veteran and sometimes even worked with him. Whenever Olka had a set-to with her mother, the whole block could hear them. The old woman would run down the stairs and out into the yard followed by Olka armed with something from the kitchen, whatever she first laid her hands on, cursing and shouting as she went. The brother would not be far behind, rushing to defend his mother, while the one-legged veteran would bring up the rear trying to re-establish peace. All this would usually happen on Sundays. The rest of the people living round our yard would be watching events unfold as if they were in the theatre. Yet when things reached boiling point, they would all retreat inside, so as to avoid the next round, but usually there was no next round. Then things would be quiet for a while, although sometimes there would be shouting and swearing going on inside their flat as well.

THE BLACK STAIRCASE

The apartment building we lived in was large and it had two stairwells, one at the front and the other leading upstairs from the yard. It was known as the black staircase. All the other residents, apart from the Odessa family, tried to live quietly and keep a low profile. Under our flat was an enormous apartment, occupying the whole of the first floor. At one time it had been lived in by Mr Genis, who now lived on the fourth floor, reached via the black staircase. He kept very quiet and was frightened that people would remember his wealthy past. His elderly parents had gone one step further, taking refuge in a little house at the back of the yard. Occasionally they would walk past the hordes of playing children. They were like a vision from the past. Above us lived the Petrauskas family: a mother, her student sister and two children, a boy and a girl. They never came out into the yard or tried to make friends with the other children, neither did they ever visit anyone or invite anyone in. They tried to stay completely out of sight, but occasionally the sound of a piano could be heard coming from their flat. After the war their father disappeared when new Soviet authority was in place.

Our house was often the object of unannounced raids, with officers of the NKVD and Alsatian dogs running up and down the stairs. They would rush in through the main entrance and then make their way up and down the black staircase to individual flats. They would check people out, searching through all the rooms. Sometimes they would have militiamen in tow as well. They were looking for 'Green Brothers' – Lithuanian nationalists. They would turn up after having been tipped off by one of the residents. Our neighbour Denisov would be among the militiamen. Denisov's wife was a Lithuanian woman called Aldona and they had an Alsatian chained up to their shed, guarding their treasures. When there was a flood, the dog began to drown, but its owners did not even go out to rescue it. Either they were not at home or did not care about it. It was my father who swam out to save the dog. He first walked through the water in his rubber boots and then swam over to the dog. Everyone was watching. The 'grateful' dog later bit me, very hard. Its masters used to beat the dog mercilessly and Father would go and plead its case. The Denisovs used to store onions, various other things and a large wooden suitcase under their bed. Denisov could hardly write and although he went on going to courses at the militia training school and gained some qualifications, whenever he actually had to write something, he would ask for my mother's help.

In the flat at the front of the house on our floor lived Aunty Polina, a pious old spinster, sister of the woman who had previously owned the whole house, the sausage shop and the sausage factory. Mrs Kazenas and her husband who had enjoyed all that wealth in the past were now living in the country village of Kacherginai and they only came to visit Aunty Polina on rare occasions. They would hardly speak to anyone, merely greet our father in the softest of voices. The husband used to wear a black pre-war coat and a felt hat. He had a white moustache and sideburns, a character from bygone days, while his wife was always dressed in black, wearing a little hat. They were people from a vanished era.

After my bout of scarlet fever I stayed for a whole month in Aunty Polina's flat, in order not to infect my brothers and Anya. Under her roof everything was quiet and peaceful, only clocks striking as required every half hour. I was isolated from everyone there, as if I was in prison, but there were advantages. Aunty Polina was a remarkable cook and, in secret, used to provide lunch for two young students, one training to be an architect, the other a sportswoman. At six o'clock in the morning Aunty Polina would go off to the Catholic Church, returning at nine o'clock to prepare lunch. She would often forget to buy some ingredient or other and have to go out to the shops. That was when I would start spooning soup out of the saucepan, often a wonderful borscht or mushroom soup with homemade noodles. It was important that the change in the level of soup in the saucepan was not noticeable. Then I would move onto the main course. My favourites were beef stroganoff and goulash. I could take something from both those dishes without it showing, as I could lazanki, small flat pieces of dough with a sour cream sauce and crisp chicken skin. Although I did not really like fatty foods, in Aunty Polina's kitchen everything was irresistibly tasty. The really difficult dishes to taste were those laid out in ready-made portions – a hopeless venture. Each individual share would be clearly visible. My mother would bring round apple purée, mashed potato and curd cheese three times a day. My parents were unable to understand why I did not eat what they used to make for me. At the same time they were well aware that I was not losing weight.

Aunty Polina lived a long time. While we were growing up, she was growing old. The former house-owner, Mr Kazenas, died fairly young and it was his wife who lived longest of all. Throughout those post-war years Mrs Kazenas had grown used to living quietly and keeping a low profile. In the end she was issued with a permit to leave the country and go and live with her daughter in Sweden. Her daughter had left Lithuania with the Germans as a young woman, ending up in Sweden. She qualified as a doctor there, married, had children and started trying to get both her parents out of Lithuania. Just before we left Kaunas ourselves, Mrs. Kazenas left Soviet Lithuania for Sweden. She had very little luggage with her – just a small suitcase containing a housecoat, a pair of slippers and one dress. She looked the part of a poor elderly pensioner, but my father had stuck her remaining diamonds and other stones inside her ear canals with plasticine. She had been saving the diamonds for her daughter. To repay him, Mrs Kazenas had given him a beautiful silver teapot. It was larger than the official silver allowance and the Soviet customs officials confiscated it when my brother eventually left the country. Our resident militiaman, Denisov, separated from his wife and went to live somewhere in Russia. Aunty Olka and her family applied to leave for what was now Israel.

My pretty little friend Niele grew up to become an actress. She was the only girl in our whole courtyard who had become a close friend. At first she lived on the first floor in a wretched little flat at the back of the yard, which had a dark, narrow and unlit wooden staircase. On the ground floor there were buckets with holes in and parts of broken bicycles lying around. Upstairs there was a small bed-sit with a kitchen alcove. Niele was looked after by her grandmother, while her mother hardly ever appeared. She was the director of a small food-shop in Vilampol, a suburb which had contained the Ghetto during the war. Her mother's admirer was the supplies manager for the whole hospital where our father was head of the ENT department. They kept their heads down just like everyone else. The supplies manager had a sick wife and when she eventually died, he and Niele's mother married. Thanks to their joint commercial efforts, the whole family moved into a new and beautiful detached house in keeping with the latest fashions. It even had a garden. They never had to stand and queue for sugar or flour. Sometimes Niele's mother would get hold of shortage items for us like butter, smoked sausage or coffee. Once there was even a pineapple. Niele's mother always had a sack of sugar standing near the cupboard in her larder. Next to it there would be a barrel of water. After the family had moved house, Niele only came round to see us occasionally, and she would always be well dressed. Her mother used to buy her anything she wanted. In this way she was trying to compensate her daughter for all the time she'd not been there for her. Niele's mother and stepfather no longer felt they needed to hide their newfound prosperity.

The only person who stayed on in the house was Mrs Petrauskas. I visited her ten years ago after Lithuania's independence from the Soviet Union. Her children had become doctors and her sister a well-known sports coach. They were all now living in flats of their own, yet Mrs Petrauskas was still living quietly in our building. But she was a sick elderly woman. I brought her a cake and flowers and she was very pleased to see me. She was glad to learn that our family had flourished after leaving Lithuania, yet distressed that my parents had both died relatively young. She said that we had been the best neighbours in the whole building. Our flat had been beneath hers and had had exactly the same layout. The flat, which had once seemed so enormous, was in fact quite small. How had we managed to squeeze in seven people in those days, and, for a time an extra aunt and uncle? Yet all the same, our yard, our big communal house, (our small flat within it) and our neighbours were all splendid, leaving me with many happy memories.

SUMMER HOLIDAYS

Every May Mirvits comes to our home with his large lorry and helps us move out to the dacha. Mattresses are packed complete with wooden trestles laid out with pillows and blankets, bed linen, saucepans and plates. All of that is carefully assembled in the lorry and by the end of the morning everything is packed up and ready to go. Then we all sit down with Mirvits to have a meal before setting out. We have to use the best plates because the everyday ones are already packed up to be taken out to the dacha. My parents would always get round to renting a cottage late in the year, which meant that we always ended up with one that was not particularly satisfactory, and where there would be a whole tribe of neighbours.

The most colourful and noisy collection of neighbours were to be found on our holiday in Kacherginai, near an air-base which was strictly out of bounds. It was 'top secret', so very intriguing to us children. The smaller children started bickering and Anya soon started biting them. Their parents would angrily complain to our father, who only turned up on Saturday evening for the weekend. It was opportune then, that Mother had to set off in July to show Anya to her real mother, still in prison camp in Mordovia. Anya still had no idea that our Aunt Lily was her real mother. All the summer visitors heaved a sigh of relief after Anya had left. All they needed to do was to make sure that none of the children wandered into the air-base.

The year after that we were lucky enough to have a whole house to ourselves in Lampedžiai, next to the river, deep in the forest. Our parents were very happy with it, but we children were bored. There was nobody else around, just our Nanny. She was clearly unable to control us and we used to go down to the river by ourselves. Anya and

Solomon would push our little brother's pram and one day, when Ben started crying, interrupting their game, Anya decided it would be best for him to float in the river in his pram. Heaven knows how we managed to rescue him and who came along to help us! Our Nanny? Someone doing their washing nearby? After that we were only allowed down to the river at weekends with our parents. The nearest neighbours lived some distance away but sometimes, at our parents' request, they would come and visit us or even invite us back to their house.

It was out there in the country, rather than at my Jewish school, that I learnt some Yiddish, especially in 1956, when there was a football match between the USSR and Israel. All the local men set off to Moscow to see the match, while those left behind sat round their television sets listening to excited commentaries. The women grew very agitated. For every goal scored against the Israelis they were ready to tear apart anyone who happened to be standing nearby. Only the wise old men would calm them down, pointing out that they were hardly evenly matched, the Israeli team not being a full time professional one, unlike the Soviets.

One year we struck lucky, all our friends asking who had helped us rent half a house in Palanga on the main street leading straight down to the pier – Basanavichaus Street. That year, my seventh, just as in all the previous ones, the indispensable Mirvits came to fetch us with his lorry. We embarked on the solemn task of carrying out our vital belongings. Everyone joined in. The children carried out boxes, and the adults the mattresses and bundles of bed-linen. There was only room for Mother and little Ben in the driver's cab. Everyone else and Nanny had to climb in the back. The journey took four hours, perhaps even five. Father had not been able to come with us. It was the first time we had seen the sea. So as not to miss a single day on the beach, we would all be taken down to the sea every morning after breakfast. We went to the women's beach, where our well-endowed mother and Nanny used to strip off and sunbathe in the nude like all the other women. It was a truly female domain and woe to any unfortunate man who might wander in by mistake!

The women's beach was next to Smilchu Street, where most of the cottages were rented out by Jewish families. Many of the Jewish mothers would be walking along the beach armed with spoons, ready at

Figure 23. Ariela's father on the Baltic beach in Palanga, 1949.

every opportunity to stuff something extra into their little darlings' mouths. At every turn you could hear the exhortation: '*Schling arop, schling arop*' (swallow it down, swallow it down). Possibly a reflection on their parents psychological past. The only person who used to go in for that kind of 'forced feeding' was our Nanny Onute, to whom my younger brother Ben was entrusted, at that time a round little boy with spare tyres round his wrists and ankles.

After the beach and our afternoon rest, an essential part of our day was the walk to Tyshkevich Park, where we could breathe in the forest air. Photographs were often taken of us next to the lions in our little summer dresses and cotton playsuits. They were specially made from leftover pieces of material, which Aunt Lily would bring home from work after her release from prison. For those summer holidays our mother and Nanny used to have identical georgette dresses embellished with life-size pansies.

Palanga holidays were to become a family tradition. While we were renting that wonderful house on Basanavichaus Street, our relatives

Figure 24. Ariela with her family in Palanga, 1953.

from Moscow used to come and visit us. Mother's cousin, Tamara Kolmanovskaya, who had married a composer, used to come with her two children. Father's two cousins used to come too. Before arriving in Palanga they would go to Kaunas for a few days to have dresses made by our pre-war tailors.

Later, that house was no longer rented out, or at least not to us. We were that much older by then and could therefore qualify for holiday vouchers from the Polytechnic where Mother taught. This meant that we no longer had to take mattresses or bed linen with us, and the era of children on the women's beach was over. Father would join us there for a short time. Sometimes he would manage to extend our original holiday voucher or would rent a room for us all somewhere else. It was no easy task to feed such a large family. There were endless queues in Palanga during the summer season, in both its expensive restaurants and humble eating places. The smaller children would be fractious after their morning on the beach and we were privileged to be provided with lunches in the house of a pious old lady.

Figure 25. Ariela with her brothers and cousin on the beach in
Palanga, 1954

The only other people to be served lunch by her were priests. They
would sit down in decorous fashion, make the sign of the Cross and
then eat their meal in silence. Our behaviour was not always in tune
with their polite manners. We would start asking for second helpings
although, as small children and on the basis of the money already
paid upfront, we were only entitled to half portions. I do not think
that we were a source of much profit for the old lady, but she would
have felt embarrassed if she'd turned down our requests. We were
moved into the second shift however, and Mother was reluctant to
pay for full portions for everyone. Yet we ate adult portions, only paying for children's.

As we were growing up Mother would get to know many of the
people from Moscow and Leningrad who came to the Lithuanian
coastal resorts for holidays. One of those families, the Pechalins,
even helped me to obtain a place later at the Maurice Thorez Institute of Foreign Languages in Moscow. One of the professor's wives
at the resort started trying to marry me off to her red-haired student son, but by this time I was already imagining my future as a
student in Moscow. I had no urge whatsoever to be married off to
anyone at the tender age of 17. I did not even bother to look twice

at the 'fiancé', much to the distress of my mother and the professor's wife. The youth was clumsy and always blushing. He was useless at dancing as well but Mother used to say: 'The main thing is for you to do the dancing and for him to concentrate on his studies. He'll turn into a professor, perhaps even an academician.' She was right. He did indeed become a professor, also an academician at a very young age.

My parents were loath to let me go to Palanga on my own, but when accompanied by my tall younger brothers they had no more objections. We used to hitchhike. First of all I would step out at the edge of the road, while my brothers hid in the nearby bushes. As soon as I had poked my toe into whatever car slowed down, Solomon and Ben would come leaping out of the bushes with my large suitcase full of clothes. Usually the driver felt awkward about refusing to give all three of us a lift and we would all manage to reach our beloved Palanga. In those days nobody had any inhibitions about hitchhiking and it was even a thing for students to do.

Figure 26. Ariela in the park of the stately home of Count Tishkevich, Palanga 1953.

Figure 27. Ariela with her cousin Anya and her brothers next to the statue of a lion in the stately home of Count Tishkevich, Palanga 1953.

A few years later Solomon qualified as a doctor, and for his holidays used to work as a locum hygiene-inspector during the summer holiday on the coast in Palanga. By then I was no longer spending my holidays with them. Solomon told me that he would be offered meals in all the restaurants and never had to queue. He was given the chance to bring along all his friends and relatives and offered various bribes, but as far as I can see he did not really understand what everyone was up to.

AUNT LILY AND UNCLE NAUM RETURN

At the end of the summer of 1953 there was a ring at the door. I ran to answer it. I had been expecting one of my friends but in walked this woman in coarse leather boots. The woman and the boots had taken me by surprise, but then, in a well-meaning voice with an unfamiliar accent, she said, 'Hello, Ariela dear, I'm your Aunt Lily.' The wife of my Mother's brother had returned from prison camp. Only 35, she was a toothless bent figure of a woman with grey hair. She had brought presents – a black-lacquer dip-pen with a broad nib, and a little cushion with a girl's head with *To dear Ariela from Aunt Lily* embroidered on it.

I liked my aunt right from the start. She was installed in our father's study, where she slept on the black leather couch. When patients occasionally came to see Father, her things had to be cleared away. She began looking for work. In the camp she had worked as a sewing-machine operator. Before the ghetto she had been a student, the daughter of rich parents. She spoke Russian with a strong accent, yet before her time in the camp she had not known Russian. To the end of her days she would confuse Polish and Russian and could hardly understand Lithuanian. So this was the unlikely job-candidate, who wanted something light but well paid.

Anya was told that her real mother had come back – not easy for a 7-year-old girl – and she had to help her get used to the new situation. There was an intuitive empathy between them. Anya felt drawn to Lily, which made Lily melt with emotion. My parents were more worried by it all than anyone else, and children's doctors were consulted. My father was really fond of Anya. My mother was too, but she started to grow jealous, arguing with Lily. Outwardly our Father encouraged Lily in her efforts to bond with her daughter, but he was not at ease in this new situation. As for us children, we felt jealous too. Why did Lily love Anya more than the rest of us? She tried to be equally affectionate towards all of us, but failed.

Lily had a weak stomach and liver, and swollen legs. She could hardly manage to eat anything although she was desperately hungry. She would take a piece of something and then be writhing in pain. She only seemed to possess one blouse and whenever we had to go and visit anyone – something Lily hated – our mother would lend her something from her own very limited wardrobe and that made Lily embarrassed. When everybody had gone off to work or school, Lily would start smoking and would often weep. She would only calm down when she was helping Anya with her schoolwork. That autumn Anya would have to start school. Solomon had not been withdrawn like she had and was a much more competent pupil. That also upset Lily. Jealousy – that most disruptive of emotions – seemed to be the order of the day.

Father managed to find Lily work in the warehouse of a textile factory, where the director led a counter-intelligence unit during the war – and who was now one of Father's patients. At night Lily would start crying. She was useless at discarding the fabric leftovers that needed to be documented, and which the rest of the staff would then take home after work. In the end they taught her how to do it their way, and then even we children began walking around in clothes made up from those splendid scraps. Some of them were so lovely that we only wore them for special occasions, or when photographs were being taken. Special outfits were even made for relatives from Moscow when they visited us on their holiday trips away from the capital 'to the West'. But the work was stressful, and Lily's old stomach ulcer started giving her trouble. She would rush home at lunchtime, grab hold of anything she could find to eat and then begin writhing in pain. Father could not bear to see her suffer, and would come home before her, strain her a plate of soup and then rush back to work. This annoyed my mother. (If my father had been interested in finding another woman, he could have done a lot better than poor Aunt Lily!) In family arguments Lily used to take his side and they used to give each other advice. The two of them used to get on very well, but when Anya began to call Lily 'Mama' and our mother 'Bronya', it made him inwardly wince. Anya did go on calling our father 'Papa' though. Lily felt like an intruder and would often start arguing with our mother. I would always take Lily's side and Mother would say 'Just you wait. One day Lily will show you what's what.'

In November 1954, Uncle Naum returned from the labour camp. This was a few months before his ten years was finally served. At first Lily and Naum lived in our flat. They were given my bed instead of the leather couch. After ten years in the camps Naum found it far harder to adapt to normal life than Lily did. He loved taking medicines. Access to them would appear to have been one of the privileges reserved for prisoners who worked as doctor's assistants, and he had completed the training for that in the camps. He was incapable of any physical work because of his high blood pressure. Uncle Naum's last camp had been in the Kemerovo Region in Siberia, where his health was undermined.

Work also had to be found for him. That proved a much more daunting task as there had been no rehabilitation for Uncle Naum. He was just a recently released 'Enemy of the People'. Before the War Uncle Naum had been a brilliant lawyer, but any kind of work as a lawyer was out of the question at this time. He was fluent in six or seven languages and was found a job as a translator at the Inkaras tyre factory. The director was a handsome engineer, one of our mother's former admirers, and married since before the war to a half-demented Frenchwoman who'd lost the remains of her wits. There were four children in the director's family, just as in ours, children for whom he had to play the role of both mother and father. Before Naum's return Mother had occasionally translated academic articles or dissertations into Lithuanian for him. What a stroke of luck! Mother's brother could now stand in for her.

Uncle Naum was incapable of working an eight or ten-hour day, for that would have brought on his chest pains. Part of the director's office was partitioned off so that a couch could be set up in the corner where he would be able to lie down as soon as it proved necessary. Soon there was no end to the amount of work he was having to do. Apart from his work in the factory he had to write petitions and applications in various languages for private clients. He would compose appeals, complaints and official requests. Uncle Naum was very much in demand. He and Aunt Lily eventually rented a room and moved, taking Anya with them. Later they were given legal entitlement to the room and Anya used to come and see us at weekends. My parents often asked her how she was getting on, hoping that she would find fault with things in her new home, but she was becoming more and more at ease with her new family.

Meanwhile our father had managed to fix Aunt Lily up with a new job as a shop assistant in the Kaunas branch of the Military Stores. She still found it difficult to understand Lithuanian, but there was no particular need for it in that shop and she was at last coping with Russian. Aunt Lily was now well involved in the retail world and already working in a department store selling goods not available elsewhere. The director there was a certain Maria Ivanovna, who had been an officer in the security services in the past. Her height and build would have been appropriate for a grenadier. She had two extremely skinny daughters and it was difficult to say which of them was the taller or the paler. Our father used to treat them for their endless sore throats and operate when necessary. He had operated on Maria Ivanovna in the past and, out of gratitude, she had been prepared to take Lily on, even before her rehabilitation document had come through, which had been an extraordinarily brave gesture on her part. After her German and extremely law-abiding upbringing, it was difficult for Lily to come to terms with the way in which she was expected to mislead customers. She simply could not grasp how first class prices could be charged for second class goods at a time when plenty of goods in short supply were only being sold under the counter. She was made a cashier instead, and would often start crying. That whole environment was something she could not equate with her up bringing and character. All the while she would seek diversion through sentimental novels, drink coffee and eat 'Kooochen and Kaaayse' (cake and cheese). That was the name we used for her when making fun of her Saxon accent.

Aunt Lily used to try and teach me German, making sure I had a proper accent. She succeeded, but it was something I found embarrassing because I was afraid of being mistaken for a German. Uncle Naum never really found his feet in his post-camp world. He chose for himself the role of 'poor prince', although he enjoyed the respect of all those around him. He and Lily led separate lives. After a few months of a shared existence before their arrest followed by ten years apart, two people with very different mentalities had been thrown together again – a bourgeois young lady from Germany and a well-read intellectual.

In 1972 they left for Israel after receiving an invitation from relatives there. In Israel they were allocated a good three room flat and were due to receive some reparation money. But Uncle Naum died a year after they arrived. Lily lived a few years longer and had time to marry off Anya before Lily too was brought low by all the illness she had fallen prey to in the camps. We all remained very fond of Anya: she really was our sister. When my parents eventually followed them to Israel, Lily and Anya had already found their feet. My father had forwarded the books from his library to their address, and as soon as he and our mother arrived, Lily lost no time in demanding that they should remove their books straightaway. Anyone would have thought that she and her daughter were short of space in their three-room flat lived in by only two people.

SPECIAL OCCASIONS

Our mother used to be out at work all day, six days a week. She could cook, but showed a talent for it on special occasions. It was important not to get in her way – me in particular – otherwise there was bound to be a slap or a push or she'd start shouting. But Mama would be in her element. She also set the tables beautifully. That is something she learnt from our grandmother or when she was in England. Our family was not devout, but people always wanted invitations to our Passover or Rosh Hashanah gatherings.

One of the regular guests was my music teacher, a small man with a limp called Josif Romanovich Stupel, with his wife Klavdia Ivanovna, a six foot academic from Moscow with nothing Jewish about her at all. They would come with their Pomeranian dog called Murik. The other guests would vary. There was Professor Odinov from Moscow, who had either been exiled to Lithuania or had fled there during the harassment after the 'Doctors' Plot' of 1952 – an alleged conspiracy to eliminate the leadership of the Soviet Union by several identified Jewish doctors which unleashed a strong wave of anti-Semitism. After Stalin's death in 1953, the case was declared to have been fabricated. Professor Odinov was a handsome man of majestic appearance, extremely erudite and a wonderful raconteur. Sometimes his imagination would run away with him – natural for a man from Baku. His whole family had stayed behind in Moscow. Then there was Tatyana Naumova – a typical Jewish Russian beauty with a long plait, with her husband Dr Pyotr Naumovich Reznikov who worked in the military hospital. Many others would have come as well, but we did not want to spread the net too wide.

For birthdays and New Year, however, we enjoyed our revelry. Twenty or thirty people would be invited. We would assemble all the tables and chairs from our flat as well as Aunty Polina's. Then my parents' friends would come, including some they had been with in the Ghetto. All the women would be smartly dressed and would have had their hair set for the occasion. Professor Rosenblum would take his seat at the piano. The wife of Brun, the well-known architect, would sing. If it had not been for the war she would have graduated from the Conservatoire with honours. Aba Grossman would keep everyone entertained with his anecdotes, and would be the master of ceremonies. As I recall, at least half the Jewish intelligentsia of Kaunas used to be present at those occasions. Sometimes each of the guests would bring along a dish for all to share.

At the beginning of the party the windows would be wide open and everyone would raise loud toasts to Comrade Stalin, Lenin and our wonderful Soviet life, so that there would be no risk of denunciation of quite a large gathering from passers by. The assembled company would also sing *How Broad is my Homeland* and some Jewish song or other from which I only remember part of the chorus: '*Haver [comrade] Stalin! Haver Lenin! Ai-yai-yai-yai-ya-ya!*', which had a stirring ring to it. Music to the ears of any passing KGB officers.

After that little performance, the windows would be shut tight and there would be an abrupt change in the repertoire. Brun's wife would start singing and would be joined by the wife of Doctor Livshin. As a duo they would sing songs like *Mein shtetele Belts* (My Shtetl Belts), *A Yidishe mama* (A Yiddish Mama) or *Ofen pripechek brent* (In the stove a fire glows) and then *Lo mir ale in einem, in einem* (Let us all together now, all together...). The others would gradually start to join in, thinking back to the war. They would drink for those who had perished and for their parents.

MOTHER, FATHER AND LEAVING HOME

My mother was generally a gentle, diplomatic woman but that did not always apply when it came to me. I am all too grateful to her for that. As a small child she had considered me clever, beautiful and unusually talented when it came to ballet – yet I was to disappoint her. I stopped going to ballet lessons at the age of 8 after my bout of scarlet fever and by the age of 12 my graceful shape had gone. I was no longer the pretty little girl and, worst of all, my lips were starting to turn blue. It had happened before on occasions but Mother had managed to hide it or rather disguise it, saying to astonished friends and acquaintances that I had been eating piles of blueberries or cherries. What could she do in the winter though, when there were no berries around and I was keen to go out skating? Mother thought that I could choose a warmer past-time but blue lips did not worry me. All the girls out skating had rosy cheeks and were dancing on the ice with the boys, but I had blue lips and had only the girls who had been overlooked for company. Mother used to say that nothing could be done about it, that I was already turning into an old maid, a blue stocking. She would have to reconcile herself to it all.

My rating improved a little in the summer, but one year when I was 14 and lying on the beach in Palanga, I nearly died. My brother Solomon and mother's colleague started looking for medics there and then on the beach and forty minutes later I eventually came round. That incident became the talk of the villas where people from the Polytechnic and the Medical Institute were spending their holidays, if not the whole of Palanga. Mother had not been expecting any such embarrassment and the following year, instead of going to Palanga, we set off to Moscow armed with letters of recommendation for the luminaries among the capital's cardiologists and paediatricians. By then I had grown up a little more and was more attractive, which meant that our mother's cousin, Aunt Tamara, and her husband Eduard Kolmanovsky the composer (with whom we spent that summer in Moscow and at their *dacha* in Ruza) were at a loss to understand why a young girl, fit as a fiddle, was spending so much time visiting doctors.

The professors we went to were also baffled. In general the children in the waiting rooms were mostly weak and sad-looking, some of them with Down's syndrome, and I would stick out like a sore thumb. So much so that it was often assumed we were not patients at all. My mother would come away from those visits convinced that she would after all definitely be a grandmother with beautiful grandchildren and that all the heart murmurs would stop after my teens and disappear. In general she was advised to devote her loving care to her other children too.

They failed to convince Mother however and she used to pick up the slightest hint of blue whenever it appeared. That was when she decided to follow the Russian gardener Michurin's maxim: 'We cannot expect favours from Nature, so our task is to take them from her ourselves.' While in Moscow Mother bought some lip-gloss and rouge at the shop in the All-Union Theatrical Society, which she would apply discreetly before dispatching me to school. I used to cry, worrying that people would realise that I was wearing make-up and put me to shame. What would they think of me? That I was a good-time girl? Mother had decided that such an accusation would be a lesser evil than going to school as a pathetic figure, looking pale and sickly with blue lips.

At the end of the school year my straggly plaits were cut off and I had a dress made out of turquoise taffeta specially requested by our hunchbacked dressmaker, Nesya, from the relatives in America. I looked like the queen of the ball! Mother frowned as she looked at me: 'It's fine, but could have been better'. After that I set off with my father to a medical congress in Leningrad in a bright red suit with pleats at the back and a wide-cut collar in the latest fashion, ordered once again from Nesya our dressmaker, and high-heeled suede shoes, also made to measure. My father would set off to his congress in the morning and, after making up my eye-lashes so that I looked like a soulful cow, I would stroll up and down Nevskii Prospekt arousing wide-eyed curiosity among the passers-by. Father's colleagues also thought that I had grown into a striking and attractive young woman. That made me feel inestimably proud, but even that was not enough for Mother. She went on bewailing my situation – but at least less than before.

A year later I left for Moscow to study at the Foreign Languages Institute and, after a further twelve months, I married a Frenchman, Pierre, from the cultural mission of his embassy. Not blessed with a dowry or even a flat in Moscow, I was perfectly happy with how things were going, but not Mother. She started insisting that a year previously I had been a regular beauty, but now that could no longer be said of me at all. It was the same story every year when we met up again. The year before I had looked pretty, but now things were no longer the same. She would never let me relax and be satisfied with things as they were. Later, when I divorced, she commented that 25 was very young for a married woman but rather elderly for a bride.

Figure 28. Ariela as a student at the Institute of Foreign Languages in Moscow, 1959.

She would not allow me to wear glasses, although I was extremely short-sighted and could hardly see anything without them. She used to say: 'But what do you want to see? Let people see *you*. The one thing that's beautiful in your face that's your eyes and then you go and hide them.' Nor was I allowed to be round-shouldered. Mother would even remind me about that in her letters. On one occasion when I was visiting my parents, I was waiting for people to bring round a parcel for me to take to their relatives and came out to speak to them without putting smart clothes on first. Mother began pestering me and I remonstrated: 'What does it matter, they're not so special that I have to dress up for them?!' 'It doesn't matter who they are! What matters is who you are.' Mother was untiring in her efforts to 'train' me and almost succeeded. Thank you mother...

Father, on the other hand, was perfectly happy with my appearance. All he demanded was that make-up should not be too blatant and that I was in good health. But I shall always be grateful to my mother. I almost overcame my health problems thanks to her and stopped feeling inferior. She is lovingly remembered.

My father had been a handsome man in his youth: tall, thin with a spring in his step – and a good dancer. There was an air of innate elegance about him. He always used to wear a suit and tie, although he only had one suit, and it was not until I was much older that a second one appeared. I always thought he looked most impressive. So did many other women, regardless of their age. I had felt proud of him as a child and I felt important stepping out with him. When I was a young woman, I never felt put out when people thought we were a couple: indeed the one time when he visited me at the institute where I was a student, everyone assumed that he was my mature admirer. I felt incredibly proud. Father only began to look his age after he had fallen seriously ill at the age of 55.

He was very impulsive and hated any kind of dirty tricks, deception or cunning. He did not like it when people pretended to be what they were not. He never made a secret of his origins or his Jewishness. When I reached 16 and had left school, I went to the local militia office to be issued with an internal passport. A former patient of my father's was working in the passport section and she offered to do me a favour: 'Why don't I put you down as Lithuanian – it'll make life easier for you later on?' (The internal USSR passport included details of ethnicity.) I told her that I needed to go and talk it over with my parents and went to ask my father. Without a moment's hesitation he said: 'After the Ghetto and everything that you went through, could you do that?' I turned the offer down much to the amazement of the woman issuing passports. Father was a role model for us children. While it was Mother who worried about my outward appearance, Father was more concerned with our ideas and our health. He was put out seeing my face made up or if I used false eyelashes. Yet he was keen to draw me away from all that was grey and ordinary: he gave me books to read about great travellers and discoveries. He found people to teach me French and German. He would always find time for us and would drop by during the day to make sure that everything was all right, lie down for half an hour's rest and then hurry back to work again. On Sunday morning we would all – including the cat and the dog – climb into his bed.

Looking back now, it seems that Father was like a mother to us and Mother more like a father. Father was the one whom we used to ask for money. If something important needed doing he was also the one we would turn to. Half the town used to turn to him with requests although he was a surgeon and head of a large department. It was a model department which ran like clockwork, the best in the hospital. By then Father was earning good money, but money was something he never took an interest in for himself and often there would be very little left over for him. He might be using it to get hold of medicines for a little boy from the orphanage or for helping the Gravlin family repatriated from France to settle in – an illiterate mother with four children, one of whom was in Ben's class.

Father was extremely easy to deceive though and could be taken for a ride. His gullibility, as she saw it, used to incense our mother. He was far from being a fool though. Father simply used to take people on trust. Every time they deceived him, he got upset like a young schoolboy. He was a good doctor and a well-known one. One of the methods he used for nasal sinus surgery is even described in the Greater Soviet Medical Encyclopaedia. Yet it took him a long time to write his doctorate. But there were four devoted children to show for it all. He was always there for us, our 'green light', right up till the time he left Lithuania.

DISCHARGED AND EXPELLED

By 1961 we were living comfortably. I had also married Pierre. That summer, a few weeks before the beginning of the new academic year, we crossed the boulevard where we lived to Moscow Hospital No.24 and I was admitted with acute lower abdominal pain. On admission the doctors thought that there was also something seriously wrong with my heart.

I was left there in a ward for sixteen people. My husband took fright when he saw it and the next day the doctor from the French Embassy appeared there. His visit was followed by visits from other French people I knew, including the commercial attaché, whose father had been France's ambassador to Lithuania before the War. Friends of my husband from the cultural mission also came to see me, and I felt that it was not so much how I was feeling that interested them, as my surroundings. It was highly unlikely that they would have had the chance to see inside a district Soviet hospital in 1961.

There was great consternation in my part of the hospital. Without waiting for the results of my tests they decided to operate under local rather than general anaesthetic, and removed a cyst. They discharged me immediately after my operation, much to the horror of my foreign visitors. I could hardly stand. By then my husband had to return to France without me when his visa had run out.

Just after my husband had flown home, I was called to the offices of the District Committee of the Komsomol (Soviet youth organisation), where a very kind, good-looking young man with blue eyes and an open face asked me: 'What a pretty girl you are. Do you really mean to say there aren't enough Russian lads here for you? What do you need that capitalist French fellow for?' I muttered something to the effect that he had left-wing views but it made no difference. An unscheduled meeting of my branch of the Komsomol was called. The students in my year didn't have much idea of what advice from 'senior comrades' implied – neither did they respond by expelling me. They merely issued a reprimand. I no longer recall what for. After that the Party organization convened a Komsomol meeting for the whole Institute and I was expelled on grounds of 'moral instability'. I went home in a state of despair, not even capable of explaining properly to my father, who had come down from Kaunas to see what had happened. He thought that the stitching from my operation must have burst. When he learnt what had really happened, he was furious: 'How could you frighten your father like that? Anyone would think you'd had your throat cut!'

THE BAKULEV HEART INSTITUTE

I was then referred to Dr Burakovsky, a specialist in children's heart defects at the Bakulev Institute. I did not check into that hospital straightaway, there was no time. First I waited till my husband had left and then I prepared all my documents for my own trip to Paris. Only after all that did I agree to my parents' request that I should go and find out what kind of heart defect I was suffering from. The building gleamed, everything in it was new, with only two or three patients to a ward. Vladimir Burakovsky was a rising star in children's cardiac surgery and all the diagnostic equipment purchased by the Soviet Union was delivered to him.

In April 1959 (at the height of Cold War) a team of doctors from London's Hammersmith Hospital had come to set up the equipment and brought with them the 'heart-lung machine' developed by Denis Melrose, and to teach our people how to use it. These wonder doctors demonstrated cardiac catheterisation – where the heart was examined by inserting a tube through the arteries. They also demonstrated the latest techniques in open-heart surgery and we had learned about their pioneering work, reading about them in the newspaper. The patients in the wards had enormous scars on their arms from catheterisation. The rib cages of the child patients were swollen after they'd been sawed through for their operations, not all of which were successful. I started to feel scared, my mother even more so. She decided wisely that cardiac catheterisation was not going to cure me and, if it was to prove necessary, then I could have it done in London by those same English doctors. After all, she reminded me, they had more experience and there was no urgent hurry for a diagnosis. But they gave us two possibilities: one operable and the other not. So I left for Paris to join my husband with a heart 'riddle'.

PARIS

I don't remember anything about packing. My parents prepared a suitcase full of linen: tablecloths, duvet-covers and pillow-cases. I stamped my foot, shouting that I refused to take all that clutter to Paris, that people would laugh at me, because nobody there needed things like that. Father, who had spent his student years in France, calmed me down, saying: 'All right then … What you don't need, you can bring back: we can make good use of it.'

There was always some money in the desk drawer and whoever had need of money could take some. When it ran out, occasionally we used to borrow from the home-help. Yet it turned out that we did not have enough for my send off to Paris and we borrowed from my uncle and aunt, who by then had returned from the camps. They were better organised by then and had managed to build some savings.

Figure 29. Just before setting off to Paris, December 1960.

The whole family accompanied me as far as the border station Brest-Litovsk. It was the first and only time in my life that I saw my father's tears. He was the first to cry, and then everybody else joined in, including the conductresses on the train and the woman from customs; they must have felt sorry for my family left behind, wondering if we would ever meet again. She allowed all those seeing me off to stay in the coach until it was time for the train to leave. That was rare for those days.

The journey to Paris lasted more than two days but already when we reached Berlin I was able to see the difference between the two worlds. We approached the solid wall dividing off East Berlin. Everything was grey and deserted, and border-guards were running up and down the train with Alsatians. Meanwhile, in West Berlin I saw a Christmas tree right in the station. There were decorations and advertisements everywhere and one could sense the atmosphere of the lead-up to Christmas with people running around bare-headed despite the frosty weather.

I was met at the Gare du Nord by my husband and his cousin, and we set off straightaway to celebrate Christmas with the cousin's family. It was unusually cold in Paris that year and my heavy tweed coat with its thick quilted lining and fox-fur collar, complete with matching hat didn't look ridiculous, although in France, it would only have been possible to see that amount of fur in Hollywood films. I was definitely the main attraction of that Christmas gathering, distributing the presents I had brought: caviar and vodka.

My husband's cousin had recently been sent back wounded from the war in Algeria. I was very surprised to see how within a single family at holiday time people could argue so heatedly. It seemed that a fight might break out at any moment over whether it was legitimate for France to be ruling Algeria. 'You're a reactionary, a fascist!' shouted the cousin.' 'You're an enemy of France!' shouted the head of the household at his son, almost foaming at the mouth by this time. It all ended, however, with a Christmas turkey and a wonderful chocolate 'Bûche de Noël' followed by goodbye kisses.

On the evening of the next day we set off to the Café Flore. I assumed that this watering-hole of the existentialists, and one of the most famous cafés in the world, was typical, that they were all like that. The place was full of its very colourful characters: elderly men with long hair, crumpled faces and enormous bags under their eyes, not to mention all the women talking loudly and smoking. People there turned out to be well-known writers, musicians and journalists. They were greeting and embracing, wishing one another a happy Christmas. That same evening my husband introduced me to a young Russian girl, Nelly Cournot, the pretty wife of a well-known journalist. So straight after arriving in Paris I made a friend. A friend for life.

Just before New Year my husband and I travelled by car to Nantes where his parents lived. It was a long journey and -12°C when we arrived. Everyone was talking about those who'd got caught in the snow. Some had died from the cold or been stranded without heating. My husband's family had been waiting impatiently to meet me. They'd apparently been expecting a plump woman with small feet, as previously I had sent them my measurements which they'd wanted so they could buy me a wedding dress. I had not known that there was a difference of four sizes between Russian and French dress sizes, and two sizes for shoes. They heaved a sigh of relief when I took off my enormous tweed coat.

During the week before my arrival, my husband's relatives had been seeking advice from their priest. How should they respond? Should they accept me? Not only was I from the Soviet Union, but was Jewish. They were devout Catholics and, what was more, the family had lost half its money in bonds in pre-revolution Russia. The priest permitted them to receive me and advised them to be kind. After all I had arrived from that 'terrible' country and they should show me compassion. So they started to take care of me and spoil me. Everyone had been helping to prepare for the New Year celebrations, and I could have had no idea at that stage that a lunch starting at one o'clock in the afternoon could last until well into the night – that lunch would turn into afternoon tea and then dinner. Neither did I know that French people were capable of remembering at New Year precisely what they had eaten at the same occasion the previous year. People were talking about nothing but food.

My husband had two sisters. One of them, Germaine, had become a nun and on New Year's Day we went to a Dominican convent to visit her. I was wearing my thick winter outfit and she came out to meet us in a long black habit, with nothing but clogs on her bare feet. I felt frozen standing there in that cold monastery in my winter coat with its quilted lining, so I had no idea how she survived. The nuns used to spend eight hours of each day at prayer, another eight hours working and eight asleep in their unheated cells. Germaine fell seriously ill and had to leave the convent. My husband's younger sister was still a school-girl and regarded me as a thief who'd stolen away her older brother. In general, however, the family was well-disposed towards me, even though marrying a woman from the Soviet Union had robbed him of the chance to become a diplomat. He also had to leave the cultural mission, despite graduating from the Institut des Études Politiques with a virtually flawless command of Russian and Czech.

HAMMERSMITH HOSPITAL

My heart was still a riddle. Six month later when the summer was nearly upon us, Father's brother, Uncle Arno, who lived in Manchester, invited me to stay. He then arranged and accompanied me to a consultation in Hammersmith Hospital, London. I arrived in May 1962 to seek a diagnosis from the experts. I could have seen exactly the same kind of specialists in Paris of course, I spoke French and had social insurance, but for me and my family, only the English doctors who'd visited the Bakulev Institute in Moscow would do. We sat quietly in a queue, waiting to be called to see Professor Melrose, head of the team. Finally a modest-looking young man quietly ushered us in: 'Please come through'. I looked at him rather condescendingly, wondering who this puny young lad might be. I replied to him in French, saying that I was waiting to see Professor Melrose. 'That's me', he replied. My uncle was not translating very well and they called in a Yugoslav trainee doctor.

Then they admitted me to the Hammersmith Hospital and we were offered the same diagnostic tests as in Moscow. I was to have a catheterisation. The ward was enormous, just like Moscow's Hospital No.24, but even larger, more like a hall. The only difference was that the bed of each patient could be divided off from the rest of the ward by screens. It was in that ward that I got to know other young people using gestures and, if I found someone who could speak it – French. There was a door in the wall of the ward leading on to a huge terrace. A few hours before the catheterization was carried out, I was injected with a tranquillizer. Out on the terrace someone had put on a tape recorder, and the 'walking wounded' began dancing the twist. Despite my injection I ran out to join them. What an opportunity! It would be great fun to learn to dance the twist! I didn't notice the nurse and my consultant, Dr Arthur Holman, coming out to find me. They couldn't believe their eyes when they saw me dancing wildly with the others. Dr Holman decided that you would probably only find patients like that in Russia. The procedure was unpleasant. The whole team commented on the results, convinced that I didn't understand what they were saying. I understood enough to know that what they had found was the second, inoperable situation. I began to sob. Melrose left altogether, saying that they should finish the procedure without him. The Yugoslav doctor began reassuring me in his poor Russian, saying that nothing was definite. That they needed to complete the catheterisation. I was eventually taken back on to the ward, worn out and red-eyed. The screens were pulled round my bed and I fell asleep.

When I woke up, Dr Holman was standing next to the bed with a nurse, asking very kindly how I felt and whether I wanted a drink. 'Perhaps I could have some juice?' By that time supper was being handed out to the other patients. I asked what they were being given as it smelt so nice. It was roast beef and vegetables and I asked: 'Can I have the same as the others, I don't need the juice'. Their eyes almost feel out of their head in surprise. So, Russian patients recovered from their anaesthetics like lightning too? Uncle Arno went back to Manchester and I remained alone in the hospital, in a city where I didn't know a soul and could not speak the language. After his visit to Moscow, Dr Holman had worked hard at his Russian, and sent his Russian teacher to see me every day. She was a remarkable woman, an émigré of the 'first wave', who spoke with a St Petersburg accent. I was very grateful to them, and learned that Dr Holman remembered me till the end of his days. When I saw him years later, he was already a senior consultant working at the University College Hospital (UCH), but I always went to him for consultations. On the desk in his office there was a wooden pyramid-shaped model of the Kremlin, of the kind that used to be sold in Moscow in the 'Children's World' department store. I commented on it and when he retired, he sent it to me as a present.

Figure 30. First summer in France.

I returned to Paris feeling very sad. There was to be no operation and I had to make do with things as they were. A twist of fate brought me back to Professor Melrose. In 1977 my brother Solomon was training in the Hammersmith Hospital and met him while he was there. It turned out that Professor Melrose remembered the girl from Russia from among the hundreds of his patients: he was glad to learn that I was still alive and said that he would like to see me. I have always had the warmest memories of those doctors who looked after me so well and never charged a penny. I went to see him the next time I came to London. The professor had been expecting to see a pale and wan young person. But I took him completely by surprise. He had not thought that I would survive, let alone turn into an energetic and attractive woman. He told me that immediately after the catheterisation he'd written to my parents saying that, in his opinion, I did not have much longer to live and that it would be best if they could be at my side during the difficult times. Uncle Arno had also written to my father to say that my days were numbered and that operating would be out of the question even in America, where Father's second brother, Uncle Leon, worked as a doctor. Father tried to persuade me to come home, but I chose to stay in Paris.

DISASTERS STRIKE

Then my husband left me for somebody else. I also failed all my exams at the university, and would have to take them again in the autumn. On top of all that, one unbearably hot Friday evening, when all the Parisians seemed to have left town for the weekend – I walked home to find the *concierge* waiting for me: 'There's been a fire'. The door had been broken down, the walls were covered in soot and water stains, and there was no light in the corridor. In the bedroom there was a burnt blanket and burnt feathers everywhere. The dressing-table was burnt and the mirror was covered with a black film. There was nobody who could give me a shoulder to cry on.

My only close friend, Nelly, had gone away for a few days and on Saturday I was due to receive my first-ever language student – Dr Morin, a cardiologist with an interest in Russian. Nelly had found him so that I should not die of hunger. I was unable to contact him to change the time however, as the *concierge* warned me that, until the insurers came on Monday, I should not touch anything, not even change the lock. The next day, at six in the evening, sitting in my soot-stained flat with a door that would not shut, and covered in soot myself, my student appeared. I tried to explain and put him off, but he walked further into the flat in his elegant pale-coloured suit, catching sight of the layer of soot on the dining room table and chairs. I picked up a clean towel to wipe it away, but only made things worse. He behaved as if he was deaf to everything I said, brought out a neat file and Dictaphone and sat down. He'd already been learning Russian for several years, but was keen to improve. I thought he must be mad. Yet the lesson lasted two hours – one hour on grammar and the second devoted to translating texts and conversation. I had never in my life seen such an industrious and well-organised pupil. After the lesson he put money on the table, more – thank God – than I had expected.

We arranged to meet again the following week, and I promised that by then the flat would have been cleaned up. He paid no attention, asking 'What are you going to eat?' I muttered something about having some food but he was persistent: 'Where?' he said. 'Over there in the fridge and the cupboard.' He went into the kitchen, finding no food. 'Off we go, I'll feed you in a restaurant.' 'I won't be going anywhere. I'm covered in black and my face is filthy. How could you imagine doing any such thing? Anyway, I'm not hungry.' 'You need to eat', he went on, trying to persuade me, but I refused to give in. I was about to collapse after those two hours with him. In the end he went down to the neighbourhood shop and asked me to set two places. He put down some pieces of clean paper bearing his official doctor's stamp and we ate at the table out of boxes.

A week later everything, including myself, was cleaned up. As on the previous occasion the cardiologist brought out his file and Dictaphone, took his two-hour lesson, paid the same amount of money, and then suggested we should go to a restaurant and have a look at his new car. It turned out that apart from the Russian language he also had a passion for sports cars. 'I've only just fetched it from the garage, you will be my first passenger.' I did not protest. Down in the street stood a shining beauty of a Lancia. All the customers in the café on the ground floor of our building were craning their necks to have a better look at the car and at me. At least they now had something new to talk about. In Paris in my little patch, life was like a village: everybody knew everything. On the third Saturday, early in the morning, my husband turned up. The 'news' had reached him. He sat there during the whole lesson with my student, but in another room. After that he did not go out – either at the weekends or during the week. It would appear that he had taken some leave and that his new girlfriend had disappeared forever. Sitting around on my own in that terrible charred flat was more than I could bear. I rang up some of the friends I had met at the very beginning of my sojourn in Paris. So we went on living a Moscow life, going out to a Russian cabaret almost every evening. That was how my husband tried to blow away any last trace of my homesickness. We spent almost all his money.

THE NOVI CABARET

At the 'Novi' cabaret I made the acquaintance of a couple: the husband was a bass singer and his wife used to sing folk songs and *chastushki* – topical jingles. They'd both ended up in Paris after some very hard times in various parts of Europe. The wife had been driven out to Germany when little more than a child and the husband had been a POW. The wife would sometimes visit her family in the Soviet Union, but the husband never went there and never talked about his past. They lived in a cul-de-sac not far from the Avenue Victor Hugo in a semi-basement in a very bourgeois apartment building. They used to get home when it was almost morning and get up again at three or four o'clock in the afternoon – and then get back to work after a few hours at home. When they found out I was in trouble, they invited me back to their place and took me to the cabaret the next evening. The wife took me under her wing and used to comfort me saying: 'Once you've passed your exams, there'll be no need to worry about your Frenchman. Push him out of your life, he'll be no great loss. A man like that is not what you need. We'll find you another one.'

They'd been together for a long time. He was enormously tall and strong and looked like a bass singer. If life had turned out differently for him, he would probably have known fame and fortune. His wife, on the other hand, was tiny and frail and didn't appear to be in good health. When she was in pain, he'd carry her from room to room. But once evening came, they would be busy in their separate parts of the cabaret, hardly noticing each other. She was a lively dancer, refusing to give in to pain. On stage she looked like a young girl, yet up close you could see she was a middle-aged woman who'd had some difficult times. 'Why don't you watch us at the cabaret? You haven't got anything to do or anywhere else to go.' I agreed, and they sat me down in a corner, ordering tea and cakes. The owners recognized me, or pretended to, as I had been there two or three times with my husband. I sat there almost the whole evening, my friends taking it in turns to come over to talk to me.

When it was nearly closing time, some of their customers at one of the other tables asked a dancer who the person was they kept fussing over. The dancer explained that I had recently arrived from the Soviet Union after marrying a Frenchman and that I had problems. They invited me to their table to have a meal with them. I was led over, wearing my light short dress, totally unsuitable for a cabaret of that era. I was given a chair next to Volodya Polyakov, a guitar player specialising in gypsy songs, brother of the well-known modernist painter, Serge Polyakov. They asked what they should order for me. I felt embarrassed and began muttering that I'd already had my dinner. They then offered me a drink: 'Champagne, vodka?' 'No, thank you, I've already had some tea.' At that Volodya Polyakov hissed at me: 'If you don't want to eat, and don't drink, don't stop others.' 'A glass of champagne for the lady! Pink champagne!' A new bottle was opened. There was already a good deal of champagne on the table, but none of the pink variety. In those days such a bottle would cost 800 francs, and for each bottle opened the *artiste* performing at the time would get 10 per cent. On that particular evening it all went Vladimir's (Volodia's) way. Then they ordered caviar for me, which I did not even look at.

My new friends took me back to their flat in the small hours, and I spent the rest of the night and the following morning with them, returning with them to the 'Novi' when evening came. It was only a few days before the cabaret shut down for the summer season. It was noisy, and I was invited to go over and sit with their guests. Once again I was offered food and drink. They used to tell the customers I was from Moscow, and people would be amazed and start asking questions, plying me with food and drink. Once more I earned a percentage, but this time my 'patron' the dancer accepted them. I was young and shy. Then the owner of the cabaret asked. 'Come round again after the summer. By the way, can you sing?' 'No, not really.' 'Not at all?' 'Well a little...' 'And dance?' 'No, it exhausts me.' Back in the past I trained at the musical theatre, but only for a short time, when I was still a child. There was amateur singing and dancing at school. I went to lessons at the Isadora Duncan School as well, but dancing made me very tired.' 'All right, come back in the autumn. And buy yourself a nice dress.' Evidently I looked out of place in my modest outfit against the background of the purple velvet chairs and couches, the candles and the waiters dressed in their red Russian shirts; I was virtually invisible in those settings.

In July I went away with my husband to the family home in the Vendée. He had told his parents a little about his gallivanting, so they were bending over backwards to please me, to earn forgiveness for his sins. His mother would start cooking early every morning. First there was breakfast with warm croissants, which would be served to me in bed because of my health. Immediately after that she would start working on lunch. By midday I would come crawling out of bed in a lace night-dress and a light dressing-gown, which had been bought in the not-very-expensive department store 'Marks and Spencers' by my aunt in England. They called me 'Madame de Pompadour'. We would all set off to Sables d'Olonnes at the seaside every day as I loved swimming and sun-bathing. Meanwhile my mother-in-law would continue cooking. By this time the whole day's timetable had changed. They only began to eat when we came back from the beach. To everyone's great relief this only lasted a month.

In the course of that month my husband's sister, Germaine the nun, fell ill with TB and she had to decide whether to leave the convent or not. If she stayed, she could be an invalid for life or even die. It was decided by everyone at a family council that her health was a sufficient reason for her to abandon her total commitment to the service of the Lord. It was seen as a disgrace to choose the monastic way of life and then to renounce it. But her illness was getting worse, and before she took her final vows it was as if the family was in mourning. Yet it was shame in front of their neighbours. Two years later she gave birth to the child of a passing black sailor. I felt truly sorry for her. Bringing up a black child of an unidentified father in provincial Nantes in the 1960s was a dreadful prospect. By that time though, I was no longer in touch with her.

After the summer holidays I went back to the 'Novi' cabaret in a new dress: black, long and tight-fitting and with a low-cut oval neck. I had bought it with my friend Nelly at the boutique of the magazine *Elle*. It was cheap and stylish, and in my new dress and false eyelashes I now stood out. The old owner of the establishment, Monsieur Novsky, who'd been a young officer in the White Russian army, and his wife – an imposing woman with expensive jewellery, who was always stressing her

high-class, aristocratic origins which nobody could verify –both encouraged me. 'All right, Mademoiselle, you shall sing, but in the chorus'. The
chorus consisted of ten people, not counting the orchestra. There wasn't
a stage in the real sense of the word and all the entertainment went on in
a very small space next to the guests' tables. I started singing the song
'*Polyushko, pole, polyushko shirokoye pole...*' in my thin falsetto voice
(this appeared in English under various titles including 'The Cossack
Patrol' and 'Cavalry of the Steppes'. A literal translation of the Russian
opening line would be: 'Field, my field, my wide field...'). After that the
rest of the chorus joined in and my modest efforts no longer mattered.

By the middle of the evening customers started inviting performers
to their tables – Volodya with his famous guitar, the singers Valentin
and Alexei Dmitrievich. People would come specially to hear them, to
have a good time, enjoy the company and spend money. Many Paris
celebrities used to come along: Yves Montand with Simone Signoret,
Alain Delon, Romy Schneider – and Brigitte Bardot. Excited French
customers would throw empty champagne glasses over their shoulders
and smash them, convinced this was an obligatory Russian custom.
The best customers though were the American Jews with Russian
roots. They were the ones suffering from real nostalgia and I appeared
to bring out their fatherly feelings. Sometimes they would come along
a number of times during their visit to Paris – sometimes with their
stout wives and sometimes with their twittering girlfriends. There
would also be Russians who'd stayed on in the West after the War and
who'd made their fortune in Latin American countries. I remember a
Vladimir Ivanovich with his hard yet watery gaze, an enormous diamond ring and beautiful wife Anna, the daughter of pre-war White
Russian émigrés. Anna's parents had no money at all, so Anna married him. She always wore earrings with nut-sized diamonds and a
diamond necklace. If Turgenev's Gerasim had hung all of that round
Mumu's neck instead of the stone, she'd have drowned without question (Mumu was a title of a short story by Ivan Turgenev about a serf
and his dog). Vladimir Ivanovich would take his resplendent wife to
society balls. Everyone would gasp. When the couple went home
again, he would remove all the diamonds and lock them away in his
safe. Sometimes he would get drunk and hit her in a rage; anyone, even
an inert pillar, could arouse his jealousy. Anna told me this when we
were sitting on our own in a corner in deep arm-chairs.

They had to train me, so that I could at least manage to sing something when I was sitting at a table. I was horribly out of tune. The only thing that I could manage was a song of Bulat Okudzhava's *Vy slyshite, grokhochut sapogi* [D'you hear them, the boots thundering by']. I used to sing that with such feeling that the guests would have tears in their eyes and start smiling. I also knew a song by my uncle Eduard Kolmanovsky (the husband of my mother's cousin) *Tishina* [Calm], which I had heard hundreds of times. They called out the band-leader and he was duly given instructions: 'Mikhail, you need to work with Ariela, so that she can at least sing her *Tishina* in tune and then something else as well. It doesn't need to be very much.' The results were middle-of-the-road, but I could now manage to sing while sitting at a table, especially if Vladimir accompanied me. I was offered money for my performances, although I didn't collect it myself. The musicians thought I was not up to it as it made me feel awkward and embarrassed. Nobody ever asked me for my opinion on the subject.

People started inviting me to enjoy oysters with them in the all-night restaurants of Les Halles or Montmartre, after the cabaret closed. Especially Menier, the King of *chocolatiers*. The Russian couple who had taken me under their wing used to drag me along too. We would eat and drink till morning with whoever had invited us, paying for everything. I would be feeling ill and over tired by this time, and would be taking the drug Valocordin for my heart, so I ate lemon to stop me smelling like a pharmacy. I became skilled at pushing my full glass towards my neighbour, at swapping my full glass with an empty one and working out whether a restaurant customer was mean or generous from the way he brought out his wallet. Before long though, I started taking a taxi home. The doorman, Prince Orlov, used to order the taxis for me. He felt very sympathetic, because we both had heart problems. And he liked the kind of Valocordin I used to take. Most of the taxi drivers who came to fetch me were elderly tired Russians, who looked at me disapprovingly, frowning when they caught the 'pharmacy' smell, 'That's not the right place for you, young lady. It'll be the death of you'.

On 7 November 1962 for the October Revolution Holiday I was due to travel as part of an organised tourist group to Moscow to meet up with my parents. I made careful preparations and when the cabaret guests heard about it, they started giving me money to buy presents for my relatives. I was reluctant to take it, but I was persuaded: 'You're going to your parents. They're letting you in. Buy presents for everyone.' At that time the cabaret was visited by an American, who everyone seemed to be on good terms with. When he came across a woman from the Soviet Union, he started showing interest. He invited me over to America and gave me his card. He was a sugar-baron by the name of Tereshchenko. When he learnt that I was going back to the USSR he asked me to pass on a considerable sum of money to his relatives. The cabaret was also visited by Solomon a fur-baron, who wanted to give me a present of a fur coat for my trip, but I did not collect it. I encountered him a second time ten years later, but in very different circumstances. He insisted that he could remember how I used to dance. But I explained to him that I did not dance because, as he was well aware, it made me too tired. Yet he insisted: 'You danced very well, so don't argue.' We were both trying hard to remember. Then I got it. On one occasion the Russian dancer had fallen sick and some customers had turned up who'd come specially to see her dance to the music of *Ekh, polnym- polna moya korobochka* (An old Russian song about a pedlar selling his wares: 'My try tray is full, I play my trade. Here is chintz and fine brocade...'.). I had to take her place as there was nobody else available. Madame Novskaya was around 65 and the other woman sang well, but was fat and awkward. I was dressed up in the real dancer's costume, took some Valocordin and went on. Everything was OK, and I managed to keep going to the end.

I started practicing conscientiously and my student cardiologist friend – to who I taught Russian – brought along an enormous tape recorder, a novelty in those days. Nelly and I played and practiced music on it like two monkeys, and listened to what we recorded. Nelly said I had made noticeable progress. My appearance on the scene, although it had been low-key, spoilt the atmosphere in the cabaret. The guests started to notice me: although I was no great singer or Russian beauty, I was a young student from the USSR and this intrigued them. People started giving me more money, even though I didn't ask for it. There was a woman of about 45 working there who had a child to bring up. She sang far better than I did but her earnings began to shrink. Things could not go on like this. My cardiologist friend, who I used to invite to the cabaret, thought that things would soon come to a head. He advised me to be on my way using imminent exams as an excuse. I left in the spring.

DO I STAY OR GO?

Meanwhile I was getting on with my life and my studies in Paris, getting to know new people and unaware of what 'bright future' was in store for me. Things were difficult at first and then started becoming more and more interesting. I became very friendly with Nelly Cournot, Elena Cardenas and their husbands who introduced me to the gallery-owner Edouard Loeb and his photographer sister, Denise Colomb. I came to know Max Ernst and the writer Pierre Daninos – in short, the Paris artistic elite. I did have collapses due to my heart problems but not often enough to make my life really difficult. My Paris friends divided into two 'camps': some felt that I ought to go back to the USSR, others thought I should stay in France. My friend Nelly even went to the Soviet Embassy, showed the people there the letters from my doctor and, appealing to their humanity, asked them to give me a permit for permanent residence in the USSR. Lena, on the other hand, did not understand why I should go back.

The application for a visa was under consideration for eighteen months. Over that period I'd settled in France and had no urge to go anywhere any more, or for only a month at the most. My mother realised that it was a young girl who had left home, while after six years it was an adult with very different tastes and habits who would be coming back. She wrote to convey all this to me albeit indirectly: 'Darling daughter! ... I obtained a holiday voucher for the sanatorium in Druskeniki ... I have bought myself a chintz house-coat to go down to take the waters in and almost everyone has similar one. You would definitely like them...' Father, meanwhile, wanted me back home, but said that if I wanted to go back to France again, they would not stand in my way. He didn't realise that if I used a visa of the kind planned,

Figure 31. Ariela in Paris in the 1960s

I'd be obliged to apply for the exit visa just as I had the first time, need-ing a new invitation from my husband. He'd been called up for his military service, which all university graduates had to complete before they were 30. He was also undecided about what to do. Summer was about to begin and I had a choice: go and spend the holidays with my friend Lena and her family in Carrara or to visit my parents. I threw a coin. Heads or tails? It turned out that I was going. 'I'll be coming back after the summer anyway', I thought to myself.

While I'd been thinking things over, everyone had left for their sum-mer holiday. The only people who came to see me off were my uncle and the cardiologist, who turned up just before the train left. The train stopped at Brest-Litovsk while the wheels were being changed for the wide-gauge track. That's where Mother came to meet me. She'd bought a ticket in the same sleeping compartment and we were due to travel on together to Moscow. Yet I was not allowed into Moscow. Because the invitation had been from my parents, I had to travel to their place of residence. That was the first unexpected shock. I had no choice. We turned up in Kaunas with two suitcases, a box of French prunes and cracker biscuits, neither obtainable in the USSR. It wasn't clear what was I going to do in Kaunas. I decided to take a holiday in

Sochi, but I could not travel there either, unless I handed in my passport for foreign travel in exchange for an internal one (an essential identity document). So that is what I did. I turned up in Moscow, but my relatives there gave me a rather muted reception, not understanding why I had come back. My former friend and landlady, Lydia Pavlovna Lezhneva (who did translations from Russian into French and at the time was working on a book about Cézanne), took me in. I was able to help her a little with the translation, but this could not be a long-term arrangement as I had no registration in Moscow. I never got as far as Sochi and returned to Kaunas to prepare for my return journey to Paris. But it turned out that my visa was for permanent residence in the USSR! 'But I'm married', I protested. 'Get your husband to send you an invitation and we can start the process all over again', was the officials' response.

My husband was cross that I had left for the USSR before he was demobbed and did not reply. He'd gone back to his former girl-friend who was ten years older than he was. She was also pregnant, so my return definitely did not fit her plans. Nelly and our friend Edouard went to see my husband and explained to him that I would not be making any demands on him, all I needed was an invitation. That proved not to have been the most diplomatic approach. He immediately filed for divorce, with me cited as the guilty party. It was I, after all, who had walked out of the marital home. The divorce was granted, and I was high and dry in the USSR for the next seven years.

BACK IN THE USSR

It was all too clear. I was not going to be able to return to France that easily. I needed to reinstate myself at the University, otherwise any chance of seeing Moscow would go up in smoke. It would be as well to do it by the beginning of the academic year. The Dean – one-eyed Alexeyev – was not prepared to see me, saying that he did not want internal enemies at the Institute, that I had learnt French by now anyway, and that I would have a bad influence on the other students. 'Why?' I asked. The Rector, Sidorov, who'd previously been in the secret service, explained 'You look different'. 'I think I'm modestly dressed'. 'Whether modestly or not, your appearance is non-Soviet'. Indeed, my boats seemed well and truly burnt. 'What has my appearance got to do with it? And what's non-Soviet about it?'

I did not have to think back further than to the other first year students in my previous group before I left for Paris. Apart from Liza Muravyova, who had been repatriated from France with her parents, and myself, there had been three 'followers of fashion' studying with us in the old days: two of them offspring of the well-heeled and powerful – Natasha Likhachova, grand-daughter of the director of the Likhachov automobile plant, and Lidia Timofeyeva, daughter of some kind of attaché in Switzerland. The only true representative of the people had been Lidia Safronova, who used to struggle to keep up with the others. Those two were interested, above all, in diamonds. They used to bring out their sparklers in break-time and start swapping or selling them. Liza Muravyova and I did not feel we were part of their set. Liza was much more interesting with her knowledge of the poet Mallarmé. She'd compare him with Victor Hugo, and explaining why Mallarmé was the better poet. Her opinions seemed to interest the boys in our extremely advanced group that year. We were a strange mixture: brainy fashion addicts. The boys had been pupils in a French special school and had an excellent command of the language, but had not been taken on for inter-preters' courses either because they had poor eye-sight or because their political credentials on the application form had not been up to scratch. (At the Foreign Languages Institute there were two faculties: the presti-gious one for interpreters and another for language teachers.) They also preferred Liza with her aristocratic beauty and intellect to the 'Babettes' (this was the name used for those who imitated Brigitte Bardot's hair-style which had become famous after the film *Babette goes off to War!* had been released in Russia). I was on friendly terms with those boys until I married. Anyway, despite my promising past as a student it was no longer advisable to have anything to do with me. However the other girls started quietly offering me the chance to buy diamonds. What did I need them for? After all that, how could people possibly say I was not modest and might have a bad influence on other students!

Protesting wasn't going to get me anywhere, and I realised by now that the Rector might even admire me in my hand-tailored little muslin dress, but that would not change anything. They were not going to take me back. So I went to Father, our 'green light' in any situation. He went to see the First Secretary of the City Committee of the Party in Kaunas – Narkevich. He had saved the life of her only daughter, born when she was no longer in her first youth, and Secretary Narkevich was prepared to do anything for him. Various telephone calls were made, even to KGB people, but by this time the academic year had already begun and there was nothing left for me to do but accept a place in the external students' department and go out and find some work. I could only obtain regis-tration to live in Moscow for one or two months, to cover the time I would be preparing for and actually taking exams. I had no plans to leave for anywhere just yet though, but Lydia Pavlovna, from whom I had rented accommodation in the past, was about to rent out a room to jour-nalist Vladimir Posner and his new wife – far more promising tenants and able to pay their rent. I turned to another acquaintance, the widow of the well-known lawyer by the name of Barsky. She was a woman on her own who'd moved out of her own flat into a room in a communal one because she was afraid of being by herself when she was old. She tried to register me with the right to live in Moscow as her official ward, but the request was turned down. The neighbours had started giving her strange looks. Staying in Moscow was starting to look problematic.

KAUNAS AND MOSCOW

I left for Kaunas, since by the exam season in Moscow, I needed to have acquired a form from my place of work. Father found me a position as a French teacher at the Agricultural College. It was outside Kaunas in Aleksotai, where Father had, in the Ghetto days, dismantled the planes and lorries known as *Stalintsy*. I had to travel a long way on a rickety old bus. French, I thought, was exactly what those future agronomists from peasant families needed! But I did manage to attract their attention. They now had a young teacher, rumoured to have turned up from Paris, wearing interesting clothes. At any rate, the marks of the students in my group improved considerably. Meanwhile I was going out of my mind. In order to fall asleep at night I would surreptitiously drink Father's reserves of home-made apple wine. After all nobody else drank it - or counted the number of bottles left. But eventually, the exam season arrived and I was able to rent a room from Lydia Pavlovna in Moscow for the whole summer. She was going to a sanatorium and her other tenants had been allocated a flat of their own. What luck! An individual flat in a block reserved for writers in Lavrushinskii Lane! Wonderful.

Everyone was keen to come and visit me in a flat like that. There was a whole study-library full of works that had once belonged to the *Smenovekhovets* Lezhnev and all the books put out by 'Akademia' publishers. The *Smenovekhovets* were supporters of the views advocated in the émigré publication *Smena vekh* (Change of Landmarks) – a collection of six essays (1921), which appealed to the authors' fellow émigrés to revise their earlier attitudes to the 1917 Revolution, Bolshevism and the Soviet authorities, cease armed struggle against them and start cooperating with them. There were books by the poets Khlebnikov, Akhmatova and Kruchenykh and I generously handed them out to those who wanted to read them. Some went missing and I had no idea who to blame. Fortunately, Lydia Pavlovna didn't notice. My friend, Janna, a model who I'd known for years and introduced to a Frenchman (who had *not* married her), found me a job in a clothes designer's office, where I was to model new creations. I hardly had time to cope with my various commitments, so between shows I went to lessons at the Institute with my hair in curlers concealed under a plastic cap. In Moscow that would be seen as just another hair-style, even a fashionable one. Occasionally I'd have to pick up a false eyelash that had come adrift. One of our teachers – Aleshnikova – was very fond of me, despite me always turning up late. She used to comment without the slightest hint of malice: 'Well, at least she's turned up. Our star has appeared: we can start the test'. She knew about my situation and advised me to do all I could to register as resident in Moscow. She promised that once that was sorted out she would get me a university job. 'But how?' I asked. 'The fewer questions you ask about that the better.'

That summer, as an external student, I required neither registration nor accommodation and was able to enjoy a whole crowd of friends. Some of my modelling friends would borrow French outfits when they had an important date. After that it would be difficult to get them back and, if I ever did, they would be virtually unwearable. The modelling work brought in very little money, especially if I turned up late. I was thinner than the others and was always needing to have things taken in with safety pins. In the sports club *Soviet Wings* I was advised to walk sideways so that the safety-pins would not be seen.

The exams were now over and by this time only fear of a death sentence or a police escort would have made me go back to the Agricultural College in Kaunus. I had met a girl named Larissa Elyutina at the Institute, who'd studied in the parallel group to mine before I'd left for Paris. She came round to see me at the flat in Lavrushinskii Lane and we became close friends. She started inviting me round to her home, telling me that she and her husband – the son of the Minister for the Food Industry – were soon leaving for a sanatorium in Sochi. Larissa herself was the daughter of the Minister of Higher Education. The children of such people naturally married within their own circle. I have seldom met any woman more beautiful than Larissa: she was tall, with long legs, slim ankles and wrists – and beautiful hands with decadently elegant fingers. Her face was almost child-like and she had languid blue eyes. She also sang magnificently. Her mother had re-married and her new husband was a smart operator with whom she had had a second daughter with very weak health. She made no time for Larissa. Her father had also re-married and had little to do with his daughter, who might as well be an orphan – but his name could work wonders. Larissa had gained a place at the Languages Institute hardly knowing a word of French. Initially she had no plans to learn any. When the teachers asked her: 'Elyutina, aren't you ashamed of yourself?' she would casually stand, pulling herself up to her full height and say: 'You're the ones who should be ashamed of yourselves. You gave me a place!' No-one was ever brave enough to complain to her father. By the time we met, Larissa was a post-graduate student, had visited Paris and had a competent command of French.

She and her husband were going to visit Sochi. So I decided that I would go too, planning to rent a room on arrival, deciding that it was more tactful not to get in the way of Larissa and her husband. I reached Sochi's bus-station from Adler airport in the evening. A woman took me by the hand and dragged me off to rent a room in her house 'just round the corner'. At first I carried my large case myself, but then the woman took over. Eventually we turned up at her house totally exhausted. The room was a room like any other, but there was already someone else sitting on the bed, a tipsy blonde. 'But where is my room and my bed?' I asked. 'You girls are skinny young things, you'll be able to fit into one bed ... and the rent's cheap'. I was almost in tears and my 'room mate' started consoling me: 'There's no need to bawl like that. I go out in the evenings and come back late, if at all. Anyway, I'm not planning to stay here long.' There was no telephone in the house and I had no energy to go out to ring Larissa from a public one. In the morning the young woman turned up with a young Georgian, paid what she owed in rent, collected her things and I ran out to telephone Larissa. She came rushing round and was even more horrified by the place than I had been. We packed my case and set off to her sanatorium. The young couple's room was modest. After all, it was their fathers that were ministers, not Larissa and her husband. They made up a bed for me on the settee, their bed being at the opposite end of the room and screened off by a row of chairs. I fell asleep straightaway while they went to the beach. I spent three days there, then they asked their friend from Sukhumi to come over and fetch me, since he ran a holiday hotel or some kind of tourist centre. We set off together with the friend, had supper in the 'Caucasian Aul' (the name often used for a village in the Caucasus or Central Asia) restaurant, then left for his town. The friend's parents were pleased to welcome the ministers' children but could not understand what I was doing there. Immediately after sharing a meal with them, I moved into the tourist centre, which was more luxurious than the average one, but didn't like it and soon returned to Moscow - all my illusions about holidays in Sochi shattered.

It was cool in Moscow by the time I returned. A new tenant had moved into Lydia Pavlovna's study, a young post-graduate from Tbilisi, David Ioseliani, from a well-connected Georgian family. He is now Moscow's chief cardiologist. Once again I had to find somewhere to live. I must have changed rooms at least ten times. The first one, near the Kursk railway station, was rented to me by a young photographer who was living at his girlfriend's place. Three other families also lived in that communal flat. Next to me there were two rooms lived in by the first family of the famous airman Prokofiev. They were intrigued to know who the girl in the next room was, who was always receiving telephone calls: one moment it would be her parents from Kaunas and the next a girlfriend from Paris. My brother Ben who was studying at Moscow's Power Institute, would also appear. Things hotted up when the local militia-man came round, saying that he was looking for the man officially registered as living there. He did not even ask me for my registration papers, which I still had at the time.

As soon as my registration ran out, the photographer refused to continue letting the room to me. Friends helped me to find another room, or rather a corner of one behind a partition. I promised my landlady I would sort out my registration papers, but was unable to keep my promise. It was not possible for me to stay with Aunt Tamara, because by now her sons had grown up and the house was full of singers, with rehearsals going on all day. On a couple of occasions I was found temporary accommodation in some wretched little rooms. But because of registration problems I never managed to stay anywhere for long. For a short time I stayed in Larissa's flat, while her husband had gone to stay out at his parents' *dacha* near Moscow in Serebryanyi Bor, while her grandmother, who had brought her up, made do with a bed in the kitchen.

Our university course was drawing to a close. Larissa rang the Rector of our Institute, who by then was the formidable Marfuta Borodulina. She too had worked in the secret service in the past. Larissa was able to talk to her as an equal and asked her over the telephone to take me on as a post-graduate, promising to sort things out with her father. The Rector replied (and I heard her say so myself) that no father anywhere would help her and that nobody would take up the case of a Jewess who had spent such a long time in France. 'For then everybody will start doing it: marrying some kind of foreigner, leaving, coming back – straight into graduate studies. What kind of precedent would that set? People should think what they're doing before they leave their country. Anyway, what made her come back all of a sudden?' Something sinister had obviously occurred to her and she warned Larissa: 'Don't get yourself mixed up with her.'

I did, however, receive an offer of a post-graduate place from a specialist in Chinese at the Institute of Oriental Languages in Professor Pozdneyeva's Chinese department. She needed someone with a good knowledge of French and French literature. At the time she was studying the influence of Confucianism on the French Encyclopaedists. Initially I had to translate a Papal Bulla of Pius II from the Latin, which touched upon that particular subject. I had forgotten a good deal of my Latin and so asked my mother to translate. She completed it fairly quickly and Professor Pozdneyeva was delighted. There was one major disadvantage. I didn't know a single word of Chinese, not one hieroglyph. The professor, however, managed to find me a Chinese teacher from among her post-graduates, convincing the staff committee that very soon, by the end of the first semester, I would know enough Chinese and that in all other respects my level of knowledge was excellent. I began to acquire more friends, but still did not have anywhere to live. Through Janna I came to know Nikita Krivosheinyi, who helped me get translation work from 'Progress Publishers' and introduced me to 'non-conformist' artists. Only people like that would not be afraid of being on friendly terms with a girl who for some reason had come back to the USSR from France. I also made friends with Anna Kozlovskaya, daughter of the singer Ivan Kozlovskii. Her mother, the actress Galina Kozlovskaya, allowed me to live in their flat on Gorky Street in Anna's part of their flat.

Eventually though, I felt that they had all had enough of the arrangement. Anna's mother – a decisive woman – finally found a solution. She arranged a fictitious marriage for me with a good friend of hers. She had been the love of his life and so he was prepared to take that 'terrible' step. It was our big secret. My teacher Aleshnikova kept her word: I was immediately given a job in the foreign languages section attached to Moscow State University's natural science faculties. Yet, as I'd been taken on in the middle of the academic year, had to be paid by the hour. Straightaway I was given a group of post-graduates and scholars, who were about to set off for abroad for various kinds of academic training. I had to train them in conversational French as quickly as possible. I was also entrusted with a group of professors from the law faculty, who were interested in French language and culture. Professor Mishin used to come hurrying on long crutches, desperate to be in time for lessons. They were all so keen to be in my classes. For them it was a respite or perhaps even entertainment. 'The students will envy us having a teacher like you!' Young as I was at the time, I did not remember all their surnames – a pity. They were so full of praise for my French and for my appearance. I acquired some private pupils as a result: the daughter of Academician Mandelshtam, two post-graduate mathematicians from Tbilisi and their academic supervisor. Plenty of offers for work came in from various departments offering foreign languages. Sometimes invitations came from admirers.

I now felt well and truly part of the capital's cultural life. One of my closest friends at that time was the actress, Olga Yakovleva, so I had the chance to see all the plays being put on by Anatolii Efros several times over. I rented a room in the so-called 'House of Young Actors' on Chekhov Street and later rented a whole flat next to the 'Molodyozhnaya' metro station. I no longer had the urge to go away. Why would I need to? I had work, I was friendly with local artists, reading unofficial *Samizdat* books (banned by the Soviet authorities and censors as being politically or ideologically unacceptable) and able to go to concerts at the Conservatoire. My friend Sonya Ardashnikova brought Galich along to my birthday party in 1971. He spent the whole evening singing for us. I also met my future husband, Roman Sef, after giving him a photograph of his now dead friend, the painter Yulo Sooster. They'd been in a prison camp together.

Roman was a children's poet. He was an elegant witty man, always full of jokes and impromptus. To look at Roman you'd never think that he'd been through the camps like so many people in the Soviet Union. He'd been in the same camp as Andrei Schimkewitsch, who became our great friend in Paris. He was born in 1931 in Moscow. His father was shot during the period of Stalin's notorious repressions in the 1930s and his older brother was killed defending Moscow when the Nazis approached it in 1941. After the war, when Roman was just a teenager, his mother, despite being a communist, was sent to a Stalinist labour camp to work on a pig farm as the wife of an 'enemy of the people'. In 1951 Roman himself was arrested too, but after the death of Stalin in 1956 he was fully rehabilitated. Distinguished Russian writer Kornei Chukovsky gave Roman a piece of advice, when he came back from the camps: 'Write children's poems – they don't lock you up for that.' During his life-time Roman published many collections of poems and they were translated into a number of languages. The wife of the Japanese Emperor was so enamoured of Roman's children's verses that she invited him to her palace.

Roman Sef was also a playwright and translator, translating many English, Australian and American modernist poets into Russian. His translation of George Bernard Shaw's *My Fair Lady* was a great success on Russian stages. He became a President of the Union of Children and Youth Literature, Head of Children and Youth Creative Writing in the Literary Institute (named after Gorky) and the Chairman of the Association of Children Writers in Moscow and was head of the Children's Theatre Section of Russia. He was bestowed the title of the Merited Artist of Russia in 2000.

Figure 32. Ariela and her husband Roman Sef at the Louvre, 1991.

KITTY

One day in Alabyan Street in Moscow I saw an old man and a little girl with a dog the size of a poodle trotting next to them. It had long hair along its black and white back, a spaniel's ears, a terrier's little beard and aristocratic grey in its fringe. I took an immediate fancy to it and followed them. The man looked nervous and kept turning round. I went up to him and asked: 'Is it your dog? Do you need her, because she doesn't have a lead?' The old man looked at me as if I was mad. Then I asked: 'Will she be having puppies? I should love to buy one?' 'No, we're not planning to sell her and if she does have puppies, it won't be for a long time.' I left my telephone number with him, just in case, even though the last thing I needed was a dog. I had no flat and was living in a rented room. I soon forgot all about it. Five or six months later the dog-owner telephoned me out of the blue. He explained that although he loved the dog very much, his daughter and her husband couldn't stand it and the child was making its life miserable. 'Perhaps you'll take the dog?' he asked hopefully. It was so unexpected. The spring holidays were about to begin, my landlady wanted me to move out and now along comes a dog. Nevertheless, I said 'Yes!' I went to fetch her immediately. They asked fifty roubles for her at a time when I was living on a hundred a month. I took the money round straightaway and collected the dog. But where could she go?

I telephoned my brother Ben, who was on the point of flying up to see our parents. She settled comfortably and trustingly on his lap and they set off there and then for the airport. My father was in Sochi at the time, so it was our astonished mother who met Ben at the airport. 'This is Ariela's dog', he explained. 'She is very attached to her and wants you to take good care of her.' The dog went down well. Everyone could see that she was well-bred – we simply did not know which breed. We called her Kitty. Two days later Kitty disappeared. Ben had let her out while he was lacing up his shoes. When I rang up later to ask how they liked my Kitty, the answer I received was a cautious 'Very nice'. Meanwhile, notices were going up all over the town about the lost dog, promising a generous reward. Mother's acquaintances, her students, family friends, friends of my brothers were all sticking up notices. They'd lost all hope of finding Kitty, when a woman telephoned and asked: 'Does the dog belong to the doctor?' The woman had recently come across a soggy notice stuck to a lamp-post. The woman was infinitely grateful to my father, who had operated on her daughter and, realizing that the owner of the dog was that very same doctor, the family had decided to bring her back.

That was how a new member of our family appeared on the scene. Kitty used to stride proudly along the central avenue of our town with my father, making a handsome pair. Mother, who was always more cautious and sceptical about new acquaintances, grew fond of Kitty. Our father was offered large sums for her, but replied that he did not sell members of his family. Father used to take Kitty out to the *dacha* by bus, hiding her under a seat. The conductor would only catch sight of her as she got out. Kitty also shared several of our father's tastes. He loved swimming and so did she. He used to go out to his allotment after work to plant strawberries. Kitty would follow him and then trample over them.

While away at the *dacha*, Kitty embarked on an affair: it was a disastrous mismatch with an ugly dog that looked like a short-legged fox, even though there had been plenty of competition from the finest poodles in Kaunas. She had a litter of six, which kept us all busy. For the first four weeks Kitty was a model mother, but after five weeks she stopped noticing her young. Homes had to be found for the puppies quickly, but Father refused to give them away for nothing. 'With a lineage like that, you can't just give them away!' he said: 'Especially in Lithuania. They'd be abandoned. If we're going to take money for them, then we have to ask for quite a lot. Then people will think twice about turning them out.' Many would-be customers came along. Father divided them into three groups according to his own special system: the maximum price should be charged to shop managers and just a token price for teachers. Only three of the puppies bore any resemblance to Kitty, while the other three turned into enormous 'watchdogs'. When Mother was asked why they were so big and why their fur was not curly, she would reply, 'It's early days yet.' They kept Motya, the most attractive one, back for me to take to Moscow. Later he would become the *raison d'être* in the life of my Parisian friend Andrei. Kitty began to put on weight and soon resembled a hairy barrel. She took the place of us children now that we were grown-up. She was often naughty and would beg for food. But Kitty did not like small children (she obviously had bad memories of them) or men with high, thin voices. She would bite anyone of either category without any warning. But people would forgive her and come to her defence.

Figure 33. Ariela's mother with their dog Kitty, Kaunas, 1973.

Everything in Kitty's life was going well until my parents and brothers decided to leave the USSR for Israel. Things were going well for me too, but they wouldn't leave either of us behind. Given my health problems I needed to be part of the family luggage. By this time my brother Solomon had already interrupted his post-graduate studies at Moscow's First Medical Institute and my mother had left her job. Father had renounced his responsibilities as head of department. They were going to set off somewhere new at a time when everything was going well for me. If only they had had the opportunity to do it earlier. At any rate I brought out my French passport, and in fear and trembling set off to the Consulate hoping that the militia-man at the entrance would not notice that it had expired. In the French Consulate I was informed that the Moscow consulate did not deal with people from the Baltic republics and that I would have to go to Leningrad to sort the matter out. With similar trepidation I went to the Leningrad consulate, but there found a very pleasant man. He understood my worries and promised to have all my French documents sent to my friend Nelly Cournot's Paris address and to issue me with a Laissez Passer travel document which would be valid for three months. We set off together in his car to get the necessary photographs taken, so I should not have to go back in again through the gate.Armed with that document, which I hid carefully away, I could set off calmly to France.

The time came for us to prepare for our emigration. Kitty could sense the atmosphere and began to grow agitated. We left on the train from Vilnius to Brest-Litovsk. As far as Brest she travelled like a queen and nobody disturbed her in the train. The nightmare began in Brest. Kitty's papers were in perfect order. Her passport read as follows: 'Sex – Female; Known as – Kitty; Breed – Mixed; Surname – Abramovich; Ethnic category – (not required).' We also had forms confirming her state of health and the inoculations she had had. But we had been warned that in Brest we would have to exchange all these documents for their international equivalents in the vet's office. Since we had to reckon with one or two days for the customs people to inspect our luggage and dispatch it, we'd booked hotel accommodation in advance. It had all sounded straightforward … But we arrived in the hotel at the end of the day and it turned out that there was no room for a family complete with dog. Mother had recently had a heart attack and her friend (since the liberation of Kaunas) Hanna Levinson was taking care of her. During the war Hanna had been working in reconnaissance for the XVI Lithuanian Division and she had gone on to become a well-known lawyer. Eventually they took pity on us and gave us one large room with eight beds in it. There were six of us, not counting Kitty. The other two beds were taken by people from Minsk, whom we had never seen in our lives. It was not possible to take Kitty through into the hotel 'legally', so we stuffed the 'fat barrel' into a bag and the bag into a cupboard. When the woman from Minsk sharing our room looked into the cupboard, she nearly had a heart attack ... Kitty was sitting there quietly.

It turned out that neither one nor even two days would be enough for all the customs formalities. People started queuing at five in the morning and everything depended upon which day your turn would come. It was September and the weather was still quite pleasant. We were sitting around in shabby railway carriages in sidings, five hundred metres from the main customs hall. Some people from Transcaucasia, dripping with money, were allowed to queue-jump – arranged by bribed luggage-handlers who were becoming quite shameless. The bribes did not always help when people's luggage was being inspected. Some people were not let through, others were even arrested. We decided that, whatever happened, we would have to give the luggage-handlers something, but that we would not give them anything for 'additional services'. If we did that they would blackmail us for every sneeze. We couldn't leave Kitty in our hotel-room, because there would be hotel staff walking up and down our corridor checking everything was in order. So we took her with us. This meant that she had to spend the whole day and eat with my father and Solomon in a workmen's temporary shelter.

The international permits for Kitty could only be drawn up on the eve of our departure. The seats we'd reserved in a sleeping compartment were useless and we had to book new ones, but it was not clear which day we would need them for. At last we were called for the customs inspection. We all went over, taking Kitty with us. The containers with our furniture were quickly unloaded and the customs men rummaged about in the enormous wooden boxes looking for stolen goods. As soon as any of them asked a question in a raised voice, Kitty would growl menacingly. Apart from some photographs of my father's taken at the end of his course for officers at his university, and awards he'd been given, they didn't find anything suspect. The photographs and awards had to be left behind though. Father protested that he would not be going anywhere without them. Kitty started barking and in the end he was able to hold on to the photos. The only items in our luggage they would not let through were six silver spoons. We already had six and twelve were not allowed: that would be over the silver allowance. The customs officials would eventually turn away, tempting people to throw something prohibited back into a container, before it had been nailed shut. But then they would start checking again and find the 'contraband'. Roman had warned me about this: I had wanted to throw in a small ring, which the customs men had forbidden. When the containers were already being nailed up again, one of the customs officials came over and asked me to show him the ring. I obediently showed him the ring. The faces of the customs men turned sour – bitterly disappointed not to have caught out a 'smuggler'.

The next morning we set out to deal with Kitty's papers. The woman at the relevant window said: 'You can't take the dog.' 'But we've got all the documents. Everyone passed them.' 'You can't take a dog in a sleeping compartment, in fact not on a train at all. You have to leave your dog behind.' By this time Mother was about to have a second heart attack. She was wearing her one and only little diamond ring and pushed it through the window at the woman. That softened her look, but she slammed the window shut and told us to come back after the break. Mother was at the end of her tether by then. Father went back later taking the small ring with him. There was another woman sitting there by that time who didn't require any rings. Instead, she calmly wrote out all the documents Kitty needed, not for a small sleeping compartment but for a large basic one. This meant that Father and Kitty had to travel separately with an enormous crowd of women and children – a whole tribe of Jews from Bukhara. After a time Solomon changed places with him. When we were waiting at a station in Poland the conductor caught sight of Kitty and invited her back into our coach. That was how Kitty managed to travel in style, while one of the Abramovich men had to travel in the large compartment with the Bukharans.

Just before we climbed into the train, which was only waiting for a few minutes, we had to have our personal luggage inspected. When they caught sight of Mother with the dog, the luggage-handlers took pity on us and quickly moved us forward in the queue. There was plenty of time left, but for some reason they were hurrying us along, saying: 'If that tribe comes along, you'll know what's hit you. If you don't get in ahead of them, you won't be going anywhere.' The customs men shook everything out of our cases and demanded that our shattered mother walk over to them. She could hardly stand. They started to hurry her – and then Kitty went for them, barking her head off! At first they were angry, but then started smiling. Our indignant father started to calm down as well. Just as we repacked our suitcases, a whole caravan of people appeared without a single suitcase between them – with nothing but bundles. There were perhaps as many as fifty. The men strode out in front looking important, then came the women wrapped up from head to foot and finally an endless swarm of children, all speaking a language we didn't understand. How grateful we felt to the luggage-handlers. One even said to us: 'You're educated people and we felt sorry for you. We weren't going to make much out of you now, were we?'

In Vienna we alighted on to a platform guarded by men armed with sub-machine guns. Then some lively young people started loading our parents on to a bus heading for Schönau Castle. The situation was almost military, as a few days prior to that a bus of newly arrived Jews had been blown up. After seeing my parents off I was to travel on to Paris and wanted us all to be together a little longer, before they flew on to Israel. None of us knew when we would see each other again, so I climbed on to the bus as well and spent two more days with my family. We were given a large room with a shower and toilet. The first of us to settle down to sleep on a bed was Kitty. In the evening dinner was organized for everyone at an enormous table seating about a hundred people. There were many Jews from Bukhara. The next morning everyone was taken off to have their luggage packed away. Each person was only allowed to take two small cases for the next stage of the journey. Everything else was to be dispatched separately. We had to admit that Sokhnut had organised everything to perfection. Sokhnut was known in English as the Jewish Agency (created in 1929). It served as the pre-State Jewish government before the establishment of Israel and later became the mandated organization in charge of immigration and absorption of Jews from the Diaspora. All the Jews from Bukhara were given tidy cardboard suitcases for their most important belongings. All bundles vanished.

After that a bus full of American 'sponsors' drove up, coming to look at those they had 'helped on their way'. For the most part they were heavily made-up elderly ladies with smiles of dazzlingly white false teeth like ceramic tiles. There were young girls there as well with eyelids brighter than the feathers of African parrots, who went into raptures when they saw their 'saved' brothers and sisters. They felt a special 'affinity' with the Bukharans with their long skirts and mouthfuls of gold and silver teeth. There were also well-mannered professionals who wanted to 'make friends' with the new arrivals and boost their morale. On that particular day, however, there was nobody apart from our family who seemed to fit the bill. My father and brother chatted away with them pleasantly enough. Kitty offered each member of the company a paw. The overseas visitors did not seem to find anything odd about us. A shared supper that evening was organised for the new arrivals and the Americans, and all the 'newcomers' had to thank the Americans in one voice for their help and the concern they had shown. 'So, let us thank our brothers from America! Hurrah!' shouted a representative of Sokhnut. Everyone repeated what he had said, as if we were on the parade-ground. The next day my family flew off to Israel and I left for Paris with my two suitcases. I was supposed to have arrived a week earlier, so Nelly had given up and set off on her holidays. Everyone was away. Parisians had yet to come home. Where could I go? I went to look up another friend, but she was not in town either. They let me into the house though and I sat it out till they came back.

There was no news from my family. Later I discovered that they'd been given somewhere to live near Haifa in a temporary flat, rather like a hostel. In Israel flats all had stone floors and Kitty developed pneumonia. Vets were expensive and Kitty's was a serious case. But my father treated her as if she'd been a human being, using human medicines. Some kind neighbours from Britain brought a vet round, free of charge. Kitty recovered and even outlived my parents. Eventually they were given a proper flat and Kitty did not get sick again, unlike Mother. Kitty stayed with our parents and had more puppies after she reached Israel. That time they ended up as small poodles and were quickly taken off our hands. My parents kept back the two smallest and weakest of the bunch, Drolly and Jolly. After the death of my father and countless upheavals, the smallest and most sickly of the puppies was taken in by my school friend Sonya, who prior to that could not stand the dogs, but took the puppy to Canada where she thrived for eighteen years.

My Father worked as an ENT surgeon in Tel Aviv and Mother as a part-time English teacher. My father was involved in a dreadful car accident on the way home from work and he was taken to Tel Ha-Shomer Hospital, where he had an emergency operation. However a few days later he died. It was 1977. My mother was unwell for some time and moved to London to be with my brothers. She passed away three years later from breast cancer.

After my parents died, my husband Roman and I inherited Kitty. She travelled to almost all the countries of Europe, spending time in Cannes, Antibes and Rome. And in Venice she was even helped out of *vaporetti* by doormen in livery and white gloves. She loved restaurants, particularly the 'Lipp' *brasserie* in Paris, where she would be given beef and vegetables. She knew the way there. Kitty even flew 'back home' to Moscow several times. She was loyal and friendly, but would not put up with any undue familiarity. When I was ill, she was perfectly prepared to go out with my friends to see to her immediate requirements, but never further than the nearest pavement corner. My friend Elena Cardenas would walk her up and down, hoping to spur her into action and extend the outing, but Kitty sat down at the threshold of the house like a sphinx. Kitty often used to stay over in the house of Nelly Cournot. Her husband Michel was a journalist working for *Le Monde* and he would always refer to her as 'black rubbish'. Kitty did not really take offence, well aware that he liked her really. In general though, she preferred to remain in her own territory. She died of pneumonia after all, but in a Paris clinic – at the grand old age of 13.

RETURNING TO PARIS

I had returned to France in September 1973 with two suitcases and four hundred dollars, half of which my father had given me before leaving Vienna. I was hoping for a bright future and was counting on support from my friends. I had to re-register at the university, find work and somewhere to live. I went to stay with my friend Nelly Cournot outside the city, in Sceaux. The flat only had three rooms. Nelly's husband, the journalist, occasionally needed peace and quiet to concentrate. Their son Ivan was away on holiday, so at first I slept in his room, but on his return I had to move into the hall. Each morning Ivan and Michel would walk past my bed on their way to school and work. I too needed to get into town as I had all sorts of paper-work to attend to, but I felt I could not get up straightaway, as they needed to organise themselves for the day ahead.

We decided that it was best for me to find a hotel room somewhere in the Latin Quarter, near the university – and I found one – The Hotel du Danube was in Rue Jacob – for 26 francs a night. (Nowadays you can't check in unless you have at least 260 euros.) I left my suitcases with Nelly, since there was no room for them in the hotel room. I'd also been given a little money by my friends Nelly, Lena and Edouard Loeb, whom I did not yet know very well, but who'd paid me for three pictures by Edik Steinberg, which the wife of his nephew had bought in Moscow. I had had to pay for them and she'd promised that her husband would pay me back in Paris. Her husband, Edouard's nephew, refused to give me the money, saying that he was not responsible for his crazy wife, and that he did not collect rubbish like those pictures. Yet they had been my main asset – a thousand dollars' worth! Edouard was fond of his nephew and did at least know me a little. He had even visited me once with his young girlfriend in Moscow and eventually he paid me. The money however, melted away. My friend Lena had a house, four children, a husband (a Cuban surrealist sculptor), a nanny and a few other relatives. Lena herself worked at UNESCO, in the Russian department, and was the object of close police attention. So it was out of the question that she take in a friend who'd just come back from the Soviet Union.

Everybody started looking for someone to put me up. A French couple came to the rescue – Monsieur and Madame Bauer. They had a large house next to Parc de Monceau, two small boys aged 8 and 11, and a spare room complete with a bathroom on the top floor. They wanted to have a young girl living in the house so that, occasionally in the evening, she could keep an eye on the children while they went out. They didn't go out very often, and besides, I needed to stay at home to study. They even arranged a party in my honour at Russian New Year in the old style calendar. They tried to help me find work and were very enthusiastic in their efforts. They printed out my modest curriculum vitae on smart sheets of paper, putting them into envelopes.

Monsieur Bauer was a man of the world and at that time he was working as an advisor to Air Canada. Before that he had been the manager of the *Comédie Française*. Madame Bauer was a beautiful fashionable woman from a French bourgeois family, slightly younger than her husband. The most interesting part of the house was Monsieur Bauer's floor with a bathroom consisting entirely of black marble and an almost identical bedroom with black sheets, towels and enormous pictures by artists known to no-one apart from the master and mistress of the house. The floor with the sitting-room was even more interesting. On two walls were paintings depicting exotic plants, with unreal multicoloured birds tall enough to stretch from floor to ceiling. The walls opposite the birds consisted of mirrors. The finishing touch was a snow-white leather settee in the shape of an enormous double bed. My little room with its separate bathroom and kitchen was also on that floor. I was allowed to bring my friends home, it was even encouraged. The couple were very keen to be seen as belonging to the Bohemian intelligentsia and were only too pleased to know that their house was being visited by famous journalists, sculptors, dealers and gallery-owners: for (although I was penniless) the people I mixed with were interesting. But after my friends had seen the décor, they refused to come back.

One Sunday I brought Nelly's son, Ivan – who was 8, the same age as their youngest – to have lunch with the Bauers' children. These children were beautifully brought up and sat demurely at the table, while Ivan started jumping around in his trainers on the settee after lunch, much to the consternation of the Bauer boys. Stopping him was impossible, as at home he was allowed to do what he liked. The more I begged him to stop, the worse he behaved.

Relations between Monsieur and Madame Bauer were going downhill. He had found himself a mistress and she an admirer. They started having rows and they used to set off for separate destinations, leaving me to care for the children. In the morning they had to be taken to school and in the evening I had to look after them till it was quite late – this was now every day – and sometimes make their supper. It was becoming impossible to do all that and find time for my studies and work. I was also becoming an easy target for the couple's bitterness and resentment. I was not cut out for the role of professional nanny and they started finding fault with me. By this time they really did need a proper nanny.

It was at that point that my friend Jana, ever a champion of justice, gathered up my things and took me off to a small room at the top of a house close to the Boulevard Saint-Germain-des-Près. The room had no real window, just a skylight in the roof. When it rained, water dripped straight on to the bed. I had six square metres, into which were squeezed a sink, a stove and a bidet, but I don't remember ever being happier than I was there. What is happiness? Everyone has his own answer to that question. The whole district of St Germain was so lively. My mood was free and relaxed as I went out with my friends to the nearby cafés. On top of all that, Edouard left me the key to his flat over the summer. He and his girlfriend had gone to spend two whole months in Spain and I could invite my friends to his wonderful cool flat. My cousin Anya even came to visit me all the way from Israel. When she saw his enormous dark studio, she was horrified: 'How can you live in this ramshackle place? The furniture's shabby. Have you completely run out of money?' Yet in that flat were hanging pictures by Max Ernst, Wilfredo Lam, Roberto Matta and Picasso; sculptures by Arp, and Henry Moore. There were also remarkable rare books, including some illustrated with engravings by Ernst and Picasso. My cousin advised me to put up some new wallpaper or at least paint the place.

The summer sped by and I was not keen to return to my dovecote. I had an urgent need to rent a flat, but who would rent anything to a young woman without a regular salary? I needed guarantors. My own girl-friends could hardly make ends meet for themselves. So I turned to the well-known antiquarian, Lev Adolfovich Grinberg and my friend Edouard who both agreed to be guarantors. However each time we turned up things turned sour. One landlady said: 'And if those old fellows give up on you, what then?' Neither they, nor I, had given any thought to the impression that the three of us made...

In the end a flat was found. A young couple was renting out a flat. He was an artist in advertising and she a well-known photo-model. They were moving into the Marais district and were prepared to rent out their former studio flat. What a stroke of luck! I had never seen anything so gorgeous. It was all on the ground floor and very light. One floor consisted almost entirely of glass except at the very bottom. The tiled floor positively shone. The studio was enormous and a third of it was made of white-painted wood. At the back there was a platform stage raised forty centimetres from the main floor. The walls at the sides of the stage opened up as cupboards in which pictures, suitcases and frames could be stored away. There was room here to sleep, lie about and eat. The platform served as both giant-sized bed and table. Opposite it was a double mattress laid out straight on to the tiled floor, so there was a second bed – a good place to sleep in the summer when it was hot. In the winter the tiles were terribly cold and the flat was only heated during weekdays. From Friday through to Sunday the neighbours who stoked the boiler would be away for the weekend in the country and I would freeze. The only solution was to put the bedding on the stage-platform, or better still on the mezzanine floor. So there were three different places to sleep in this large room. The mezzanine floor was supported on pillars and it was easy to climb up there using a step-ladder. Inside the mezzanine the mattress was fixed firmly to a large board laid out over the pillars about one and a half metres from the ceiling. The total height of the room was four metres. The ceiling was painted dark blue and full of golden stars, the walls were lined with pieces of chintz forming a patchwork and on top of the wallpaper everything was covered with feathers the colour of cyclamen or lettuce. Similar feathers had been stuck all over two of the walls, on which there were also white shelves. On these, delicate plaster eggs of all different sizes had been laid out – ranging from ostrich-size eggs to ones that were a metre high. The last remaining wall was also white, consisting of one large built-in cupboard. I used to wake up in the morning in a world of pink and green feathers. It was fantastic. There was no furniture in the small second room, just another grand bed right up by the ceiling, on a surface supported by two pillars, just as in the main room. Again, there was a step-ladder. It was warmer to sleep there during cold weather. The kitchen was just another kitchen, but the bathroom was varnished red – albeit rather carelessly applied – with a black bath and basin.

The space was more than ample and I could lie back and relax, watch television or invite my friends round. The 'stage' could serve both as table and performance area. I did not yet have enough money for curtains to shut myself off from the street, because the amount of material required would be phenomenal. It was like living in a shop-window at the end of an arcade. People rarely walked by and, when I needed to change, I moved into the small room. When I lost my keys, I climbed into the flat through the window in that room. Once, Lev Adolfovich Grinberg, at the age of 77, came round to see me with my friend Asya Muratova, and calmly climbed in through the window, finding the whole episode extremely amusing. I used to give parties, enjoying all sorts of escapades. But I fell ill from the cold in the winter, ending up in hospital, after which I had to take steps to improve my wonderful abode. My parents, brothers and friends from every corner of the globe came to visit me there. The family of the legendary Soviet Jewish actor and Moscow State Jewish Theatre artistic director Solomon Mikhoels also came to stay. The Moscow State Jewish Theatre was a Yiddish theatre company established after the Russian revolution in 1919 and shut down by the Soviet Authorities in 1948. Decorations sets and costumes for its first productions were done by Marc Chagall. Solomon Mikhoels also performed Shakespeare's *King Lear* to great international acclaim. He was chairman of Jewish Anti-Fascist Committee during the Second World War. Mikhoels was assassinated on Stalin's direct orders in 1948, seen as the most visible of the intellectual Jewish leadership. When his family arrived at the flat, at first they couldn't get over the shock of the décor but soon grew used to sleeping on the mattresses, and even began to find the feathered walls pleasantly bright to look at. Nor was I likely to be robbed by anyone, since my small terrier, Motya (the off spring of Kitty) would hurl himself at the door barking loudly whenever he heard the slightest rustle. If only the place had been heated I would not have needed alternative accommodation.

THE LOEB TWINS

I first met Edouard Loeb in his huge studio flat at a lively gathering after the *vernissage* for the Mexican artist Camacho. There were a large number of people there from the world of Latin-American bohemia. There were also well-known collectors and the artists Max Ernst, Dora Maar and Jean Arp. It would have been impossible to arrange such a splendid reception in the gallery itself because of lack of space. I had been taken there by my friend Lena, who was married to the Cuban sculptor Cárdenas. It was the first time I had encountered famous artists in such large numbers. They were all in good spirits, apart from their host. Edouard had been upset by his girlfriend Françoise whom he loved desperately, but who had fallen for another. And his twin-brother Pierre had fallen ill. The two brothers were identical –only close friends could tell them apart – yet they were quite distinct characters. Both wore grey felt hats with a pipe in the corner of their mouths. They were tall and well-built, with slightly hunched shoulders: yet elegant with a youthful gait and aristocratic hands. Pierre was a tougher, more decisive individual.

They were both enamoured of new art, and had been involved with the Surrealist movement. They devoted their lives to promoting new artists, drawing up contracts with them which every now and then lost them money – as they did with Joan Miró. The twins had travelled to Spain, to a remote farm, where Miró lived with his mother. The mother decided that they were engaging but crazy, as they were prepared to pay her son money for his 'daubings' – even offering him a monthly allowance. She actually felt sorry for them. But they were ahead of their times.

Edouard seemed the calmer of the two, tolerant and more able to distance himself from events. He also had a subtle sense of humour. If asked, for instance: 'Edouard, how do you like my girlfriend's book?', he might reply: 'Remarkable, like a coffee-grinder without the coffee'. The two brothers lived in a state of constant inner existential anxiety, often encountered in Jews. Pierre kept this under control through incessant movement and action. Edouard however, remained a Romantic. He'd once written: 'To be born a Jew is a destiny.' They came from an old Jewish family in Alsace, where their mother ruled. What softened her was her sense of humour. Their father was a gentle artistic man, who had a lace business in Paris. In the First World War, the twins set off as volunteers for the Front. When they came back they worked as travelling salesmen for their father's company. Edouard managed to pass his baccalaureate, hoping to become a doctor. But Pierre had no qualifications at all. He was far more interested in the latest art than in lace, and became a member of a Surrealist circle. He was also very keen to become an artist. He went out to buy brushes and paints and set off to work, but returned home, announcing to his father: 'I'm not going to make it as an artist!' His father responded with the advice: 'If you like artists so much, go out and sell them.' So with his limited resources Pierre began buying pictures. He spent a large amount of his capital on publishing André Breton's manifestos and helping the members of his circle prosper.

The twins had a younger brother who had a bent for mathematics and the sciences. He was very different from Edouard and Pierre, graduating from the Ecole Polytechnique. Later he was to become the chief engineer of France's *Ministère des Ponts et Chausées*. Their sister, Denise, the youngest in the family, looked very different from her tall brothers: she was small and thin. She was later to become the well-known photographer, Denise Colomb. Her husband, Jules Verne's Paganel, a naval engineer and rear admiral, was the director of Saigon port, while the French still governed Vietnam. He used to run round after his wife like a loyal dog carrying her heavy photographic equipment. Thanks to her brothers, Denise was able to take photographs of every well-known artist of the twentieth century. Particularly striking are her portraits of Picasso, Dora Maar, Giacometti, Max Ernst, Calder, Nicolas de Stael, Sophie Tauber, a double portrait of Leonor Fini and Leonora Carrington, Marc Chagall, Braque and my friend Elena.

In 1924 Pierre opened his 'Galère Pierre' in the Rue Bonaparte. Back in 1925, he exhibited Miro's works and organised a surrealist exhibition including works by Man Ray, Picasso, Arp, Paul Klee, de

Figure 34. Ariela in Paris. The photo taken by her friend photographer Denise Colomb, 1961.

Chirico, André Masson and Max Ernst – with a catalogue and introduction by André Breton. In 1930 he exhibited Matisse's sculpture; in 1931, Giacometti; in 1934, Balthus and Manielli; in 1938, Henri Michaux; and in 1939, Lam. During the German occupation Pierre left with his wife and two children for America. After the war he discovered Riopelle and Viera da Silva. Success and money were to be a constant part of his life and he was an expansive, generous man.

Edouard went on helping his father, still working in lace production, and spent the war years in France hiding from Germans, going hungry and seeking shelter in villages. He was a romantic and true poet, contemplating the world around him, writing and travelling. He published a number of memoirs and short essays, such as *Island* and *My Century on a Wire [Thread]* (Mon siècle sur un fil). He later travelled throughout the USA and Latin America, visiting Panama, Mexico, Venezuela and Cuba. He spent time in the Antilles islands and made friends with the poet Aimé Césaire. A companion of the Surrealists at the age of 30 (using the pseudonym Edouard Kazeyev), he printed 350 copies of a book called *Reason for Retaining an Irrational Organ* and *a Letter to André Breton, leader of Surrealism*. It was not until 1953 that he opened his own gallery. He too exhibited works by great artists, including Max Ernst, Natalia Goncharova, Albert Manielli and Wols. And, like his brother Pierre, he collected art from Africa and Oceania. Pierre died in 1964 and in great pain from lung cancer. After his death Edouard wrote: 'We were one being. Now, after my brother's death, am I aware of my individuality. I have got my second wind.' Yet nothing changed in his life. Pierre simply lived on in Edouard.

I don't think Edouard would have ever noticed me in that crowd at the preview. He wouldn't have taken any notice, if it hadn't been for Lena, who told him that I was from Russia, had married a Frenchman, had a weak heart and was soon to return to the USSR. That sparked his interest. Edouard was fascinated by women with problems. Healthy, beautiful women with no 'hang-ups' were of no interest to him. He'd been married just once in his youth to a dancer from the island of Madagascar, from whom he had separated during the war – to the relief of his parents. I saw Edouard once or twice before leaving again for the Soviet Union in 1965. He even suggested to my friend that he would be prepared to pay for a medical examination and operation for me in America if necessary, but my mind was made up and I went back home.

Eighteen months later Edouard came to visit me for Russian New Year, bringing his new girlfriend – a 24-year-old American. He'd scooped her up somewhere near his house in Spain, on the beach in a hippy hostel. She was a girl who had run away from a typical, rather ordinary American family and had had a nervous breakdown. I took them both to the celebrations in the Sovietskaya Hotel, the most fashionable place for celebrating Old New Year. The girl had never seen such beautiful, smartly dressed women. Even Edouard was impressed to see something like that in the 'poverty-stricken' Soviet Union. It was 1968 and they had brought me a georgette greenish dress, low-cut at the back and with gathers round the décolleté. This dress still looks like a work of art today, and the daughter of my friend Lydia, who works in the cinema industry, was to wear it to her first Cannes festival twenty-five years later.

The next time we met was in 1973 in Paris, where we saw each other often. I fulfilled all his requirements: I was young, attractive, ill and poor. Edouard had a weakness for beauty and his three Russian friends – Elena, Nelly and Ariela – were like Chekhov's three sisters to him. We used to accompany him to restaurants and cabarets. He was very proud of his bouquet of beauties. The whole of Saint Germain knew him and when he came into the Lipp brasserie, those present grew more animated, even though it was frequented by many of the rich and famous, including Mendes-France, Mitterand, before he became President, and Francois Giroux. Romain Gary the novelist also used to visit the Lipp and during the last year of his life I used to go there with Edouard and my friend from America, Lena Shchapova-de Carli, a poetess and the ex-wife of Eduard Limonov. She is described in his novel, *I'm Edik!* and would come in simply dressed but with a long cigarette-holder and enormous cowboy hat. She was tall, slim and blue-eyed and everyone would turn round to look at her. It was at that time that Edouard introduced her to Romain Gary, and they had a brief affair.

At the end of his life Edouard was a very sick man, but his sense of humour never deserted him. Once he lent an artist a thousand francs, which he promised to return the very next day. But he did not. Whenever he caught sight of him he would cross to the other side of the street. Edouard went up to him one day and started to thank him effusively. 'What are you thanking me for?' the artist asked. 'Thank you for asking me for only one thousand. If you had asked for two, I would have given you that as well.' Shortly before he died he began studying Japanese and everyone asked, 'What for?' Edouard replied, calm until the end: 'Because I will never, but never, need to make use of it.'

ANDREI

Roman had told me a great deal about his friend Andrei, a Russian who now lived in Paris, and who'd spent over twenty-five years in Russia, for most part in Soviet prisons and camps. Since Roman used to tell me many stories about unusual people – Japanese commanders-in-chief, princes of the royal line, Hitler's chauffeur, prominent Banderites (members of the Ukrainian nationalist movement led by Stefan Bandera 1909–59), nationalist partisans from the Baltic region – the so-called 'Green (or Forest) Brothers', guerrilla units based in rural areas and the forests (many of whose members sought to avoid conscription into the Soviet Army) which actively opposed the Soviet regime in Lithuania between 1944 and 1953, during which period 30,000 of those involved and their supporters are estimated to have died. They were offered an amnesty in 1953 after Stalin's death – I had no clear memories of an Andrei. Yet now we were in Paris sitting with our limited funds in a modest little Italian restaurant. Roman, recently from Moscow, kept on ringing up this Andrei, he was so keen to see him. I decided that the telephone number must have been changed a long time ago. Then, success at last – he got through. An hour later Andrei came rushing into the Rue des Cannettes in Saint-Germain-des-Pres where we were waiting for him.

Andrei Schimkewitch was a short, elderly, balding but very lively man with a small moustache. What hair he had was shining and sleek, with a generous dose of brilliantine. His blue eyes were extremely alive – a real '*titi parisien*' (a cheeky Parisian kid). He would speak in poor Russian and then switch over to exquisite French as he talked to the waiter, criticised the food and behaved rather noisily. He could be very happy sometimes, coming out with Russian obscenities learned in the camps, the only words he ever declined properly, then lurching back into French. He was also hyper-active; telling jokes and slapping Roman on the shoulder. In the end Andrei said we were sitting in too modest a place and he wanted to take us – by this time utterly replete - to eat oysters in a fine restaurant. So he did, and would not let us pay. We drove in his English hand-assembled car to a wonderful bar where all his friends were waiting. But I decided to go home, letting them reminisce about the things they had in common. Roman returned at four in the morning, telling me about the smart cabaret, where Andrei – shouting that he was a prince – had ordered nothing but champagne. After that they had moved on to a run-down bar, where some other 'friends' of his were meant to be hanging out. But there was nobody there apart from two elderly prostitutes, who were treated to champagne by Andrei.

The next day he came round for us to show us the city he loved. He knew every little corner and monument of Paris; who had lived where, and when. I found him to be a highly educated and cultured man, who would suddenly turn into some kind of louche travelling salesman. I soon discovered that this complexity was an intrinsic part of him. He'd take us to expensive restaurants, treating us to cognac bottled in the year of his birth (1913), then invite us back to his house. This was a house which Le Corbusier had built in 1924 for his friend, the Cubist sculptor Jacques Lipchitz and his beautiful wife Berta – Andrei's mother. It was a classic Le Corbusier building with two enormous workshops with ceilings that were ten metres high, with just one brick wall interlinking the two rooms. All the other walls were glass – joined like stained-glass windows with lead partitions. The house was bitterly cold. There was sculpture covered in dust, piles of clutter; crates, old saucepans, boxes, rickety chairs, and a shabby chests of drawers which after restoring I kept in my flat. On the landing between the ground and first floors was a small room with a narrow bed, books shelves full of books right up to the ceiling and a chair. It was ascetic in the extreme and had been Andrei's childhood bedroom. To save money on fuel, he no longer used that floor. In any case, you needed to be sober to get up to it, as the spiral staircase was incredibly steep. He lived in an enormous room with a smouldering stove. Next to it was a bucket of coal, a bundle of firewood and his bed. He used to heat water in a bucket. There was a peasant table in the centre, with teapots and plates, and lovely Spanish chairs, which could be seen in all the photos ever taken in the studio by his artists friends. Some of the enormous windows were cracked and had been pasted over with sticky tape. On the walls were abstract drawings of his mother, and there was a plaster cast by Lipchitz on a wobbly table. Paper had been shoved under its legs to try and steady it. Everywhere lay magazines and newspapers, more bookcases full of books – with separate ones for French and Russian classics and another with books about secret service organisations, particularly the KGB. His mother's small bedroom, containing an enormous bed, a small set of shelves and a broken bedside cupboard, lay beyond the large room. Downstairs, the small kitchen contained his store of condensed milk and tinned food – enough to see him through a year. He lived in poverty, yet everything was clean.

There was a wonderful view from the flat roof, a lime tree growing in the garden and stone benches for visitors. Dishes of food and milk were laid out for the cat in the garden, where ancient trees lined the path. When the lock clicked and the high, heavy gates opened lots of alley-cats appeared. The house used to host famous artists' parties with Modigliani, Soutine, Kremegne, Kikoin, Zadkine, Brancusi, Max Jacob, Maria Vasilieva, and others. The whole *Ecole de Paris*, in fact. Modigliani had painted a portrait of Andrei's mother with Lipchitz and he'd given her a lucky horse-shoe, which Andrei showed us on the evening of our first visit. He talked about that picture many times. I first saw it at a Modigliani exhibition in the Pushkin Museum in Moscow.

Andrei had been born in 1913 in the 14th *arrondissement* of Paris near Montparnasse. His father, Mikhail, was the son of a famous research biologist, Vladimir Shimkevich, who became the first elected Dean of the Physics and Mathematics Faculty, later becoming an Academician. In the first few years after the October Revolution he was Rector of Petrograd University and one of the leaders of KUBU (Committee for improving Scholars' Living Conditions). He also protested about the arrests of various professors. Andrei's father Michail Shimkevich, a talented young officer in the Tsarist army, had also campaigned against injustice. He was arrested on several occasions, fled Russia and eventually found himself in France where he met the young poetess and artist Berta Kitrosser (Kitrosky), daughter of a sugar manufacturer from Kiev. They married and Andrei was born. After the 1917 revolution Andrei's father returned to Russia to build a new life. He was a military expert and was given a high position in the Red

Army. Yet his wife and son did not join him. Berta divorced Mikhail, then met and married the sculptor Jacques Lipchitz. Andrei was an attractive child, but with a nervous nature. He attended the *Lycée Janson de Sailly* in Paris until he was 15, where he'd been a difficult pupil.

Eventually Berta and Lipchitz decided to send him to live with his father, to try and instil some discipline into him. Mikhail asked the secretary of state for education, Lunacharsky, to accompany his son to Russia. So Andrei arrived in Moscow, in the special coach of a special train, with Anatolii Lunacharsky, the first Commissar for Education after the 1917 Revolution until 1929, and his wife. 'This curly-haired blue-eyed blond in short trousers, a young pupil from a French *lycée* did not know any Russian at all', recalled Galina Alpers, a neighbour of Andrei's father and the wife of a well-known critic. Andrei did not like his handsome father's new wife, his endless carousing, the cold, or life there in general. He started visiting anti-Soviet students, who promised him the position of Ambassador to France once they'd overthrown the Soviet regime. All he had to do was to take some forms somewhere, which had been stamped with false seals. They were all arrested and Andrei was convicted, albeit as a minor. He managed to escape and returned to his father's flat, where he took a pistol and some maps of border areas. He got as far as Turkey, where he was caught and exchanged for two sheep. Beria himself interrogated the unfortunate youth, and he was sent back to prison. Then came the show trials of 1937 and his father was shot. So Andrei, in addition to his own misdemeanours, was the son of an 'Enemy of the People'. Yet once again he escaped and even got as far as the French Embassy in Moscow. He spent a few days there, but was handed back to the Soviet authorities.

Roman met Andrei in Karaganda camp. By that time Andrei had already been in prison camps for twenty-three years. His nickname was 'Conspirance'. When asked what nationality he was, he used to say 'Russk'. He told me later that he had never tried to learn Russian properly, because he was afraid of forgetting his native French. What he liked doing most of all was quoting Baudelaire by heart. In camp he behaved very honourably, helping his friends as best he could. He was well loved by the more educated prisoners, by former followers of Bandera and the partisan 'Green Brothers' from the Baltic states. Over the course of twenty-six years he saw many different camps: Solovki prison camp located on the Solovetsky Island in the White Sea was a large forced labour camp for political prisoners. It became a model where NKVD developed and tested security measures, 'living conditions', work production norms for prisoners and different measures of repression; in the Krasnoyarsk region, Magadan, Karaganda, and Pechora. He also had two stays in Lubyanka prison which was the feared destination of thousands of innocent victims of Stalin's purges. After his ill-fated escape to Turkey he had even spent time in Tbilisi's Ortadzhala prison. Those 'travels' lasted till 1956. They finally released him, issuing him with a Soviet passport. He turned it down however, explaining that he was a French citizen. He then worked in Moscow for eighteen months for Progress Publishers as a proof-reader and French translator.

Figure 35. Andrei Schimkewitsch just before leaving Moscow for Paris, 1957.

In 1958 his French passport was finally returned to him from the KGB archives and he went back to Paris to his mother, who'd been desperately trying to find him. She'd written to Khrushchev, turned to the communist poet Aragon and his wife Elsa Triolet for help; then to the writer Ehrenburg, Peshkov and anyone she knew in France or Russia who might have had some influence. Andrei left Moscow very quietly, telling no-one. He did not taken the direct route from Moscow to Paris, but decided to go via Finland and Sweden. He could not come up with any straightforward explanation for this, but everyone was aware of his nick name 'Conspirance' and so did not ask many questions. Admittedly we had known he had some friends in Finland and that among his fellow camp-inmates in Russia there had been the odd Swede. It was only Roman that went to see him off. They arrived at the station in good time for the train, put his luggage in the compartment, shared a cigarette and the odd joke. Andrei was tense and nervous. A few minutes before the train left, two solidly build men with stony faces and felt hats walked into the compartment. Andrei turned pale and almost collapsed, muttering, 'They've come for me'. It turned out that they were diplomats returning after a holiday. The train moved off and there was a letter saying that Andrei had arrived in Finland, had an outburst of rage, then started to have a good time and amuse himself, before continuing his journey to Sweden to pass on an important message to the family of anti-fascist hero Raoul Wallenberg (as it later proved) before returning to Paris, and his mother.

When Andrei returned his mother was no longer with Lipchitz. During the War the two of them went to America. Lipchitz had stayed – but Berta came back to Paris in the hope that her son was alive and would return to her. Later Lipchitz divorced Berta to marry a nurse who'd been caring for him in hospital. By the time I met Andrei, his mother had been dead for two years and Lipchitz died a year later, so Andrei was living in that tumbledown house on his own, failing to make ends meet. He sold what he could and by the time we appeared on the scene, there was virtually nothing left to sell. It was not Andrei's penniless mother who'd inherited the house, but Lipchitz's second wife, despite the fact that Berta had lived there, guarding the valuables, corresponding with Jacques and looking after his European affairs for more than fifty years. Her only recompense was her right to live in the house until she died.

After being away for thirty years, Andrei found it hard to adapt. He ended up as a not very successful insurance salesman, hence some of his odd characteristics. He tried teaching and translating, but these occupations were short-lived because he found it so hard to settle. He also had a quarrelsome nature. He would spend his few francs showing off in as much style as he could: wanting to make up for all that he had missed, yet he was often cold and hungry. But we were soon like relatives, taking responsibility for him. At last I had a grandfather! Whenever we were in Paris, Andrei would spend almost all his time with us. We would go together to visit friends at Christmas, Easter and New Year, and hardly ever accepted an invitation if he was not included. I started cooking family lunches that Andrei loved, like home-made meat balls and chicken soup. He had beautiful table manners, regardless of how much he drank. He and Roman would sit down over a bottle of wine and talk for hours about their camp experiences. The rest of the world might as well not have existed.

ADVENTURES WITH ANDREI

Andrei was what one could call a character – and sometimes his behaviour was reprehensible. His twenty-seven years of experiences in the camps, where he was incarcerated as a political prisoner with some heavily criminal elements – all men – meant that he wasn't always the most respectful or civilised of guests when he'd had a drink or two. For example, a friend had invited twenty people to a formal dinner. The main guest was Madame Gallimard, wife of the well-known publisher. Although no longer young, she was a handsome woman and appeared in a smart closely fitting dress, which showed off her well-preserved figure to advantage. All the other guests were younger than she was and Madame Gallimard had decided to fit in with the young crowd at the gathering. She had brought along her grandson to stay as company for Ivan, the son of the hostess. The guests took their assigned places at the beautifully laid table, complete with starched napkins. Sophisticated conversation was the order of the evening: the latest literary publications were being discussed. Roman had brought Andrei along with us. He was clearly an educated man and was joining in the conversation, reciting Baudelaire, and telling entertaining stories about Romain Gary.

The mood became less formal and people began to feel less inhibited. There was plenty to drink. Silva, wife of the artist William Brui, had prepared wonderful carp in the Jewish style, and Nelly our hostess was an excellent cook as well. The guests started changing places and moving round. Andrei sat next to Madame Gallimard. He asked her to dance and then to a restaurant. He was soon slapping her bottom! Madame Gallimard, unused to being treated like this, tried politely to extricate herself from the situation and turned him down.

Andrei was very drunk by this time and was trying to pull the star-guest into his car, but Madame Gallimard preferred to use her own. We set off home in single file. Eventually Andrei lurched forward and blocked the road so that Madame Gallimard could not pass. He demanded that she get into his car and go with him to a Russian restaurant. Madame Gallimard was cowering by this time and with great difficulty Roman and I managed to get our lady's man to desist. By this time he had already arranged a rendezvous.

Almost the same thing happened when our friend Lena gave a party on New Year's Eve. Lena's husband was a Cuban, the well-known sculptor Cardenas. Their house was full of guests: the collector Baron Ulvator, the painter Mansurov, Edouard Loeb, Frédéric Mitterrand and a whole tribe of Latin-American artists. A Brazilian band was playing; champagne was flowing like there was no tomorrow. We all felt good, relaxed and happy. Andrei invited our hostess to dance. He was wildly drunk by this time and started slapping her bottom and squeezing her. Lena's Cuban husband, who was tall with the figure of a strong athlete, was not prepared to tolerate it, nor were his friends. Their Latin-American blood was about to boil. Lena quickly stopped dancing and asked us to make sure that Andrei left the premises. Her husband and the indignant Latin Americans were ready to tear Andrei to pieces after his insulting behaviour, but Andrei was perfectly happy and having none of it. He did not want to leave. Four of us eventually dragged him out of the house and saw him home. That was the end of our New Year celebrations.

On another occasion he set off with my husband Roman to buy a car from an old widow, Baroness Erer. Her servant took them straight out of the lift into the garage. The car was almost new. The husband of the Baroness – recently deceased – had not had time to go out in it and for the Baroness the sight of the car brought back sad memories. Andrei had lost his previous car: it had been stolen. He could not afford this new one and the Baroness was not someone with whom they could possibly haggle. So Andrei pretended to be a Russian prince. The Baroness immediately began to melt, her maid started pouring out tea from a silver pot into cups of Sèvres porcelain and the sugar tongs came out. They started bewailing in unison the way life had become so coarse, not like the old days, exclaiming in horror at the brutish ways of the modern generation. The Baroness and the 'Prince' were in their element in that magnificent setting. Roman was passed off as a relative from Russia, whom Andrei had encountered in Paris. The Baroness by this time had been prepared to surrender the car for nothing, but we had no desire to take it with us to Moscow, as that would involve too much bureaucracy and Andrei had decided by this time to give up driving. A very sensible move. The 'Prince' did not go back to visit the Baroness again. All he did was make a polite telephone call to thank her for her kind invitation which he was sadly unable to accept.

One of Roman's acquaintances was an influential business-man, who in the past had been a member of De Gaulle's government and one of his associates: he was a colonel and a war-hero, who'd fought in North Africa. He was also an arrogant man, clever and with a cunning streak. He had been carrying on some kind of dealings with the Soviet Union at a national level. He was very fond of Roman, enjoyed his company and often invited him to dine with him – alone if possible. He was less fond of me as I was less inclined to listen to all that boasting. And then there was Andrei. If Andrei was with us, Roman would refuse to go alone and so the colonel had to take on the three of us.

We went along to a private club in the Rue Presbourg. One of the halls there was for playing cards and roulette and the other set aside for dining. Colonel Moskowicz had evidently had his fill of the gaming tables by the time we arrived and calmly took a menu from the hands of an enormous black waiter dressed in the striking purple uniform of the African Zouave Rifles of the First World War. The Colonel was in a mood for reminiscing about battle in Africa. That was when Andrei chimed in: 'So colleague, where was your command? A parachute detachment? So we really are comrades-in-arms! We were serving very near each other: I was in charge of land operations.' I don't remember whether they started talking about the D-Day landings in 1944 or about battles against Rommel, but what I did register was Moskowicz's reaction: 'That's strange, I don't remember you at all. What was your command?' Andrei replied without batting an eyelid, but Moskowicz countered by remarking: 'Strange, as I remember it, someone quite different was in command of that contingent.' During the war years Andrei had been in Soviet prison camps and probably knew little of what was happening outside the barbed wire and was definitely unaware of the fighting going on in North Africa. He refused to budge though. In the end he got so drunk that Moskowicz was prepared to forgive him his fantasising and we took Andrei home.

As a small boy Andrei had dreamed of being a commander of French combat forces in the colonies. The French were not engaged in combat anywhere else in those days. Andrei was capable of marching into a café in an unfamiliar part of town when drunk and regaling strangers with tales of how he had been in command and fought in the heat and sandstorms with the troops based in Africa. He was always eager to acquire new knowledge and had read widely on the history of the Second World War in which many of his comrades participated.

One morning in 1982 there was a telephone call from Andrei: 'My love, I've just had a call from Sweden and they want me to go there.' 'Slow down, Andrei. What makes it so urgent that you have to wake me up? Who's inviting you?' 'The Royal family.' 'Are you out of your mind?' 'Here we go again!' I thought to myself. I knew he sometimes had delusions. He was terrified of being followed. Sometimes he refused to answer phone calls for a week and I'd begin to get worried, thinking he might have got drunk again, or had an accident (he was always having problems with his car, which was eventually stolen, thank God). On one occasion I had been so frightened that I asked my friend Nelly to come over. We rushed over to his house and desperately rang at the bell. There was nobody at home, just a barking dog. Nelly climbed up on to my shoulders and leapt over a fence that was a few metres high. All of a sudden Andrei came downstairs after watching everything that had been going on from his window. It turned out that he had been afraid of people trying to buy his house and had been 'living under the siege'.

Yet this was different. He told us that for three days 'they'd' been bombarding him with telephone calls and letters. That he'd been sent a first-class railway ticket. And that he was being invited to an international Wallenberg conference with letters bearing the Swedish Royal Seal. Then I remembered. He'd once told us that in December 1947, when he was in the Lubyanka Prison in Moscow for a re-examination of his case, there'd been a Swede in the cell next to him who'd not known a word of Russian. Yet he and Andrei had managed to knock out messages to each other and communicate in French. That had been

Wallenberg, who had asked Andrei to contact his family in Sweden should Andrei ever regain his freedom. He did his best to grant Wallenberg's wish, which is why he had stopped off in Stockholm on his journey back to France from the USSR. Wallenberg's sister carried on a friendly correspondence with him for many years. He was even received at the palace and presented with a remarkable watch, which he later must have either lost when drunk – or sold.

Raoul Wallenberg had been a Swedish diplomat in Hungary during the last couple of years of the Second World War. His skill, courage and commitment saved nearly 100,000 Hungarian Jews from being taken off to the death camps and the gas chambers by the Nazis and Hungarian fascists. He issued protective passports to Jews and sheltered many others in buildings designated as Swedish territory. One instance of his courage was the handing out of protective passes through the unsealed doors of a train about to leave for Auschwitz. Despite being shot at by guards and ordered to come away, he carried on, saving hundreds of lives. During the siege of Budapest by the Red Army in 1945, Wallenberg was detained under suspicion of espionage for the West and Soviet troops took him to the USSR, where he disappeared for two years. He ended up in Lubyanka prison in Moscow in 1947, after which he was never seen again. Wallenberg had realised that he might never get out of Soviet prisons and that the KGB would try to conceal the fact that they had made such a shameful error.

'But I shan't be going', Andrei told me. 'Motya my dog cannot be left alone. They told me I should bring him, but Motya has bad ears. He couldn't possibly fly.' By this time I was wide awake: 'Andrei, I'll look after Motya. You should go.' 'No, I'm too old, I don't want to go anywhere.' The next day was another call. 'They're sending a car for me. They're going to hire someone to look after Motya or pay for his board and lodging.' 'Andrei, you must go', I insisted: 'There's no need to send Motya anywhere, I'll take him.' It was obvious that I should take Motya, all the more so, since I had brought him to France from Moscow, where my mother-in-law had proved incapable of coping with him. He was a sick dog, frightened of any sudden movement and when scared, capable of biting everybody. Back in Moscow there had been plans to put him to sleep, but I had dragged him to Paris. When my father had died I had had to fly out to Israel at short notice and had given Motya to Andrei to look after. Then I brought our old dog

Kitty back with me to Paris. Motya stayed on with Andrei, brightening his life for the next fifteen years. I had paid Andrei 'alimony' for his care of Motya as well, which helped him make ends meet.

Andrei was persuaded and started packing. He flew on a special plane with the French journalists. I begged him not to get drunk or disgrace himself or say anything stupid, and every evening I rang to find out how he was getting on. Andrei did us all proud and remained sober. Indeed, he pointed out: 'How could I possibly get drunk. I don't even have time to eat. It's a good thing they chop everything finely here, because they poke microphones straight into your mouth.' 'Who's chasing you?' 'Journalists. I'm the most interesting person here!' It turned out that at the first session of the conference the witnesses had all taken an oath on the Bible to speak the truth and nothing but the truth in the presence of judges, lawyers and the Royal Family. Andrei was the only delegate who had actually seen Wallenberg in 1947. The other witnesses could merely say that their father, mother, uncle or friend of a friend had seen him. The Soviet representatives insisted initially that they knew nothing about him, but later that he had died of a heart attack in 1945. It was only after *perestroika* that it came to light that Wallenberg had been in a Soviet prison and had been killed or had died there in 1947. Wallenberg was long dead, but there was Andrei in front of the assembled company speaking faultless French. He turned into the main 'attraction' of the whole proceedings. For the journalists present, he was like a character from the novel *Papillion* or even the Count of Monte Cristo.

Then came another telephone call. 'Andrei', I exclaimed, 'You wanted to go to a museum and have a walk. Have you been? You had enjoyed yourself there in the past, hadn't you?' 'Yes I went, but they gave me a car. I told them I like walking. They let me out and I walked, but the car followed me complete with two security men. Wherever I went they would follow. It's not even possible to go to the toilet in peace.' Andrei had to have special security as he'd overturned the official version of the story presented by the accused Soviet authorities. He was the hero of the day. Members of the US Congress invited him to visit and journalists reserved appointments with him for interviews. Newspapers devoted whole pages to him and his life. It was my telephone number that Andrei handed out, turning it into a hot-line. Quite a job to note down the times for all the interviews, lunches and dinners. It was important not to double book him.

There were also countless requests for him to write a book or at least dictate one, and some of the finest publishing houses made him offers. Andrei turned them all down, saying 'No. some of those people are still alive. I can't possibly risk endangering them. I'll write it up myself.' Journalists tried to put pressure on him through me, but Andrei never put pen to paper. He did, though, let some Canadians and Australians make a film about him. The Australians almost managed to get out of paying what they'd promised. So I threatened them, telling them that their film might be taken away at customs and they wouldn't be allowed to leave as planned. The idiots believed me.

After all that drama, Andrei's social insurance in France was sorted out, as were his right to medical care and an enhanced pension due to those who had been in Soviet prison camps. Prior to that there had been nothing this old man of 70 could count on for support. He'd hardly worked in France at all and was so frightened by his previous life experience that he was scared to approach the pension authorities to make inquiries – frightened that he might be punished for not having informed them of the fact that he'd even been briefly married, then divorced, yet paying the taxes of a married man. He lived another fifteen years, enjoying the status of an honorary pensioner. As time went on, Andrei acquired a calm wisdom. He virtually stopped drinking, knowing that he was suffering from slowly developing cancer. He did not talk to anyone about it, merely complained of feeling weak. In the end he lived to the age of 86. He was the kindest of men. He went out of his way till the end of his days to help the woman to whom he had briefly been married, and wherever he went he would always take a modest present. A rascal and gentleman rolled into one, but a real Gentleman.

RETURNING TO PALANGA

I went back to Palanga in 1992, just after Lithuania had regained its independence. A room was booked for me and my husband in the Brezhnev Villa which was very different from the houses in which we had lived during our Palanga holidays. The holiday accommodation had been built for members of the privileged Politburo and the Fourth Department, the Main Directorate of the General Staff of the Armed Forces of the Russian Federation, originally set up in 1918 by Trotsky, and Russia's largest foreign intelligence agency. It was a year after the Soviet Union had collapsed, but the whole set-up and the levels of service were unchanged. Even after the various resorts we had seen in Europe and the high quality hotels, this particular villa made an indelible impression on us, with its enormous grounds and building almost at the water's edge, as by the end of his life Brezhnev was no longer able to walk over the sand dunes. Indeed, he never lived to see it all. The rooms were up to 60 square metres in size, the beds three metres wide and the armchairs easily large enough for two stout people. The materials and fittings were of good quality: the finest oak had been used and everything was upholstered in red velvet. Next to the bedroom there would be a sitting room, also measuring 60 square metres, and then another bedroom slightly smaller in size, probably designed for a secretary. That was just one suite. There were eight all together. The swimming pool was filled with heated seawater. Each guest would book a particular time, during which nobody apart from your own family or friends would be allowed to use the pool. It would be quiet around the pool, apart from the occasional knock when an attendant would bring in enormous bath sheets to replace those already used. Who did this establishment belong to? Nobody really knew.

At that particular time the new Lithuanian Minister of the Interior was staying there with his wife and teenage son, a rich businessman of the new breed with his family. There was an enormous round table in the dining room for the chief guests. People would eat in silence, occasionally whispering to each other. My husband and I felt rather awkward in this setting and made a point of greeting everyone politely, commenting on the fine weather and sea water. The next day I started talking to the son of the Interior Minister, who only ordered vegetarian dishes. I decided to join him, finding common subjects of interest. From day to day the table became more talkative, a more human place. By the end we were positively friendly. In the town buying food was difficult. The Soviet Union had just collapsed, there were queues in all the shops and they were always running out of stock. In the villa we were not served sophisticated hors d'oeuvres either – all the things that the Politburo members would have had at their disposal, caviar and various kinds of smoked fish. There was nothing like that, but what we were offered was homemade and tasty. There had been plenty of vegetables and our cook had put her heart and soul into it. The well-trained and attentive young waiters would take down our orders several days in advance, noting down everything. From the very first day to the end of your stay, they never needed to ask a second time which kind of mineral water you wished to be served. The Interior Minister, the businessman and the government official all began to greet us. People started talking more loudly and to discuss between themselves what they would order for their meals. I cannot say that they all proved compatible in their ideas, but even at that enormous formal table people began to behave towards each other in a more courteous fashion.

The following year we did not go back again and later we discovered that the building had become the official summer residence for members of the Lithuanian government. When not required by the government, the villa is now rented out to groups from America and for corporate functions. It is rare for individual visitors to spend holidays there. In 2007 we decided to go there again. We told the director what a fine holiday we had had there fifteen years previously in 1992, and after that she agreed to let us return. The décor had not changed but it was all looking rather shabby and worn. There was no seawater in the swimming pool any more. The table d'hôte menu was still allegedly available, but the food was ordinary although the staff was putting themselves out. In a word standards were gradually going downhill. The Soviet system for the privileged Politburo was also now a thing of the past.

A SITTING TENANT

The Le Corbusier house had been up for sale for twenty years and Andrei lived in the house on sufferance rather than with any firm rights to it. Lipchitz never got on with Andrei and could not understand how anyone could possibly have remained locked up for 27 years without having done something. He left him virtually nothing. After his death, his heirs – the second Madame Lipchitz and her grown-up children – decided to sell the house which they did not need. But for Andrei, the house contained memories of his happy childhood, and of his mother. It was the home he had dreamt of coming back to during all those long years in Siberia. Turning him out was not straightforward, and neither was the conscience of the second Madame Lipchitz stirred.

At first they offered him some wretched accommodation in exchange for moving out. Then, making out that Andrei was incapable of ensuring that their property was adequately maintained, stopped sending him money for the upkeep of the house, along with the monthly payment of a hundred dollars that Lipchitz had earlier provided for Andrei. The family started complaining that it was experiencing financial difficulties, although Lipchitz by this time was a sculptor with an international reputation and had left his family wealthy. They lived and prospered in New York, did not need another house in Europe and even managed to get their hands on the Modigliani portrait of Andrei's mother, pretending they needed it for an exhibition. They never returned it, saying it was re-imbursement for the money they alleged Andrei owed them.

They started sending prospective buyers to view the house. Andrei would try and hide from them, but sometimes they would catch him unawares. Andrei's nerves, weak at the best of times, were undermined by all of this and he began to suffer from a persecution complex. A tenant like that frightened off plenty of buyers. But sometimes, when he liked the people who came to view, he would give them an honest account of the house's history and ask them not to buy. And that was how almost all of them responded. If buyers made him feel uneasy, he'd start splashing water over the ceiling and walls, turning their attention to its dilapidated condition. This also had the desired effect. On one occasion when I went there with Roman, there was water dripping from the ceiling and patches of damp on the walls. 'Andrei what's happened?' I asked: 'Has a pipe burst?' 'No, my dearest. Don't worry, it's all for the buyers. One of them is too interested.'

He started involving me in his game. Andrei asked me to write a letter to Madame Lipchitz saying that I admired Jacques' work, that I too was from Lithuania, that my father had known Jacques and been a friend of his in the 1930s, when he had been studying at the medical faculty in Paris. I agreed, writing that Jacques and my father had often met up in Montparnasse and that for those sentimental reasons I should like to acquire the house, to prevent it from falling into the hands of complete strangers. I asked her to let me know the price and once again stressed the sentimental attraction the house had for me. The letter produced the desired effect. Madame Lipchitz sent me a touching reply with the news that the house cost a million francs, but that she was prepared to wait for me to make my final decision. I replied that I needed time to assemble the money but that my intentions were serious. In the meantime we succeeded in getting another would-be buyer off Andrei's back. Madame Lipchitz felt I was the more promising candidate and she had no doubt about my credit-worthiness. At the time I would not have been able to afford even one of the cellars, but Madame Lipchitz waited for me to come back to her for over a year.

Andrei managed to hold off buyers for almost twenty years but was finally 'sentenced' to re-housing in spite of the efforts of the lawyers. In France it is impossible to evict anyone during the winter months and the legal executors had more sympathy with Andrei's situation than with the *bourgeoise Américaine*. In the end the city authorities found him a modest one-room flat, which had mod-cons and proper heating and cost next to nothing.

When he moved into his new flat he was already seriously ill. He said to me one day: 'It's a good thing that Motya died first. I shan't have to worry about him.' One of my very good deeds had been leaving our dog Motya to Andrei. It was meant to be temporary, but ended up for keeps. Andrei devoted all his reserves of tender feeling to that dog with shattered nerves. Motya hated drunks and as soon as Andrei started drinking, he would bite him. Andrei would turn up at our place with bandaged fingers. 'Has the bastard been biting you again?' 'He's absolutely right. I'd been drinking you see. Motya doesn't like it.' Motya completely reorganised Andrei's life. He had to be fed at regular intervals, be taken out for a walk three times a day and visit the vet for medical advice. Andrei would take him off into the Bois de Boulogne for almost the whole day once the summer came round. They would sit down on a bench and stare silently into the distance. 'You mustn't disturb Motya, he's composing poems.' Motya lived with Andrei until he was eighteen. Andrei used to bandage his paws, carry him up the spiral staircase to the first floor and feed him with fresh meat, but when visitors came Motya would start biting them mercilessly. Andrei would always make excused for him, as Andrei's life had acquired a purpose.

We thought that he would not survive the move he'd fought so heroically against for twenty years, but now that he had finally decided to go, he gave most of his belongings away. I was astonished by the greed of his 'friends' and how unfeeling they were. To my surprise many of them suddenly appeared. They pretended to be so sympathetic about Andrei's plight, while they collected up books of his, took down the original lamps in the studio, trying to oblige him and help in every way they could, until such time as they managed to load up the extremely valuable easel that had belonged to Lipchitz, and other valuable items. I had not wanted to take anything, but did take home one piece of furniture that he insisted on giving me – a chest of drawers. It now stands opposite my bed. Restoring and moving it from his house to mine cost a good deal more than it was actually worth, yet now it is all I have to remember him by. This large mahogany chest of drawers with its austere straight lines, devoid of any decoration stands just as it did in the household of the internationally famous sculptor Jacques Lipchitz and my friend Andrei.

BIRTHDAYS AND GOODBYE

We always celebrated Andrei's special occasions. When he was 70 we gave an enormous party where people dressed to kill. Even Limonov turned up in evening dress. But Andrei criticised them all. An enormous vintage car had driven up and the chauffeur had marched in with Pierre Cardin gifts (for a brief period I had been the representative of that fashion house in Moscow). We had such a good time that night that the neighbours called the police. When the policemen caught sight of all of us and the 'birthday boy', they congratulated him, raising glasses to wish him the best of health. For his 75th birthday there were just the two of us – and Andrei – in the Hotel Crillon on the Place de la Concorde. Yet Andrei started making a fuss about everything in Les Ambassadeurs, one of the most exclusive restaurants in Paris, even insisting that the sommelier change the wine, and giving 'advice' to the chef. I was so embarrassed. His eightieth birthday was celebrated in the Lipp brasserie in Saint-Germain-des-Prés among close friends. By that time he was feeling really weak although he used to come regularly to my bedside that year as I was having a bad time with my heart. On one occasion, when Roman and I had failed to locate Andrei, I got almost all my friends in Paris searching for him, even though I was in hospital with heart failure in London. Andrei in the meantime had been suffering from a diabetic crisis and was taken to hospital in a coma, after which he was never in his right mind.

During last few months of his life Andrei was a very ill and very confused man. We celebrated his eighty-sixth – and last – birthday on the 20th of February in his room in Saint Geneviève. He was just about conscious. We had brought a cake and some sparklers, which we lit at his bedside. Suddenly a siren started whining. The staff came rushing

Figure 36. Ariela and Roman Sef in her favorite Brasserie Lipp,
Paris, 2006.

in, and we were pushed out along with the cake. We'd inadvertently
set off the fire alarm and were even threatened with the Police. When
they saw how bewildered we looked they left us alone. Andrei died a
few days later with me and Roman each holding one of his hands.

PART II
MEMORIES OF ARIELA

KAMA GINKAS:
I TOO WAS BORN IN THE GHETTO

Every time you open a book, particularly a biography, you are inevitably drawn into someone's life story. You cannot change anything in that story, you cannot call out: 'Be careful – over there round the corner!' You cannot influence it, leave any imprint on it. Yet that life story leaves its mark on you and it may very slightly, almost imperceptibly, alter your view of the world. The person whose book you have just read is unique by virtue of her very birth, of the time *when* she was born and most of all the *place*. There are perhaps only dozens of such people, or at most a hundred.

Ariela was born in the Kaunas Ghetto. Everything seemed to conspire against her being born at all – even more so against her surviving. We have known each other since childhood. We came out of the same Ghetto. I used to go to her birthday parties. When I was 6 or 7 I used to be annoyed by how well brought up she was, by her frailty, her big hair-ribbons, by the way she stared out of her great big eyes and by the fact that she could even say things in French. I preferred my mates from my yard back home – and the street fights. My parents, however, were good friends with Ariela's and so, after putting on a little suit sent over by relatives in America, I would plod over to visit them. For some reason I did not like Ariela's father. Perhaps it was because of his unusually refined nature – a kind I was not used to – or because of his elegant, carefree air. I always remember him with his stylish tie. Just imagine that immediately after the war, the occupation and the Ghetto!

I had no idea in those days that the man in the tie, who used to play *belotte* with my father on Saturdays, was busy trying to find Jewish children who had survived by working as cowherds for Lithuanian peasants. It was an extremely difficult and dangerous occupation. The peasants would often refuse to give up their 'little Jews' who were extremely useful, helping out on the farms. Often people searching for such children were killed. Ariela's father – Dr Abramovich – comes over as an amazing individual in this book. As a child, I had thought that the words associated with him – ears, nose and throat – was his second, most unpleasant surname. He had always appeared carefree and relaxed with a warm glow about him, but the doctor was at the same time amazingly natural. There was never anything forced or over-dramatic in his personality, despite the fact that he was involved in extremely hazardous, altruistic activities. Ariela was simply in love with her father and I can understand it. I did not know at the time that the doctor and his wife had adopted the daughter of their relatives who were accused of betraying the Motherland and banished to camps in Mordovia soon after she had been born in prison. Something must have been going on in the life of frail Ariela, taking her first in one direction and then in another.

In recent years we made contact again and it was then that I realised how long she had been ill, the hardship and pain she had been through and with what courage – truly amazing courage – she had coped with her illness. She adored going to see plays at the theatre, but every now and then she would ring up and say: 'I can't come today, things are worse.' But more often than not though, she would say: 'I'm coming'. Then we would go through the stage door, because she could not manage the stairs leading up into the theatre at the front of the building. Then she would sit and watch the play with the rest of the audience. Or perhaps not quite in the way the others did...

Ariela's wide knowledge of international theatre, and her long friendship with Alla Demidova (which had given her an intimate knowledge of Moscow's Taganka Theatre in its heyday) meant that her approach to the theatre was highly individual. Her circle of friends included many extremely interesting and talented people in various cities and countries. Her own rich life story had also been a contributing factor.

As the years went by I used to see Ariela less and less frequently and our contact would often be by phone. On one occasion she told me about her plan to collect the reminiscences of child survivors from the

Kaunas Ghetto. She suggested I should write down everything I knew about it. The idea was to have the book published in England and in English. I wrote my contribution and sent it to her. We discussed our impressions of the various chapters. I was convinced that there were only seven of us children from the Ghetto who had survived, but I discovered through her that there were nearly a hundred still alive around the world who were prepared to write up their memories. How she managed to find them all I don't know, but find them she did.

What matters most of all? The flow of life itself ... encounters, regardless of whether they are fleeting, long-term, enduring. Even meaningless encounters are presented as significant. They can be inspiring and exhausting. They are all part of life itself. Ariela's life, despite all its bewildering zigzags, the tragic setbacks, the injustices and cruelty along the way, is, for some reason that is hard to explain, extremely gripping, despite its minor key. In December 2008 I was telephoned from Paris with the news that Ariela was no more. So her Odyssey was over at last. But we still have her book.

SOLOMON ABRAMOVICH: SISTER ARIELA

I was 8 when my older sister Ariela brought home two foils from school, where she had enrolled in a fencing club. She demonstrated some graceful moves with those foils, but after a few moments she was exhausted and turning blue. But Ariela told both her younger brothers about the interesting and appealing aspects of physical exertion, persuading me, the older of the two, to take up athletics. Thanks to her, our brother Ben became a basket-ball star and later on she insisted that my two daughters, Natasha and Katya take up ballet, especially as she had a great interest in ballet and had particular knowledge about the revolutionary artists of the earlier part of twentieth century designing costumes and sets for distinguished Russian ballet and theatres. She had discussed the matter with our friend Maya Plisetskaya (Mother's relation) and talked to the girls about how to hold their necks and their backs and how to move their arms and legs as gracefully as possible.

Ariela had an intuitive feeling for the beautiful. From her earliest childhood Ariela had many physical problems to cope with. I realised that for the first time when we were spending one of our summers in Palanga. After a short swim in the Baltic, at a temperature of 17 degrees, Ariela came out of the water, saying she did not feel well and then collapsed – unconscious. Our mother called out her name in tears but Ariela did not answer. Our friend, a French teacher by the name of Soblis, a colleague from Mother's university department, ran off with me to find the doctor at the nearby first-aid post, but there was nobody there as he had been called out somewhere else. We left a note for the Rescue Service. Some friends at the beach helped lift her up and carry her into the shade opposite the Seagull Sanatorium near the park that had once been part of the Tyshkevich estate. Medics from the Rescue Service eventually turned up and revived Ariela. That was the first of Ariela's dramatic episodes and victories over ill health I was to witness. We always remembered the Seagull Sanatorium. Later on it would be one of our landmarks as we walked across the long beaches at Palanga. The last time I went there with Ariela was in the summer of 2008. Once again we recalled that episode which had given us all such a fright.

She had been born with a congenital and untreatable heart disorder – Eisenmenger's syndrome. Most children with heart trouble of that kind do not live to see their teens and are usually bedridden. But over the years Ariela developed her own 'life-struggle immunity' a blend of incredible will power, alertness and brave resolve. All her cardiologists were astonished by Ariela and they became very fond of her. After school she came home too tired to go to music lessons, so a music teacher my father knew used to come to the house. Lying on a couch Ariela would learn to recognise her thirds, fourths, sevenths and dominant sevenths. Being a very active and gifted individual by nature, Ariela tried to ignore her physical limitations. Sometimes, however, a telephone call would come through from the Children's World shop or from the dairy shop Pieno Centras on Laisves [Freedom] Avenue, which she had to walk down on her way from school, or later on from the Medical Institute, where she studied for a year to follow in the footsteps of our father. We would be informed that Ariela was unwell, but by the time we arrived to bring her home, she would have recovered. She found it particularly difficult to cope in the anatomy theatre during her year as a medical student in Kaunus in 1958 (before her finally chosen language studies in Moscow) because the formalin vapours made her oxygen deficiency even worse.

When we were older, Ariela used to turn to Ben and I for help – fondly referring to us as 'my great big strong horses'. We learnt how to keep an eye on her, to take her dogs for walks and to help her go about her business and carry her cases, bags and endless purchases as she set off on journeys. We gradually became more and more attached to her, almost as if she were our child. We lived in London and Ariela lived for most of the time in Paris, which she loved. It was there that she used to buy us shirts, ties, suits and the beautiful things that made us and our surroundings smarter. Her taste was remarkable and we were full of admiration for her aesthetic sense. We found her company interesting and each of her visits to London or ours to Paris always involved visiting exhibitions, theatres, opera houses and art auctions. My brother and I used to accompany her everywhere when we were young bachelors and sometimes our friends would come along too. In later years the visits to exhibitions would turn into outings for our growing families.

Figure 37. Solomon, Ariela and Ben in England, 1978.

Sometimes things had to be cancelled at the last minute, when Ariela suddenly had to take medicine and lie down. Then we would take a wheelchair and oxygen cylinders along with us. Our sons Alexander and Jacob even used to find it fun setting off like that to the Tate Modern, the National Gallery or the Royal Academy pushing two wheelchairs as they went – one with Ariela in it and the other with her husband Roman, who suffered from painful joints in his feet and knees. Ariela really did nurture in us all a love of art, beauty and all that was good. I remember on one occasion when we were spending a summer holiday in Portofino, my son Alexander, who was still very small at the time, said that he had doubts about whether Ariela would like the hotel, because it did not have any pictures or beautiful carpets in it.

Figure 38. Ariela with her nephew Alexander, London, 1994.

When in Paris Ariela and I used to go to one of her favourite museums, The Museum of Modern Art, which was not far from where she lived across the Seine. We went to see an exhibition there of the art movement of Ecole de Paris. Those artists came from Eastern Europe, Belarus, Lithuania and worked in Paris before the Second World War at the same time as our father studied in the Medical Faculty of the University of Paris. He knew some of them and would mention meeting them in cafes, which we also used to visit with Ariela. She mentioned with sadness how many of those young and talented artists had perished in the Holocaust.

In her last years Ariela derived particular pleasure from visits to the opera at Covent Garden in London. Renée Fleming was to become one of her idols. The atmosphere both inside the auditorium and in the foyer during champagne intervals was always uplifting. That would give Ariela new strength, especially after a long bout of illness, although the various tests she had to undergo showed that she was unable to walk more than 50 metres. There would be at least three of us as we drove up to the main entrance of the Royal Opera House. The wheelchair had to be taken out of the car complete with oxygen cylinders, a thermos with hot sweet tea, a bottle of Coca Cola, a hot-water bottle, a bag full of medicines and a device for measuring blood pressure. Either Ben or I would take all this equipment into the opera house, while the other went off to park the car. Usually I would stay behind with Ariela in the opera house, but sometimes, particularly earlier on, Ariela would quickly tire and have to leave during the first interval. A new range of drugs was at last prescribed for her and after that there was a gradual improvement in her health. However, her cylinder sometimes had to be switched on, which made a slight hissing noise as the oxygen made its way into her nose through a small tube. The tension in the seats around us would become even greater than that induced by events on stage. Our frequent visits to the Opera House were of course noticed and when the management saw us coming, complete with wheelchair and oxygen cylinders, our party was often led to the Royal Box if there were empty seats in it. Keeping us away from the people in the stalls was probably both a mark of kindness and a precautionary measure. Often Ariela and I sat there, just

Figure 39. New Year's Eve celebrated in Ben's house in London, 2000.

the two of us, greeting our friends and acquaintances below us in the stalls.

After a long course of treatment with the new drugs, tests demonstrated that Ariela was capable of walking just about 100 metres. We used to take the wheelchair with us, but Ariela was able to walk into the theatre on her own and instead of two or three oxygen cylinders we could manage with one, which I used to carry over my shoulder. It was taken along just in case, but we did not have to use it during the performance and we were not disturbing other members of the audience. Ariela's last visit to Covent Garden was on 4 December 2008 when we celebrated her birthday with friends and family after the event. I still have in my possession a letter from a Dr Holman dated 1962, in which, after performing a cardiac catheterisation for Ariela, he had predicted she did not have long to live. Fortunately he was wrong. She had an irrepressible urge to live another day, another month, another year. Each day she would not only be fighting her illness and but in the end managed to live to 67, guiding and steering the whole of our family down a wise and positive path. It is not lost on me that Ariela died in Paris exactly fifty years after she had arrived and at the same time of year, in a state of excited anticipation of joining her husband at a magical time of year. At the time of her death she had been running around the city buying presents. Always the life-affirming friend and sister.

ALLA DEMIDOVA:
I'M STILL EXPECTING HER PHONE CALL

Although Ariela had been ill for a long time, she left this life unexpectedly. Two days before she died she rang me from Paris, telling me where she was planning to have lunch with Roman – who had just arrived back from Moscow – and which exhibition they were going to visit afterwards. She mentioned in passing that she was planning to bring her friends together to see in the new year, but that she herself might not be feeling up to it and stay at home, as she had often had to do after booking theatre tickets.

Her passing was, for those close to her, unexpected, because we were used to believing that Ariela would find her way back out of yet another setback. Such was her thirst for life and eagerness to find out about all that was new; another première, a new project or a new fashion requiring the instant purchase of a garment. For me, Ariela is still alive. Every day I still find myself waiting for her telephone call – sometimes after midnight – she was a light sleeper and knew that I always went to bed late. Given that she often spent long periods in Paris, she used to ring me almost every day, asking about the latest Moscow premières and what her friends were up to. She wanted to be in touch about everything. During her last years she couldn't cope with the cold of the Russian winter, and after her birthday on 24 October would return to her Paris home.

Now that I have grasped that Ariela is no longer in this world, I experience a keen sense of abandonment. I think about the Ariela I knew long ago and have a strange feeling that I am in a time warp. I have vivid memories of meeting her back in 1977, as if it were yesterday. Those memories are etched on my mind no less than my last visit to her in her Moscow flat, when she read me some excerpts from her recollections of outings to restaurants with her parents as a young child. I remember one of those restaurants – it was as if it had been yesterday. She took me there twenty-five years ago, in 1983. We drove from Vilnius to her native town of Kaunas, and she'd shown me where the Ghetto had been during the War. We also went to the house where her family had lived and spent a whole day in Kaunas, walking through its overgrown park not far from the apartment building where the Abramovich family used to live. We also went into the shops on the main street. That was the Soviet era and the shops were empty, yet we still managed to find an incredible array of beads, scarves and brooches. 'For presents', announced Ariela. She loved giving presents: there was no end to her generosity and kindness.

When Moscow's Taganka Theatre paid its first visit to Paris, I telephoned Ariela, as someone in Moscow had given me her number. Although we hadn't met before, she immediately asked us round to her home in Rue Cognacq-Jay. I went there with two friends – Ivan Dykhovichnyi and Boris Khmelnitskii. Her flat – only recently purchased and repaired – was small, clean and devoid of furniture. We sat on the floor eating from a small coffee table. Ariela popped into the nearby shop and came back with croissants, cheese, eggs and herbs. We enjoyed a fine and speedy breakfast. What I liked about her from the beginning was her light touch and her open hospitality. She took charge of me while I was in Paris and introduced me to her close women friends. She also took me to a fashionable Paris hairdresser and made me change my hairstyle. She and her friends gave me a whole pile of their 'togs' and did not abandon me once during the whole visit. She was to become my close friend for the next thirty years.

In friendship, just as in love, relationships between people change, moving on from one stage to another. It would seem that initially Ariela had needed me as a friend – she used to listen to my advice, I introduced her to my Moscow friends, I would get hold of tickets to theatres which were virtually inaccessible to the general public and we used to visit the studios of the artists I knew. That, incidentally, was how she later acquired pictures by Slepyshev and Khamdamov. Then when I went to Paris she took charge of me and we used to go to exhibitions, plays and concerts together, as well as to her favourite shops.

By the end of our friendship Ariela's advice was something I could not do without: how should I dress? Hang my pictures? Arrange my furniture? And where I should buy what. Ariela would carry me off – one day to a luxury hotel in Vilnius, then to Cannes for the summer, where, six months in advance, she would reserve rooms at the famous Carlton Hotel or book tickets at the Opéra Bastille for the first run-through of a new opera.

Figure 40. Ariela with actress Alla Demidova at a theatre festival in Riga.

In the early days, when she still felt well, Ariela used to accompany me on tour or to film festivals in all sorts of towns, in order to get to know different places. I remember arriving in Tashkent, where I had been due to give a concert. From there we went on to Samarkand and Khiva, wandering among the unique religious buildings decorated with blue mosaics. She had always paid close attention to fine art, trying hard not to miss a single exhibition of paintings, whether she was in Moscow, Paris or London. During the many years of our friendship I was able to observe how she educated herself in the world of art and was always keen to widen her experience of painting, literature or the theatre. I always trusted her opinions. Ariela's life was a difficult, but amazingly interesting one. Her mental energy and desire to live life to the full, despite her illness, and her urge not to miss out on anything interesting led me to live life at a quicker pace than the one I was used to. In the course of a single day in Paris we might do the rounds of all the shops in the Faubourg St Honoré, lunch in a well-known restaurant and end up at a performance of *Hamlet* at the Comédie Française. Ariela's energy used to astonish many people. I think that when she and her brother Ben started manufacture of computers for the office automation systems business some twenty-five years earlier, Ariela had been the initiator of the project and the driving force behind it.

Figure 41. Ariela at a business seminar in Vilnius, 1989.

Despite her frail appearance Ariela's inner resolve was extremely tough and she always achieved the goals she set herself. She never shunned hard work. She reminded me of the heroine in Shaw's play *The Millionairess* who could not help making money wherever she went. Like Shaw's heroine, Ariela had an undeniable flair for business. The only things she lacked were health and strength. When her brother was building his hotel and spa resort outside Vilnius, Ariela was the focal point of the project. She would take countless flights to Italy or Paris in order to select the right fabric for curtains or bedspreads.

Every room in the Hotel Villon bears the mark of her taste: all have individual décor, nothing is repeated. It was Ariela with her wealth of experience who selected the pictures which you find hanging in the rooms and the foyer. She invited the artist Rustam Khamdamov to Vilnius, after commissioning from him the pictures she wanted to see hanging in Ben's hotel. Using her experience of Parisian restaurants, she planned the menus until the hotel's restaurant became one of the finest in Vilnius.

Figure 42. Ariela and the artist Rustam Khamdamov, Villon, Vilnius 1994.

She would not, of course, have had the strength or the opportunities for all of that if it had not been for Ben. He and her other brother Solomon were devoted to her. Like an infinitely caring mother, Solomon used to telephone Ariela every day, wherever she might be, to enquire about her health. Ariela, with a rather disgruntled expression on her face would mumble something by way of reply. Although Ben had become a successful businessman, he would always listen to her advice. Yet she never came over as the eldest in the family: on the contrary, her brothers used to treat her as their rather wayward daughter.

Ariela had an astonishing memory. She could remember everyone's phone number, and never forgot names – not only of friends but of people she hardly knew. Well-known specialists in a variety of fields

Figure 43. Ariela and Ben in the Hotel Villon outside Vilnius, 2006.

would often turn to her for advice or assistance. I know for instance, that John Edwards, director of the SPEC Group, persuaded Ariela to help him set up a business in Moscow, because, despite his international reputation as an outstanding engineer he had failed to make headway there. Ariela proved invaluable. She immersed herself completely in the task and the company achieved a leading position in the Soviet market providing office automation equipment and systems. This success was noted by Margaret Thatcher when she visited the Soviet Union. There is a photograph recording the event, when Mrs Thatcher personally thanked Ariela for her work. I learnt about this from others.

Once, when we were out on the road, the car's radiator developed a leak and the water poured out on to the tarmac. We had come to a halt in the middle of a stream of traffic. Ariela ran into the nearest shop to buy a bottle of water, which we poured into the right hole and we then set off. But the car ground to a halt again, this time outside a restaurant. Just at that moment the police turned up. Ariela was hurrying back as they came in and she slipped and fell down on her back just by the car. When we eventually got home she was coughing

Figure 44. Ariela and Margaret Thatcher at the British exhibition in Moscow, 1993.

blood. It was the first time we had seen her in this state and we were very scared. Ariela's doctor brother – Solomon – flew in from London immediately and she was taken to hospital. I went to visit her there every day. I think that ever since that day Ariela was haunted by a well-concealed fear of death. After that, carers appeared on the scene, along with oxygen cylinders and the wheelchair. Yet none of that stopped us from setting off to the outer limits of Paris to see a new play or to buy yet another garment from Sonia Rykiel. During her last three years we grew used to her new condition, regarding it as routine. There were even occasions when we turned her illness to our advantage, for instance at the Grand Opéra people on wheelchairs were allowed in through the stage entrance. There was a special member of the theatre staff on hand who used to take her through the wings. That gave us the chance to look at the sets and the props workshop. We could discuss all that we saw, because no-one around us spoke Russian. We were also able to leave the car right next to the restaurant where we were having lunch as Ariela had a special disability permit.

It is impossible to convey in mere words the image I have of Ariela, although she is still vividly alive in my heart. How can I explain that? I see a tree in front of my widow for example, and the image of that

Figure 45. Singer Elena Obraztsova, Ariela and Alla Demidova at the Bolshoi Theatre, Moscow, 2002.

tree lingers in my mind – the tree is the same in both cases. The tree in front of my window has been cut down, but the one in my mind's eye continues to exist. Yet for the reader to see the tree as I see it? Only a good writer can achieve that.

We often used to call Ariela a 'partisan'. One could entrust any secret to her and she would never betray it. She told people very little about herself. I was only able to guess at her past life from a few of her seemingly insignificant responses or words. When Ariela had been in better health, back in Moscow, on 9 May– Victory Day – she would always go to the square in front of the Bolshoi Theatre, or to Gorky Park where war veterans used to gather. She would go on her own. I used to ask her why. Ariela would just shrug her shoulders in that inimitable way of hers and give me some noncommittal answer. She had her own very personal response to all that was connected with the War and that Victory.

She was willing to talk about her father though. I think that she inherited her kind nature from him. She loved her parents and, when telling stories about them, she would talk very openly, answering all our questions. Yet she never talked about her French husband or her work in the cabaret. Ariela's work in the cabaret and her difficult life on her own in those early years in Paris had left their mark. Over the years, as her life gradually became more settled and she acquired more material resources, you could see the change in her face. Her features became more clearly defined, showing off to advantage her beautiful eyes, her long aristocratic nose and radiant smile. Because of her illness and Ariela's 'survival reflex' a new habit appeared. In the middle of a conversation she might suddenly cut herself off, her eyes would start 'peering into her soul' and I would realise that it was time for her blood pressure to be measured, or for her next round of pills. Yet if Ariela found something genuinely interesting during a conversation, a play, in a shop or at an exhibition, she would forget about her illness. It was only when we noticed her fingers turning blue that we realised she needed her pills.

I remember how, years ago in Vilnius, we were about to miss a bus. Ariela couldn't run of course, but I kept urging her to hurry. Her hands by this time were almost black and we realized we had to stop despite everything and wait a while. In those days Ariela's bad turns did not last very long.

On 21 December 2008 Ariela telephoned me from Paris. It was a Sunday evening. She asked me what news I had and I told her that that afternoon I had been supposed to present a prize of Rolan Bykov to the film director at the House of Cinema, but that he had not turned up. I therefore had had to take it home with me to give to him later. We laughed and Ariela said that she'd been coughing blood, as she had on the day when she'd fallen when the car had broken down. I comforted her, saying that it would pass, just as it had on the previous occasion, particularly because she had been feeling better that year. The next morning Ariela rang again, but this time from the hospital George Pompidou. She said that it did not seem as if she was going to pull through this time. Solomon was constantly by her side and on the evening of 23 December Ariela stopped breathing. When I rang Ariela's brother Ben from Moscow the next day, he answered the telephone in Paris. At the news, this tall strong brother of hers wept.

At this point I shall break off my reminiscences, because there is no end to them...

ALEXANDER AND LILIA MITTA: ARIELA AS WE REMEMBER HER

My wife Lilia and I often think about Ariela. We had known her and been her friends for fifty years. We began to notice that as we sat over our morning tea, we would recall first one and then another episode linked with Ariela. Then another ... and another. Naturally these recollections do not give a complete picture or a psychological portrait, but are episodes that remain fixed in our minds. Ariela was a fighter. Throughout her life she was warding off the early death that had been predicted by doctors. Yet time marched on and she stayed alive, maintaining that she was winning the battle. Her enemy was within her – a weak heart. Yet she lived three times longer than even the most optimistic doctors had predicted. I think that what helped her most of all was her vitality, which defied the beckoning of death. I remember seeing her at times with an ethereal blue face – and with the tips of her fingers turning blue. She would merely comment that she had not had a good night and ask you to bring her the news she wanted to hear. In the meantime she would be asking about our impressions of the latest plays, exhibitions and films. She had a resolute way of standing up to her illness, refusing to fade away and showing the keenest interest in the life all around her.

As she was not able to have children, Ariela's two brothers were like her children. As were the endless succession of stray dogs that she used to feed, wash and find good homes for. She was also an enthusiastic theatre-goer, making sure she attended all the significant Moscow premières. 'What an achievement', you might say. Yet how many theatre-goers have you come across who would attend premières complete with wheelchair and oxygen cylinders? That was all part of her intuitive strategy for life, which could be summed up as follows: Nothing can destroy an active interest in life. If that interest fades, so will the ability to resist illness. If she was having a relapse and unable to leave her home, she would telephone her friends and interrogate them until she had obtained a clear impression of how the première had gone. She wanted to know all the details. In the end I might start shouting at her: 'Ariela! You'll drive me crazy! Stop!' But she always insisted.

Women friends were a crucial part of Ariela's life. I only knew her women friends in Moscow and not even all of those, let alone the friends in Paris. Each of these women was treated by Ariela as her very best friend, becoming the object of the most solicitous attention. Yet Alla Demidova was probably the very best of the best friends. In the last years of her life in Moscow, Ariela no longer went to the Kinotavr film festival, but she still demanded the most detailed account of everything connected with it. Sometimes the details might seem merely amusing to me, but to her they were extremely important. She would ask. 'Who was the queen at the Kinotavr film festival?' I would have given the wrong answer, but women have their own view of these things. My wife answered: 'Alla Demidova.' Ariela blossomed on hearing that, 'Yes, yes, she is a queen! She's always a queen! She can't not be the Queen!' There was more to that than casual excitement however, because Alla was dressed in the latest Paris fashions and Ariela had played no small part in that.

For decades, when our country was closed to the outside world and 'fashion' had to be what the Moscow garment factory *Moskvoshvey* came up with, Ariela used to bring fashionable clothes into Moscow by the trunk-load. She always brought with her the latest, striking up-to-the-minute clothes that really make women look attractive. That was decades before Moscow women were able to distinguish one designer from another. Ariela herself was like a travelling exhibition of trends and fashions from Paris. She was one of the first people able to demonstrate that fashionable clothes not only make a woman more beautiful, but lend her confidence, set her free and, although they may not make her more intelligent, are a stimulus, encouraging her to live life to the full – to try and achieve something. For Ariela, every pleasure she was able to bring one of her women friends was like a life-enhancing vitamin. 'When I make someone happy, it makes me happy too – it makes me live.'

Our friend Lena has been Lena Brahms for almost twenty years, with a son already taller than her husband. It is worth recalling that it was Ariela who brought her and her brother Ben together. To say she married them off would be overdoing it, but Ariela used to introduce Ben to some of the beautiful women who could well become his wife and the mother of his child. If Ariela was not convinced that one of them might not want to settle down and give Ben a family, the lady in question would no longer be centre stage and someone else would be in the running. She was a truly caring person. My wife recalls how 'she once burst into our flat (our flats were off adjacent staircases in a block that had been built for artists) shouting, 'Lena's ill! She's got so weak! We must make her chicken soup straightaway!' 'All right. I've got a chicken in the freezer. I'll thaw it out and make some soup.' Ariela was literally shaking with agitation by then. 'No we must make the soup straightaway! The bird can be thawed out in boiling water!' The chicken soup was, of course, made on the spot. Ariela then took it round to Lena while it was still hot.

Figure 46. At Ben and Lena's wedding in London, 1990. From left to right: Lena, Ben, Ariela and Solomon.

Dogs were another of Ariela's passions. In Paris, Andrei's Le Corbusier designed house was turned by her into a home for mangy stray dogs from the Paris streets, many of them covered in sores. She would gather them in and then, with Andrei's help, would feed them, treat their wounds and bites suffered in street fights, and eventually find them good homes. In Moscow it would not be possible to find such humane people who would take in stray dogs. She usually had a couple of moulting dogs living in her Moscow house. She even took one of her Moscow dogs to Paris, after making untold efforts to arrange all the forms and permits required. She also always had two dogs living with her in Paris, insisting that her visitors go into raptures over their intelligence and refined manners. In the summer resort of Pitsunda, there was more scope for Ariela to indulge this mania in the grounds of the rest house for cinematographers. She would always be bringing in some dog or other from the beach and would bribe the hotel staff to let her take them inside and feed them. Psychologists might tell us what lay behind it all, but perhaps it's a perfectly normal human trait – to show compassion for the weak and the sick?

Figure 47. At a dog show in Moscow, 1989. The Afghan hound, Jardin, won three medals.

She was of course aware that what was bestowed on everyone around her as routine and free – i.e. a healthy life – was something she would have to wrest from a merciless adversary. Perhaps it was this that motivated her? Or perhaps the rest of us have such hardened hearts that simple compassion takes us by surprise and seems alien to us. Ariela's brothers were her children and she was their daughter. I know of few families whose members loved each other so dearly. Yet, at the same time, it would be hard to find three people who were so different from each other in one family.

Ben is an entrepreneur to his fingertips. He has incredible energy and is always endeavouring to reshape something, change it, improve it, to create something new. He is a classic example of someone who has established himself without any outside help or support. I remember his first undertakings in Moscow, where he started making money. As they might say on TV, 'everything hit him at once' – the usual Moscow double-dealing, the threats and the betrayals by once close collaborators. I saw how Ben quickly sorted out a situation with some business that he'd been cheated out of when a young associate, whom he had taken into his confidence, had scored a victory over an English rival. The next morning he was devastated, like a child who had been punished because he had lost everything. I witnessed his wild outbursts against negligent staff. Anyone would expect that after a confrontation of that kind, blood vessels in his brain might have burst. But no, Ben bounced back, his head full of ideas. How did Ariela help Ben? That deserves a volume of its own. I know only a tiny part of the story through his involvement in a film of mine when Ben was the producer.

Ariela's other brother Solomon is a doctor specializing in microsurgery of the ear. He is a gentle, caring man, whose most aggressive behaviour would go no further than a polite, quiet question. For a short time I lived in his house when my film *Lost in Siberia* was being edited and re-recorded. The working day for doctors in London begins at 7:00 in the morning, yet Solomon would get up even earlier, to place at the bedside of a still-sleeping Ariela a glass of freshly made carrot juice. How many other brothers would show such devotion to their sister in adult life? The two brothers loved Ariela and she loved them. That devotion was an active, productive and crucial part of their lives.

Ariela and I came together when working on the film *Lost in Siberia*. It was at the end of the 1980s. I felt that I had to make a film devoted to the members of my family – to my uncles who had been shot in the 1930s, to their wives and my aunts who'd languished in the camps in which they were given long sentences – sometimes five years, sometimes eight – in my mother's case ten. I thought up a plot and wrote a good script with Valerii Frid and Yuri Korotkov. The director of the Mosfilm Studios at that time was not prepared under any circumstances to release a film about camps under Stalin. That was when Ariela brought in Ben, who was unaware of what he was letting himself in for. He understood nothing about the film business but had the creative core of enterprise – grasping the essence of a new situation and then relying on intuition. Intuition in this case based on his conviction that when it came to investing money, Ariela would not recommend anyone who didn't know what he was doing.

Cinema is a highly speculative business. Success is celebrated everywhere, while if you fail, you die quietly. Failures are a hundred, if not a thousand times more frequent. Ben seemed bound to fail, because he had brought together an enormous army of 'outsiders'. Nobody predicted any other kind of outcome. I myself was entering the capitalist world for the first time but had acquired an intimate knowledge of Soviet working practices over the previous twenty-five years, so one thing I did know was that the person in charge is the director. Money, on the other hand, was something I had never had anything to do with. I learned all I knew about producers from Soviet propaganda about the alien world of ready cash and its villains; that they were the lowest of the low in the world of the cinema. Yet times had changed – and for the better. I had to rush into the arms of the wicked and he was planning to pounce on what was mine. MINE! Films had come to be regarded as a product, the manufacturing of which was what the producer was investing his personal capital in. What struck me right away was the sheer scale of the finance – absolutely incredible from a Soviet perspective entailing unimaginable risk. We were aspiring to something that was eminently marketable and that was the approach that eventually reaped reward. BAFTA – the British Academy of Film and Television Arts – singled out our film as the Best British Foreign-language Film of the Year in 1991, and the Cannes Festival selected our film for one of its main competitions. What might have taken many producers half a life-time, Ben achieved overnight. Moreover, his second Russian film, directed by Karen Shakhnazarov was equally successful – and selected for the Cannes Festival in 1991.

Figure 48. Ariela with her husband Roman Sef and her brother
Solomon after the film presentation at the International Film
Festival, Cannes 1991.

I need to point out that without Ariela the film would never have come
into being. It was she who gave the cart its first push, after that donning
the harness, pulling it all the way. Yet in the cinema things do not run as
smoothly as might appear from publicity releases. There was work in
store for Ariela after the film had been finished. It went the rounds of the
festivals and the high point of its success was a nomination for a Golden
Globe in Los Angeles. By this time the film crew was due to start preparing the film, which had been completed in London, for distribution in
Russia. Everything seemed to be progressing smoothly. Yet problems soon
emerged. The man in charge of the next stage assured us that the film was
ready for distribution, but then he flew off with his family to the United
States for a fortnight to show his family Disneyland. That was the last we
heard of him. When we began to investigate, it turned out that his papers
were in complete chaos and that plenty of fraud had been happening. As
the producer's trusted associate and representative, Ariela took charge of
the task. I mention all this so that nobody should have the impression that
Ariela only went in for glamorous pursuits, selecting clothes for her
friends, designing projects and the like. No – Ariela had her feet firmly
on the ground, turning her hand to many different things.

Wherever she went she left behind her people who remembered her with gratitude. How could we fail to recall her flat on the Rue Cognacq Jay, which provided a hospitable refuge for her friends in the days when none of us could have dreamt of paying for a room in a Paris hotel? So what specifically is Ariela's legacy? Under what heading can we put all her activities? Here I have stirred it all together – friends, brothers, dogs and films. This is not a rounded portrait but more an emotional outpouring. To put it simply, Ariela was a striking personality, a good friend – a person who had opted for the right path in an unremitting struggle against a congenital disease, but a struggle in which she triumphed.

YULII GUSMAN:
ARIELA - A NAME THAT MEANS LIONESS

There could not be a more unsuitable name for this delicate butter-fly. I thought at first that Ariela was a name to do with the air, flight, mist. It turned out to mean lioness. Ariela did not appear to live up to her name. She was the epitome of gentle tact, of kind sensitivity and yes, she did have an ethereal quality. Her strong, large and for-midable brother Ben was the lion. Yet her parents did not get it so wrong after all. Ariela was always a fighter, a desperately deter-mined fighter – for life, on behalf of her family and friends, people she knew and sometimes those she did not. And for her beloved brother, Ben, and his aspirations. Everyone responded to her with affection. It was impossible not to be fond of her. She looked at everyone with such a defenceless yet wise expression in her eyes – both proud and beautiful.

I met Ariela, becoming one of her friends at the Cannes Festival (that sounds very glamorous). Our company there was highly exotic. There was Ben with his leg in plaster in the most splendid of dinner jackets, me in my Hungarian suit of grey bouclé and a ridiculous bow tie (without which we would not be admitted), and Ariela in a resplen-dent outfit, making her look like all the French film-stars rolled into one. When we walked along the famous red carpet and past the guard of honour on the grand staircase of the Palais Lumière there was not a single person who did not stare at us. Our group consisting of flying Ariela, limping Ben with his impressive cane and myself looking very much like a Latino bodyguard. The highest of honours were paid to this carnival trio and we were given the very best seats.

At that time I had no idea that our outwardly carefree Ariela – a mere slip of a girl always so kind, open-hearted and smiling – was actually grappling with a serious ailment. Every day, every minute and every second of her life. At school we used to study the life stories of Soviet heroes, who – even when suffering from tuberculosis – would build railways or crawl back with frostbitten feet through the front-line to their own troops. It had always been difficult to distinguish fact from fiction, myth from real exploits. Yet all that time a gentle modest woman had been living alongside us, achieving a heroic exploit every day. We knew nothing of all that. But we know now.

MAKVALA KASRASHVILI:
A KIND HEART IS A GIFT FROM GOD

I was introduced to Ariela fifteen years ago when she asked me to find tickets for her at the Bolshoi. Since then, whenever Ariela was in Moscow, she made a point of attending every première at our theatre. She loved opera and ballet. When Ariela began coming to my performances she always presented me with a splendid bouquet. My sister and I used to receive flowers and presents from her without fail every birthday. She never forgot an important date and possessed a degree of responsiveness unusual in our country.

When she learnt that I was having a problem with my spine, finding walking difficult, Ariela played a crucial part in resolving my torment. She rang Paris, found out the address and telephone number of a Paris doctor specialising in such ailments, booked me an appointment and insisted that I fly to Paris for a consultation. As I knew nobody in Paris and Ariela was in Moscow at the time, she asked her friend Oxana to meet me and take me to her flat. After that Oxana accompanied me to the doctor's as well. By the time it had been decided (after a second consultation and several procedures) that I would have to remain in bed without getting up for three weeks, Ariela herself was back in Paris. She used to come and see me every day and either she or her devoted home help, Pani Irène, would supervise and take care of my meals and medicines.

Ariela's kindness was amazing. As was her hospitality. Even towards us Georgians. Ariela was a good cook and enjoyed feeding her guests: if she did not feel up to cooking herself, she would invite them to a restaurant and try to pay the bill herself. Her heart went out to everyone, especially those who were ill – including animals. Ariela never complained about how she felt and never talked about her ailments. All she ever said was that she would stay at home occasionally, rather than go out, commenting that 'it's probably the fault of the weather'. How selflessly she used to take care of her husband Roman! I have seen her pushing him along in a wheelchair when he was having problems with his legs. Roman died soon after Ariela, no longer able to 'recharge' his own batteries with her energy. She always had a great deal of inner strength. She used to listen patiently to all our problems during our international telephone calls and when we needed help, would respond immediately and do everything possible. When Ariela was no more, I felt as if I had lost a close relation.

NELLY BELSKAYA: THE 'BLUE DISEASE'

At the dawn of the 1960s there were four of us who – immediately after graduating from university during the thaw under Khrushchev – married Frenchmen. My case turned out to be the most complicated. I had been studying at the philosophy faculty of Moscow University – a bastion of official ideology. Most of my fellow students had been men over 30 – mostly dashing young men from the ranks of the KGB. After purging the state security services, Khrushchev had given those people the chance to brush up their ideological credentials and it was precisely those dashing young men who could have sent me off to build the Bratsk hydro-electric power station in Siberia, depriving me of the right to complete my studies and vetoing my marriage to Michel. They were organising everything within the rules of their particular 'art'.

Two others – Lyudmila and Svetlana – were students of the philological faculty. That was where they had met their husbands – French students of Slavonic languages, who had been their colleagues in and, what was more, members of the French Communist Party. But my husband Michel was of bourgeois origin and worked for the newspaper *France-Soir*. He had come to Moscow as part of a Franco-Soviet joint film project and was writing a script together with Sergei Mikhailov. The fourth woman in this position was Ariela, the youngest of us all. She was 19.

One spring, all four of us found ourselves in a Russian restaurant in St Germain. I no longer know whose idea it had been to meet up. Svetlana and Lyudmila were there with their husbands, while Ariela and I were on our own. In a cupboard on the wall there was a stuffed salmon gathering dust, and a ginger cat watched us from the cashier's desk. I had just received the first instalment of my salary from the *lycée* where I was working as a *lectrice* and ended up spending all my earnings on that meal – on condition that each of the others would pay me back their share. 'You and I will be going back in the same direction', Ariela had said to me, as we left the restaurant. In actual fact it turned out that we lived by adjacent metro stations. As we walked down the Boulevard St Michel to the Jardin de Luxembourg it was still daylight. I remember buying some food for Michel who used to spend all his evenings at film previews. By this stage he was the paper's film critic. Ariela and I walked down to the platform, stopped and waited for our train. A change suddenly came over her face and she sat gently on the ground. Her face and hands were turning blue. I asked the people standing nearby to call an ambulance. One of them started running towards a public telephone. The train drew up and its doors opened. Ariela opened her eyes, rose quickly to her feet, grabbed hold of my arm and pulled me into the carriage. The train pulled out of the station and then I asked her: 'What's the matter with you?' 'Don't worry, it happens every now and then. More often in cold weather. It's an illness I was born with, known as the blue disease. Don't take any notice. It comes and it goes.'

That was how I came to know Ariela. Strictly speaking, Ariela was never really on her own. There was Ariela and there was her difficult companion – the 'blue disease'. Later I learnt that she had been born in the Lithuanian Ghetto. People who had been through that rarely talked about it in any detail and the fact that Ariela only began to write about her past in the last years of her life is not surprising. Enough time had passed by then for her to be able to find the language she needed. But let us return to the Line B train in Paris. 'How are you feeling now? What can I do for you?' 'I need a hot bath. I have a shower at home, but it's not the same thing. I need to spend some time in a proper hot bath.' So we went back to my place, which meant climbing to the third floor. We went slowly and once we got there I ran a hot bath, putting in plenty of bath salts. Ariela was thrilled and before long the blueness had passed.

During the year that followed Ariela's phone calls became a kind of ritual. By then Ariela had separated from her husband and was renting a room in Sentier in the house of a furrier. The whole place was swimming in fur, the floor, the walls and her blanket. We would listen to

Okudzhava records and read the first of the *Samizdat* publications. Ariela was working as a *lectrice* as I was, but she found getting to work by public transport difficult, and struggled with the damp cold of the Paris winter.

Among my friends was a Dr Morin who had his own cardiology clinic. He was crazy about everything to do with Russia. In the early period of my life in Paris I used to give him Russian lessons. He declared himself ready to take on Ariela's 'case'. Medical examinations followed and Dr Morin told me: 'I can't possibly grasp how she has managed to reach the age of twenty. When children are born with this heart defect, they are usually operated on immediately. Without an operation they would die in infancy. Ariela needs to go straight back to her family in her home country.' In order to obtain a visa to return to the USSR, a special document was required. I was given the task of taking it to the Russian Consulate. I took it there and read it on the way. I could not believe my eyes when I read: *The patient has a maximum of two years to live.* That was the conclusion drawn by a group of French luminaries and Ariela undermined their prediction by 47 years.

In Moscow, which I used to visit on countless occasions, I came to know Ariela much better. I met her brothers Solomon and Ben, whom I took to at once. Ariela often used to visit my parents' house in Kuntsevo on the edge of Moscow. I think she succeeded in part in filling the gap I had left. In Moscow we were always off to the theatre together. Ariela's passion for the theatre was highly contagious. Everything I used to see in Paris seemed bland by comparison to what was happening on the stages of Moscow and Leningrad. Our second shared interest was clothes. Anyone who knew the Moscow of the Soviet period doesn't need reminding about the importance of clothes for any young woman. Ariela had a real talent for presenting herself. For a time she even worked as a mannequin in Moscow's House of Fashion. I can imagine how much she must have enjoyed it and can still see Ariela's face when she used to look through the clothes I had brought with me from Paris. It was the shining face of a child overwhelmed by Christmas presents.

My first woman friend in France was called Anne. She taught me many useful things and I visited Russia with her in the summer of 1965. According to our travel plans which we had duly reported to the

Russian Consulate in Paris, we were going to go as far as Yalta and Ariela was going to come with us. She had booked a room by the sea, which she had not seen before. We took a taxi and arrived at the place where we were meant to be, but halfway there, in the middle of vineyards, Ariela began to turn blue. I took out a multi-vitamin pill from her handbag. It helped and we reached our destination. It was very primitive. Water had to be drawn from the well and there was no phone. The landlady was not sympathetic either. 'If it's going to be as difficult as it looks to get down to the sea, how on earth are you going to get back up again?' I asked Ariela. She replied that we should get out of the place while it was still light. Climbing back up to the house from the shore took us over two hours. Every two minutes Ariela had to sit down and rest. When we got back to the main road it was difficult to wave down a car as it was already dark. Ariela managed to find a bed in some kind of guesthouse and we shared a bed head-to-tail and fell asleep.

When I came to Russia in 1972, she was on top form. We visited Moscow painters who gave us addresses of people in various Jewish organisations. We were to supply names of those who needed invitations so that they could obtain an Israeli visa allowing them to emigrate, and so we ended up with large numbers of addresses of would-be émigrés. I asked the painters to print them on thin cigarette paper. At a later stage another meeting was organised – this time a fair distance from Lubyanka – during which I was passed over documents about what was going on in the psychiatric hospitals of the USSR. I wrote down names of victims, doctors and medical establishments. I ended up with something the size of a roll of toilet paper filled with minute writing. That roll of paper was later to be transformed into an article published in the *Nouvel Observateur* under the fictitious name of an alleged dissident physicist. Getting this 'commodity' through the customs somewhere near Lvov was a hair-raising experience, but that is another story.

Ariela's disease seemed to be under control. She and her family were soon to be leaving for the West: her parents to Israel and her brothers to London. Ariela herself was going back to Paris. The address she would be using in France for the time being would be mine in Sceaux and her French papers could be reinstated. By this time there was someone new in her life – Roman Sef, her new husband. Now that they have both left us, I feel at liberty to say what a remarkable couple they made. Roman had astonishing eyes with a hint of sad irony in them. They were almost like Chekhov's in the photograph which I keep framed at home next a photograph of my son Ivan. Andrei Schimke-witsch appeared on the Paris scene as well. He was like a surrogate son, despite the fact that he was old enough to be our father.

In 1999 we buried our 'adopted son' at the age of 86 – later visit-ing his grave both together and separately. Ariela's visits to Paris were becoming less frequent by this time. Her 'blue disease' had long since stopped behaving and French doctors were recommending a new course of treatment for her. For them it was probably an intriguing experiment and I knew that Ariela would agree to it. A miracle actu-ally happened though, the second one after the Ghetto, and she survived that bout of illness. The last time we attended a concert together was in the auditorium of the Louvre. The nurse, the oxygen cylinders and the wheelchair had been mothballed by then. We even went to the restaurant afterwards on foot. Although fashion was no longer of major interest to me, I noticed that Ariela was wearing some-thing extremely avant-garde with a Japanese flavour, which nevertheless had nothing loud or over-the-top about it. It made me happy, just as it did all those years ago, when Ariela used to try on the outfits I had brought her from Paris.

I learnt about Ariela's death on the island of La Réunion in the Indian Ocean. I resolved straightaway that after my return I would travel to London to visit her brothers and go with them to the ceme-tery. Solomon and I went there with an enormous bunch of flowers, but the cemetery was closed for the Sabbath. There was even barbed wire to keep people out. Solomon immediately found a place on the fence where there was no barbed wire and leapt over it like a profes-sional gymnast, coping with the vase and the flowers as well. It made me happy again. The next day I walked through the open cemetery gate with Ben. We added some more flowers and Ben said a prayer in Hebrew. On the third day Solomon accompanied me to the grave together with his younger daughter Katya. Her resemblance to Ariela was striking. Katya looked just like the young girl in her photograph, which Ariela had given me years before. She must have been aged six or seven. Once again there was joy amidst the sadness. Ariela had a new 'shadow' allowing her to live into the future.

SERGEI NIKOLAEVICH:
A PRESENT FROM ARIELA

There was something about Ariela's appearance that reminded me of a bird, an unusual exotic bird who had flown into our part of the world. I remember her going out of her way not to miss any theatrical premières or gallery previews and she was always extremely stylish in her dress. She would follow Paris, not Muscovite fashions. So it was not immediately clear whether you were encountering a foreigner or one of our own women. The doubts were reinforced by the fact that Ariela always had a most gracious smile and would apologise, in a vague sort of way, when asked near the entrance to the Conservatoire if she had any spare tickets. What also made her seem different from Moscow women was the short-sighted way she would look round her, as she stood in some endless queue for a buffet, or to pay a cashier for some purchase, instead of pushing or using determined elbows. She came over as a foreigner living in Moscow – in Lavrushinskii Lane, no less, in a block of writers' flats opposite the Tretyakov Gallery. Her name seemed foreign too.

Ariela had other addresses; Paris, London and Vilnius. She seemed to have houses, friends and family everywhere. Her special trip to Maurice Béjart's last première in Lausanne, her dresses from the latest Sonia Rykiel collection, purchased in a Saint-Germain boutique – they were all part of another life. At the end of the 1970s when I came to know her, people in Russia could only fantasise or dream about a life like that as they struggled to gain tickets to showings of films in the Goskino centre, which would not be on general release, or leafing through journals in library departments for which special readers' permits were required. Yet Ariela never showed off about her rare opportunities. Where they had all sprung from no-one seemed to know. Ariela herself would always be the first to joke about them, telling hilarious stories about how an attendant in the Bolshoi Theatre had taken hold of her ultra-fashionable sweater with seams on the outside, whispering to her in confidence. 'My dear, you've put it on inside out – and such a beautiful garment too.'

Ariela Sef was frail-looking by nature, seeming to weigh almost nothing, like a circus performer or ballerina. The fact that she did not have to be at work by nine o'clock was something one could also sense straightaway, from her very first gesture, word or smile. Her life had a different rhythm, someone who was used to being in control of her own life and her own time – and who did not need to hurry anywhere. Yet how insistent and businesslike she could appear when she wanted to help someone, involve influential acquaintances in some project, collect money together, get hold of crucial medicines or doctors. She was passionate about being useful and went out of her way to help anyone who turned to her with a request. Where did that fighting spirit of hers come from? Not to mention her punctuality and honesty?

It was with that single-mindedness that Ariela devoted her energies to the famous project at the Stanislavsky Centre – *The Cherry Orchard* directed by Eimuntas Nekroshius using Russian actors – generously providing accommodation with five-star comfort for all the company in the famous Villon Hotel just outside Vilnius, which also provided ideal conditions for rehearsals. It was with the same enthusiasm that Ariela, despite her seriously deteriorating health, embarked upon organising an exhibition in memory of the well-known painter Lev Novikov in the House of Nashchokin Gallery. She rang round all the crucial people, making requests, cajoling and bringing in the money. Yet none of this activity had been stimulated by any ambitions of her own or hopes for financial gain. Her own name was something she forgot to mention in the lists of sponsors and well-wishers. She didn't need to. When she was asked to do something, Ariela would put her heart and soul into it. When anyone requested something of her they would find her frail hands already stretched out in a responsive gesture towards them – a gesture which seemed to say that she was ready to give of herself, to help. That was Ariela in a nutshell.

Perhaps all this came from a childhood filled with terrible darkness, danger and so much loss. Not long before her death, Ariela decided to write her reminiscences about the Kaunas Ghetto, in which all her family had been living during the War and where she miraculously survived. She recalls a life so rich in all kinds of experience. Those terrible pages written in a light, almost ironic tone are hard to reconcile with a life that turned out so well. Yet, brightly coloured feathers are often a form of camouflage and self-defence. Nobody was meant to know anything about that grim past, or ask questions about what lay hidden behind her charming smile and the somewhat bewildered short-sighted gaze behind tinted glasses in a fashionable frame.

We last met in the autumn of 2008 at a Sotheby's preview in Moscow, in the dimly lit halls of a house on Gogol Boulevard, her silhouette against the white walls appearing as little more than a shadow. She appeared almost transparently frail, an impression highlighted by her rouge, which had been applied too thickly. I knew that she was ill and that her husband, who she looked after with selfless devotion, wasn't in good health either. By now she appeared at public gatherings only rarely. This might have been explained by the fact that *the public* had changed considerably in recent years, as by now it would be difficult to astonish anyone by talking about Paris or Sonia Rykiel outfits. We walked past Impressionist paintings and those of the now more marketable nineteenth-century *Peredvizhniki* (Wanderers) worth millions. Some of the people there were discussing prices, others trying to establish the estimated prices indicated in the catalogue, while another group was talking about the auction which had recently been held in the Kremlin. All this was a very different world, one which had almost nothing to do with Ariela. She felt like the stranger in the second act of *The Cherry Orchard*. The people there were people she did not know and the pictures were not those she had any urge to buy.

Later on she invited me and my wife to spend some time in the Villon Hotel near Vilnius. 'Do come, just drop everything and come! It's nice up there and we've brought in new chefs. We also have a new spa. You'll enjoy it. If you decide to come, let me know. Perhaps I can get up there myself for the weekend.' We did not get to Vilnius and neither did Ariela. Yet I can still remember the New Year's Eve we celebrated in the restaurant of the Villon Hotel in 1996 – how the windows were suddenly ablaze with a golden rain of celebration fireworks. I can also remember how my wife and I danced to the Abba song *Happy New Year* and how we wanted all that to go on and on and on. There may well be plenty more New Year celebrations to come, but no more like that one. That was a present from Ariela.

Figure 49. Ariela in Villon, 2006.

OLGA YAKOVLEVA: OUR DISTANT YOUTH

Ariela and I met thanks to Lyusya Ponomaryova, an actress from the LenKom Theatre. It was some time in the 1970s. After her rehearsal that day Lyusya asked me to go with her to the flat of one of her friends, a French woman. After that we would go together to the theatre for the evening performance. It was a play we were both acting in, either Chekhov's *Seagull* or Eduard Radzinskii's *Film-makers*. The door was opened by a pale thin girl with long hair. She seemed to be hiding from the bright light, like Hedda Gabler in Tesman's house. She had thrown something light and flowing round her shoulders, which according to my mental picture of those days, was most appropriate for a Frenchwoman. I was to learn from Ariela that she was not French at all, but had been born in Lithuania in the town of Kaunas and had married a Frenchman, that she later separated from him and returned to Russia. Now here she was in Moscow. Later still I learned that she had been born in the Ghetto, but was always reluctant to talk about it, as people are when discussing tragic events, which, although they relate to the distant past, leave a deep mark in their soul. In my conversations with her I often returned to that subject, but Ariela's answers were always reticent, although she might add a few significant details.

I came to know Ariela's mother, Bronia Isaakovna, in London in 1978. Our Malaya Bronnaya Theatre was taking part in the Edinburgh Festival where we were performing Turgenev's *A Month in the Country* and Gogol's *Marriage*. After the festival was successfully behind us, we were brought to London to put on an evening's entertainment at the Soviet Embassy. Since I was not involved in that particular programme I was able to slip away and meet up with Ariela and her mother in Hyde Park, which was not far from the Embassy. Unlike Ariela, Bronia Isaakovna was a plump, placid woman wearing a hat. She was in mourning after the death of her husband and was herself seriously ill at that time. Before I left for Moscow, Ariela asked me to meet up with her again and give her some moral support. Just like Ariela, her mother did not refer to her recent bereavement or to the tragic blows dealt her by fate. All she said was: 'What a wonderful sunny day we're having in London. So many young lovers lying out on the grass in Hyde Park!'

I also remember how, on a May 8th, some time during the 1970s, Ariela telephoned me and asked what I was doing the next day. I told her I was free and she asked: 'Fine, would you come with me to Gorky Park?' 'You can't be serious, Ariela', I responded. 'I don't go there, or rather I went there once after gaining a place at drama school, taking a running jump into a flower-bed in my excitement.' Ariela managed to persuade me and early on the morning of 9 May she and I met by the park gates. It was hot for spring that day and by ten o'clock the sun was beating down. Ariela was standing by the park entrance, squinting into the sun, holding a large bouquet of tulips, narcissi and carnations. I bought some flowers as well, which were being sold near the gates, then Ariela led me into the park, turning right straightaway towards the banks of the Moscow River, where, in the baking sun was an enormous crowd of War veterans, walking about, standing or sitting. Others were playing accordions or *bayans* or even tambourines. They were wearing their old military uniforms that were now faded and shabby. They had long since 'grown out of' them during the twenty-five years since the War. Some were playing music, others singing and making merry. Then there were the dancers and the mourners, or people drinking, perhaps moving about – searching and finding. Some of the veterans were holding up plywood signs reading: *First Battalion, Byelorussian Front* or *Company so-and-so, Moscow Home Guard.* I can remember, as if it were yesterday, a scrawny, frail veteran holding his little board, bearing the number of his division and the name of the front where he had served. He was almost carried along by a woman (evidently his wife) hardly able to put one foot in front of the other. He was hobbling and weeping on her shoulder, as he said: 'How many years have I been coming out here with this board and over all that time nobody has ever turned up.' Ariela and I were lost for words. Not a single person from a whole division was still alive! The woman started comforting her soldier, saying: 'Never mind, Kolya, perhaps next year someone will come or perhaps they've gathered somewhere else.' Yet Kolya was inconsolable and went on crying: 'Nobody … not one of them. Surely I can't be the only one left?'

Ariela walked about among the people there, observing similar tragic little tragic documentaries. She was handing out flowers to those taking part in the brief 'life-story' scenes. Everyone was happy to receive her flowers, some with words of gratitude, others silently caught up in their grief or meeting up with friends. At last we reached the end of the riverbank and turned back, needing nerves of steel to walk through that sea of people with its tide of emotion. We lingered not among those who were happy with their rediscovered friends, but among those who had failed to find their army comrades or who were mourning those they had lost. After that Ariela and I took each other by the hand, went somewhere to cry in the shade and then walked on, wiping away our tears. What was striking was how, just from looking at their uniforms one could tell who had served where in the army, in what capacity and how they were making out in peacetime. The former military commanders were prospering better in peace time, while soldiers from the infantry were still making out as best they could in humble, poorly paid work. It was sad to observe all that and it made us feel ashamed.

Ariela insisted I follow her further, up above the riverbank towards a green lawn where a group of soldiers in dark-blue suits were standing in a circle round a single white-haired woman. They were soldiers from the Stalingrad Front. I can no longer remember which of the armed forces that uniform had belonged to, but it was definitely not the air-force. They were probably from some engineers' or communications unit. We stood at some distance from them, listening to them talking. They were soldiers who'd been wounded near Stalingrad, who were thanking this woman – an army surgeon, who had operated on them after the battle. They drew us into their circle and continued their conversation. Ariela gave each of them a flower and they introduced their surgeon to her, recounting how she had saved them. When one of the men showed us how thick the layer of lead had been, which had covered the whole battlefield it was no longer difficult to imagine that hell and the terrible price that had been paid for the victory at Stalingrad. The face of one of the veterans was covered in pockmarks from exploding shrapnel, but the military surgeon had managed to save his eyes. Another could not hold back his tears, as he told us how almost all the wounded who had been taken off the battle field had been dragged away, not by medical orderlies (they would not have been able to survive if they had got that close to the fighting) but by specially trained dogs. The dogs pulled them out, but the dogs did not survive. He himself had been pulled out by an orderly, who'd noticed that there were officers' boots sticking out of a small crater. If he had had ordinary solders' boots on, he may no longer be alive; one of the endless stories being told that day. Ariela and I walked behind the veterans towards the park's exit, then to the taxi rank opposite the gates. We froze in horror at the sight of a group of drunken young delinquents pushing war veterans with artificial limbs to one side as they commandeered the taxis, telling the old soldiers to 'hurry up and kick the bucket'. Some of the old servicemen were in tears.

A few years later, before the 'Actor' Sanatorium had been built in Sochi, Ariela and I decided to go down to the Black Sea. A symphony orchestra conducted by Yevgenii Svetlanov was giving concerts in Sochi's summer theatre at the time. The orchestra's manager was Leonid Salai, who'd previously been the deputy director of the Lenkom Theatre where I worked. The hotel did not have its own beach and we had to walk over to the Intourist beach. That was a long way away and involved walking all the way along the town's public beach first, or skirting round it via a steep hilly path, then coming down the other side, before finally reaching it. Ariela appeared to have been endowed by nature with excellent, or I would even say, uncommonly good taste and, in addition to that, she had just come back from Paris. What had long gone out of fashion there would be just coming into its own in Russia. This meant that Ariela was often the first person to introduce us to Parisian fashion. In the evenings when we went to Svetlanov's concerts, Ariela's appearance outstripped all the competition. She would don beautiful evening dresses from well-known fashion-houses and people would find it hard to take their eyes off her.

We were on holiday together once again without anything special to do in the evenings apart from the concerts and we used to spend hours talking the night away. Ariela taught me a great deal. I learnt from her that some clothes are suitable for ever, others for a particular season, and that it is a bad idea to be photographed in fashionable clothes because it will not be long before they are out of fashion again. Ariela also stressed that underlining what is fashionable can end up achieving the very opposite. Her knowledge of theatre and theatre design reinforced this. Our theatre had excellent designers but I always valued her taste and style – inviting her before anyone else to premieres.

Years later the news exploded into my life. 'Ariela died just before Christmas – peacefully and without pain. We were afraid to let you know that she is no more.' No more Ariela? What could they mean? Where was she? I understood what they were telling me but could not grasp it. She had always been there. Perhaps Ariela never slowed down, her butterfly flight ensuring that she never missed a single beautiful flower, fearing that she might be too late, miss seeing something? Only someone with a truly artistic nature could respond to her surroundings like she did.

Figure 50. Ariela and Roman Sef in Villon, Vilnius 2006.

ANDREI YAKHONTOV: THEY WERE AN IMPRESSIVE COUPLE

In 1975 Ariela married the children's poet Roman Sef. He was an elegant witty man, always bubbling over with jokes and expromptus. To look at Roman you would never think that he had been through the camps like so many people in our country. Kornei Chukovsky gave him a piece of advice when he returned from the camps: 'Write children's poetry – they don't lock you up for that.' During his lifetime Roman published many collections of poems and they were translated into a number of languages. The wife of the Japanese Emperor was so enamoured of his verses she invited him to her palace. Ariela's union with Roman was a most unusual one. They met across Life's immeasurable ocean, like two pieces of a ship that once been intact – and they could not do without one another.

Ariela wrote only one book – this one – at the end of her long and difficult journey. She never even saw it in print. After reading her manuscript, it is difficult not to be astounded by Ariela's extraordinary resolve and determination to help people around her.

Ariela and Roman departed this life almost simultaneously: Roman the good, wise man with a real sense of humour and Ariela, beautiful, responsive and sensitive to the end. You will both be missed.

KAREN SHAKHNAZAROV: RECALLING ARIELA SEF

I find myself talking about Ariela Sef, as if we had only just met. She was the sister of my friend and producer, Ben Brahms; a woman with a most unusual life-story and with rare charm. Women of this kind have a powerful influence over men, they manage to organise them and are the centre of attraction – the life and soul of the party – the star of the family.

When I was working with Ben on the film *The Assassin of the Tsar*, Ariela played an extremely important role, albeit an unofficial one. Although she was 'just' the producer's sister, she was the person with whose help it proved possible to resolve the problems that inevitably arose. Also, when it came to questions of taste, Ariela was someone with whom you could discuss anything. Thanks to her, relations within the team making that film were good.

Her own life-story was a real drama however, which would have made a good film, yet it seemed to have set her apart and kept her going at the same time. Right up to the end of her life, Ariela managed to retain incredible strength of will, love of life and those shining eyes. Many people's eyes become tired as they grow old, but not Ariela's, whose eyes were always radiant and youthful, reflecting her unusually attractive female charisma. They will live on in my memory.

KSENIA MURATOVA:
ARIELA, DEAR HEART

I often think what a pity it is that I used those words so seldom with Ariela. She herself did not go in for outward expression of deep emotion – it was alien to her and something she found quite impossible and intolerable, even at the most bitter moments of her life, those which cut her to the quick like the death of her mother. It was only in her last years that Ariela started using the word 'dear' when she addressed me. As she mellowed she began to use it when addressing her other women friends. She never mentioned the places which had caused her pain or been the cause of real heartache, and she stopped visiting the *Closerie des Lilas*, which she had loved so much, but where she'd received the news of the death of her father.

In the early years of our friendship she used to call me Aska. When one of the overwhelming catastrophes in my life hit me, Ariela brought me presents – perfume, eye make-up and home-made meat balls, which she hauled upstairs complete with hot potatoes covered with a napkin. She came rushing into my strange room, with its ceiling made of beams which made it look like a ship. As she held out what she had brought me, she said in a strict, business-like voice, avoiding my gaze, 'I thought to myself, this might make Aska happy.' At first I didn't know what to say, because she was gasping for breath after climbing all those stairs. The last thing I was prepared for was feeling happy. Then I burst out 'Ariela, dear heart!' But she shrugged her shoulders and half turned away. The perfume she had brought me was of the very best. The eye make-up she had chosen was exceptionally pretty, sparkling with all the colours of the rainbow like an artist's palette. She also gave me an extremely beautiful little casket made of black lacquer-work and said in an almost angry voice: 'This should last you till the end of your days.' She was quite right, the box still occupies a place of honour on my dressing-table. The meatballs were delicious: they were light, containing large pieces of onion, a novelty for me. How on earth had she managed to keep them so hot, as if straight from the stove? Ariela, dear heart...!

While I was ill, some amazing new antibiotics were sent by Ariela's brother Solomon from England. When I expressed caution about taking them, Ariela dispelled my doubts, declaring indignantly, 'Solomon would not send anything of low quality.' She adored her brothers and was very proud of them both. I stayed in Solomon's flat on a number of occasions, in a room that had belonged to Ariela's mother, in a Hampstead house surrounded by trees. At that time Solomon had only just begun practising as a doctor in London. Sometimes I felt it was important to talk to him about Ariela's health, about the foolhardy things she often embarked upon despite her congenital heart disease. It was not that she really wanted to hide those details from her brothers – I think she wanted to tell them – but she didn't want to worry them, knowing that they used to feel anxious about her every day and night. She was glad though that I sometimes 'told tales' to Solomon, but I would ask her to forgive me.

I can remember very clearly how I first met her. It was the summer of 1975. At the time she'd been living in the Rue Pascal, in a corner flat on the ground floor with doors opening into two different streets. It was a hot summer's day filled with sunshine and all the windows were wide open. At the time I was living in Rome and used to visit Paris occasionally. I used to stay with Lev Adolfovich Grinberg, a close friend of my great-uncle, Pavel Pavlovich Muratov. Lev Adolfovich was a renowned art historian and became like a second father to me and took me in, as if I was his own daughter. 'Today I want you to meet a very high-quality girl, Ariela Cavoleau', he said during one of my visits to Paris with his usual gentle sense of humour. After that we set off to Rue Pascal.

It has to be said that Lev Adolfovich was an extremely wise, far-sighted man with wide experience of life and extremely well disposed towards me. He not only looked after me then, but thought about my future. He wanted to make sure that not just during his lifetime, but afterwards, I should be surrounded by loyal, dependable and devoted friends. Somewhere along the way he had decided to introduce me to Ariela. 'A very high-quality girl' he repeated, on our way home. This was the highest praise he bestowed on anyone. It implied a person, on whom it would be possible to depend at the most difficult moments of one's life. I had plenty of opportunities to realise how right he had been.

I remember Ariela sitting on her window-sill with her legs dangling, wearing the most appealing light summer shoes. Now that I know her well I understand how her main aim on that occasion had been to impress a visitor from Rome with the most expensive and attractive of her recent acquisitions – beautiful, fashionable shoes made of the most delicate suede. This was to upstage the unknown newcomer, who, on top of everything else, was monopolizing the time and attention of her beloved Lev Adolfovich. Ariela's legs were also worthy of attention. I, of course, noticed the legs and the shoes and the all-conquering look, but I was struck more by the look in the eyes under the luxuriant auburn fringe – a look that was intelligent, missed nothing and was very focused. It was a look that summed everything up in an instant and was slightly ironic. It was also mature, all-knowing and sad, with something child-like about it. It made you feel that behind the young Parisian beauty lurked a frightened rabbit of a girl keeping track of me behind a sophisticated façade, anxious to make sure that I would not hurt her.

We began to see more of each other, we might go to the Lipp brasserie, or talk for hours as we stood in front of theatres hoping for returned tickets. More often than not we would prove lucky and after making our way through the crowd would find ourselves in the splendid auditorium of the Théâtre Odéon, in front of André Masson's frescoes or in the long narrow hall of the Aubervilliers, in the light corridors of Nanterre – or on the wooden benches at the Cartoucherie or Bouffes du Nord – or in amongst the metal structures at the Palais de Chaillot. The theatre was Ariela's special passion, just as it was mine. We tried to see all the new plays. We were able to enjoy new plays by Ionesco and Arrabal, and the amazing dramatic skills of Sacha Pitoeff and Delphine Seyrig. Peter Brook was at the height of his powers and his artistic inventiveness knew no bounds. Sparkling, razor-sharp Vitez had also appeared on the scene and the Piccolo Company from Milan used to visit Paris from Italy. We were able to revel in the impeccable mastery of Streller and the breathtaking brilliance of Ronconi or Pizzi or be inspired by the acting of Fanny Ardant or Niels Ardstrup. Ariela was an outstanding connoisseur of the theatre at that time, becoming totally engrossed in performances. I sometimes used to look at her during a play. She would be utterly immersed in what was happening on stage with her eyes fixed on the actors. One could sense her deep concentration and inner tension, knowing that every muscle in her mind and body was absorbed by what was happening on stage. After the play we would discuss our impressions and I was always struck by Ariela's observations which were always brief and to the point, yet complex and subtle.

In those days Paris was the artistic capital of the world both in quality and quantity. It was the ideas capital of Europe. At the Collège de France crowds would gather to hear Michel Foucault or Roland Barthes; dozens of bookshops would stay open until midnight. The city was a heady mix, like champagne. At that time we could not even imagine that this feast for the mind and eye might ever stop – that bookshops might give way to clothes stalls or the theatre sink to amateur levels of imitation rather than creation, that nobody would be laughing as they sat out in the cafés on the boulevards, that mediocrities would take over the Collège de France, that the State would take over art. We could not imagine that the impossibly heavy weight of bureaucracy, the administration and the police could dispel the miraculous and magical quality of Parisian life, which had thrilled us all.

Naturally she realised that Paris had changed and we talked about that during one of our last visits to a restaurant in the summer of 2008. On a warm sunny day we were sitting on the terrace of a restaurant in Avenue Montaigne. Ariela was beautifully dressed, making a special effort for the occasion. The customers surrounding us were rather brash people – quite indifferent to the beautiful things of this world. Despite the money those people may have had, they had no real opinions of their own, merely second-hand ones they had picked up from advertisements. We felt like aliens sitting there in our elegant suits, talking about how impossible it was for the world based on our values to have vanished once and for all, about the ability of modern men and women to live without art or the culture of *haute couture*, or without the codes of behaviour and the way of life we had been used to.

Ariela herself not only had an intimate knowledge of the art of past and present, but numbered artists among her friends. She had been Jean Arp's muse and was a real connoisseur of painting. She also attached importance to beautiful clothes, to elegance and to her appearance in general. Elegance for Ariela was an essential part of self-respect, part of her personality and the way she presented herself to the world. It was also part of her respect for other people: she was convinced that clothes were important for the first impression people make on each other, of how people might assess appearance, elegance and intelligence. She saw those three things as part of a whole, so her taste in art, clothes and even people was always spot on. Although the trappings of wealth, success and luxury were valued by her as the outward signs of achievement, she was modest and self-effacing in her dealings with others. Her keenly critical mind and constant inner need to help other people compelled her to forget wealth and fame.

When she was moving into her new flat, she turned to me for advice on several occasions. How thrilled we were to discover that the wall-paintings in the hall of the new building were the work of the Russian artist Chekhonin! The effort and caution with which Ariela bought furniture was the opposite of the unfailing recklessness with which she bought clothes. Her flat was empty, but the cupboards in it were crammed with the most amazing dresses. One of my early memories is of a long blue striped summer suit with red roses on a muslin dress designed by Sonia Rykiel. One of my last memories is of a beautiful pale-blue cashmere housecoat, which Ariela wore last winter when her poor health confined her to her Moscow flat. She did not, on the other hand, like jewellery: she didn't wear rings, watches, beads or chains. Her striking appearance did not require additional embellishment. She was only interested in real and rare jewels and only owned two pieces – an old pendant with a pearl in the middle surrounded by gold petals, and a platinum diamond shaped pendant by Cartier dating from the 1920s, strewn with tiny diamonds. Spending hours in front of the mirror, trying on and seeing how she looked in new dresses, wondering whether they suited her and how other people might respond to them, was an essential feature of Ariela's femininity.

The appearance of ready-to-wear clothes changed our lives. It was not Chanel, however, who was our idol. We were among the first followers of the confident, modern and unusually feminine style of Sonia Rykiel, which was later to conquer the world. I remember how we used to stand in a queue for hours in front of the tiny shop in Rue de Grenelle at the beginning of the January sales. Sonia Rykiel herself would be sitting on the steps of the inside staircase looking down pensively at the crazy women fighting their way into her shop. I still possess a whole collection of those famous Sonya Rykiel blouses dating from the 1970s, which even today look incredibly innovative. Ariela was, I think, less inclined than I was to keep garments she loved. She loved everything that was new, still unknown and unproven. As soon as she tried on a new garment, it would seem to belong to her like a second skin. She would wear it almost every day and often only abandon it when something new came along. Her attitude to clothes mirrored her hunger for life and all things beautiful: for luxury, new opportunities and delights, all of which helped her to forget her life-threatening heart disease.

In the late 1970s and early 1980s we used to travel to Moscow together – Ariela to be with Roman and I to visit my parents who had undergone major surgery. Each of these trips, which should have been more frequent, were horribly draining, both physically and emotionally. I was beside myself with happiness at the thought of seeing my relatives, but at the same time having to be the wrong side of the 'Iron Curtain' again was terrible. Before my departure I would walk up and down the Paris streets as if I was bidding them farewell forever, informing friends and acquaintances about my departure, just in case problems should obstruct my return to the free world. The actual formalities required for organising these trips were humiliating and unpleasant. We had to buy tourist vouchers, fill out forms, hand over our passports to a travel agency and worry that the Soviet Consulate might turn down our application. Then we'd set off for Moscow with a group of strangers, usually French communists who were naturally unable to understand our fears. After endless checking of our papers and filling out of customs declarations at Moscow, we would then have to make our way to a hotel, usually in some out-of-the way suburb. After registering our arrival – this could last several hours – we would have to leave our passports there and go through the motions of taking up residence in the hotel room allotted to us. We would then need to explain everything to the other occupants of the room – usually assigned to two or three other people. That was easy, as they'd be thrilled at the prospect of some extra space. Only after all that was it possible to go home. One of my relatives would usually be waiting for me nearby in a taxi and at my home my parents would be waiting for me. Then the endless hugs and kisses would follow: we would spend half the night talking and unwrapping Paris presents. A constant stream of friends would start coming round and there would be no end to the lavish celebration meals. Almost a whole day of this blissful reunion would have to be wasted on travelling to the hotel and retrieving my passport. We also had to return with the tourist group from the hotel, needing to get there well in advance of the scheduled departure time, which was either early in the morning or at dead of night, because the group had to assemble in the bus and wait there for a long time until it was eventually given permission to head off to the airport. Then came more endless queues, customs declarations to be filled in and luggage checked. Our cases would usually be thoroughly examined. Often some completely innocent items would be objected to and we would have to leave them behind. We were usually accompanied to the airport by my mother and Roman, who, from the far side of the customs section would be casting a philosophical, sad look at the pile of belongings that had been carefully packed the evening before. He would then take home the prohibited items. It is no wonder that it seemed like a miracle when we actually found ourselves in the air on the way home. It was enough to make us cry with happiness.

One of those trips was particularly 'memorable'. We were leaving Moscow, having already said goodbye to the relatives who had come to see us off, and had gone through the horrendous customs inspection. Ariela and I were the last people to go through passport control. She had gone through first and on into the departure hall, but I was kept back. The border-guards spent a long time examining my Italian passport, talking amongst themselves and discussing something. In the end they called their superior. He took my passport without any explanation and went off with it. All the other passengers had gone through and there was just me left behind at the barrier. Sullen silence was the only response from the border-guards to my agitated questions. An hour went by and then the best part of another. Eventually the officer came back with my passport and grudgingly returned it. They had probably decided there was no point in a minor diplomatic incident over a slip of a girl. I walked out into the large well-lit departure hall. My hands and lips were shaking and I could hardly keep upright. All the other passengers had long since gone through and the plane had taken off. Now that it was empty, the departure lounge seemed enormous. There was no-one to be seen, except a small figure curled up in a ball in the opposite corner. Ariela had refused to abandon me. Later on we were allowed to leave on the next plane to Paris. She asked me: 'Do you know what colour your face is? You need to put some make-up on. It's green.' Then she brought out her mother-of-pearl nail varnish and began to manicure her nails.

We used to go to the theatre just as we always had and even more frequently to the opera. The dust of the staid old days had been swept aside and some of the leading creative minds of the day were bringing together all that was finest in theatre, music and art. How wonderful it was to be together again in the Grand Opéra or at the Opéra Bastille, or in the front row of a box at the Bolshoi!

Figure 51. Outside the house of Count Tishkevich, Palanga 2006.

In October 2008, during the launch of my book on Pavel Pavlovich Muratov in Moscow's Museum of Fine Arts, after the exhibition devoted to Muratov which I had organised, I was sitting on the stage noticing Ariela's intelligent, attentive gaze as she sat next to Roman in the front row. She was taking in all she saw and storing it in her mind.

How thrilled she was when, later on, Roman recited some of his poems written for children, but which adults enjoyed just as much. During the last months of her life there were plenty of happy moments, although she was feeling weak by this time. The winter began early and it was very cold everywhere – cold that was to prove really dangerous for Ariela's lungs and heart. It led her to travel from Moscow to London and then on to Paris. Even in Paris that year it was extremely cold. Nevertheless, Ariela's last months were not sad. She concentrated on interesting outings and family celebrations. We met in London at exhibitions of Russian art in November and at previews. Her little black dresses with her favourite pieces of Cartier jewellery set everything off to perfection. Paris was getting ready for the New Year festivities and Roman arrived to celebrate with her. Over the telephone we discussed the dishes for the New Year's Eve menu, the wine, the champagne, the desert and where we should order the pastries. 'Do you really want a turkey?' she asked me. 'Why don't I make veal cutlets with honey sauce instead?' That was the last conversation we had.

SVETLANA AND VITALII IGNATENKO: WE REMEMBER HER

In Ariela we were aware of a subtle approach to everything, and to the people she had encountered in life. She was always observing what was going on around her – particularly in the arts. Perhaps she was searching for a new angle, thinking about it all deeply. We recall how she used to remind us that things never turn out quite as well as we might hope, but they are never as bad as they might first seem either.

Everyone knew that Ariela was seriously ill, yet we never heard her complain. It was a matter of pride for her to come to grips with the problem on her own. Her friends would notice her blue hands, her difficulties with breathing and those steps which were far from firm. But she did not allow people to feel sorry for her. She would just take her oxygen cylinder into the theatre (no problem!), or set off to exhibitions or dinner parties with piles of medicines (so what?). It was not just a question of our remarkable Ariela's character. It was also a reproach for all those who have not been endowed by life with any talent and who immerse themselves in trivialities. She was an example to us all, showing us how someone can live a courageous life, overcoming the Ghetto and other cruel blows. This is why we shall always remember her...

Figure 52. Ariela and Maria, daughter of the writer Vladas Dautartas and granddaughter of Ariela's foster mother Julia Dautartiene, Vilnius, October 2008 (last photo of Ariela).

APPENDIX 1
LETTER OF DR JACOB ABRAMOVICH TO HIS BROTHER ARNO IN ENGLAND, 1945

My dear Brother!

I wrote a few letters to you three months ago and I also wrote to Leo, and wonder if you have received them. I am writing to you again and hope that the sad news about the tragedy of our family will reach you.

In July, 1941, we were all locked up in the Ghetto in Slobodka with the exception of our brother Benno, who perished with 7,000 Jews in Kaunas on the 7th Fort.

On the 24th July[1] 1941, a few days after the Nazi attack on the Russians, I, Benno and my wife and her uncle were arrested without cause and locked up in the Yellow Prison. My wife, being pregnant, was released, and due to her efforts and those of the Director of the hospital where I used to work, I was also released. 7,000 Jews, including our brother Benno, were transferred on August 1st to the 7th Fort, and within a few weeks were all murderously killed. There they went through the worst horror and torments any human being could think of.

In the Ghetto the Nazis started a series of killings and acts of terrorism. The technique of the sadist murderers is impossible to describe in a letter. A few weeks after being locked up a part of the ghetto was surrounded and the people were driven on to the 9th Fort where they were thrown half alive into pits. The Jewish hospital was set on fire and the patients were all burned alive, amongst them our uncle Z.

Caplan, who was lying there after suffering a heart-attack while on forced labour. Our Auntie Goldie and their daughter Rebecca were visiting him there and they also perished.

We all lived next to each other in the ghetto. We used to exchange our clothes for bread with the Lithuanian workers on forced labour, but this did not last for long, as the Nazis confiscated all our clothes.

On 24th October 1941, the Nazis with the Lithuanian Fascist Police broke into my room and knocked out the windows. My wife had a shock and gave birth to a daughter. This happened at night without light and without food for her. On the 28th October 1941, the Nazis, with the help of heavily armed police, surrounded the ghetto, separated parents from children, old men and women, and eleven thousand Jews were sent on to the 9th Fort where they were all shot.[2] The majority of the children were thrown alive into pits. Our Mother came into this group with the old people, but I succeeded in prolonging her life until 26 March 1944. And so, with the exception of Benno, we all lived together in ghetto. Max, Anna and their daughter Rebecca, Ruvim and I used to go on forced labour. Our shirts, clothes, shoes, sheets and blankets we exchanged for bread. And every day we were tormented physically and morally by the threat of being killed.

On the 28th September 1943, 3,000 Jews were deported to Estonia. Our brother Ruvim, Bassia and their children were amongst them. A few people who were able to escape from Esthonia and were liberated by the Red Army have told us that they were all killed or burnt. This depended on which camp they fell into. The small children and old people were killed at the Kaunas Railway Station where the children were taken away from their parents. In any case our brother Ruvim and his family perished there.[3]

When the Red Army reached the Lithuanian Frontiers, we had messages as follows: that the ghetto in Vilno had been burned down, that the people of the ghetto in Schawel[4] were deported to Taurage and there killed.[5]

In our ghetto they had already started to separate us into groups. This was a preliminary to immediate extermination...

[Page missing]

...on the steps of a Lithuanian Orphanage under a Lithuanian name. The doctor who was Director of the Orphanage was a colleague of mine with whom I had worked in a hospital before the War. I left your address with him and Leo's and Bronia's family's, with the request that after the War they should contact you to tell you about my child. I contacted him on a dark night after crawling through the barbed wire of the ghetto. On the night of 14 December 1943, I smuggled Bronia and our child out of the ghetto, and left my child at the orphanage as arranged. There was nowhere for us to hide and the next day we smuggled ourselves back.

Meanwhile the Nazis had started to deport the people into camps. Our brother Max, Anna and their daughter, Rebecca, who had grown into a beautiful girl, were sent in December 1943 to Scanzer (Šančiai)[6] camp. In the ghetto there remained then our parents, Rebecca, Samuel,[7] Joseph,[8] Bronia and I. They also wanted to send my wife and I to Scanzer where Max was. Since our child was in the Lithuanian Orphanage we decided to run away instead of going to a camp. We knew that a camp or ghetto meant death. We also wanted to see our child for once. On 3 January 1944 we escaped. For a few days we were hiding in the cellars of Gentiles. Nobody wanted to keep us for long and we were destitute and homeless. I had got to know that our child was seriously ill and dying in the Orphanage. The Director advised me to take her away since they had got to know that she was a Jewess. It was winter and we were without money, clothes and food. At any moment the Nazis might get hold of us and shoot us.

Bronia and I set out into the villages in the hope of finding a good person who would be willing to take a dying Jewish child, and we could not find one. Wandering through the villages by night and through the woods by day we reached Kulautova. Not far from the woods was a peasant Kumpaitis (he used to help our parents to move in summer). We hid ourselves in a ditch beside his pig-sty. We used to get food at night. Meantime I also found a poor fishmonger who adopted my child from the Orphanage. For four weeks my child struggled for life. At night I used to go 15 kilometres to treat her and give her injections. She was in Rodondware.[9] At last she recovered and was there for another seven months.

On 26 March 1944, the Nazis took out a few thousand children and old people.[10] Among them were our parents. They led our Mother and Father with other old people to a horrible death with a few thousand children aged from 2 to 12 years. Before I ran away from the ghetto I said goodbye to them and I remember my father's words. He has suffered a lot and he always used to say he would like to live to see the downfall of the Nazis. Mother has suffered too but she showed no trace of it. After the horrible murder of the children when they also took our parents, a few thousand Jews still remained in the ghetto, amongst them Rebecca, Samuel and Joseph.

As I have already told you my brother Ruwin and his family were in Esthonia, Max and his family in Šančiai, my wife and I were hiding in the woods. When the Red Army crossed the Lithuanian Frontier, our sister Rebecca and her family with a few thousand other Jews were sent to Danzig, where Max and his family were sent from his camp. The people who were hiding themselves in the cellars of the Slobodka Ghetto[11] were all burnt, and there are still some corpses lying about. In Lithuania about eight to nine hundred Jews have escaped, and the remainder have all met a horrible death.

On 3 August 1944 the Red Army saved us. We collected our daughter from the fisherman and found her a nice healthy child.

This is, in short, the tragedy of our family together with another few hundred thousand Jews. I will write to you again in the near future in detail.

I work in a hospital and earn relatively enough...

[A page is missing with the end of the letter]

Notes

1. Father mixed up July and June here.
2. According to the Karl Jäger Report, 9,200 Jews were massacred in the 9th Fort on 29 October 1941, including 2,007 men, 2,920 women and 4,273 children.
3. Ruvim and his son perished there, however Ruvim's wife and daughter were sent to the concentration camp and survived, and at the time of Liberation found themselves in the American Zone of Germany. When Father wrote the letter in 1945 he did not know that Ruvim's wife Basia and her daughter Miriam have survived.
4. Now Šiauliai.
5. During the liquidation of the Kaunas Ghetto (8–13 July 1944) about 6,000–7,000 people were transported to concentration camps. On 12 July 1944 Kaunas Ghetto was set on fire. Hundreds of people died in the fire or were shot and killed. About 7,000 Šiauliai Jews as well as Jews brought to the Šiauliai Ghetto

from Vilnius, Kaunas and Smurgainys labour camps were transported to Stutthof concentration camp in four stages. From there, men were taken to Dachau concentration camp, while women and children were taken to Auschwitz.

6. In autumn of 1943, the Kaunas Ghetto was reorganised into an SS concentration camp. Around 4,000 prisoners of the ghetto were transferred to isolated labour camps in the neighbourhoods of Aleksotas and Šančiai.

7. The husband of my aunt Rebecca.

8. The son of my aunt Rebecca.

9. At the present time it is known as Raudondvaris and is near the village of Šilelis where I was living.

10. 27–28 March 1944 a cruel Children's Action took place in the Kaunas Ghetto: 1,700 children and old people were taken from the Ghetto in two days and transported to Auschwitz for annihilation.

11. Slobodka (also known by its Lithuanian name: Vilijampolé) was the district of Kaunas, in which the Ghetto was situated.

INDEX

Abramovich, Aaron *see* Abrams, Aron (Arno)

Abramovich, Alexander, 174, 175

Abramovich, Anya *see* Sigal née Maizel, Anya

Abramovich née Strassburg, Basia, Miriam, 17; and Marusia Strassburg, 17

Abramovich (Brahms), Ben *see* Brahms, Ben

Abramovich, Beno, 9, 10, 227

Abramovich, Boris, 17, 29

Abramovich, Borya, 13, 16–7, 28–9

Abramovich née Maizel, Bracha (Bronia), 45, 92, 114, 128, 131, 134, 139, 209; as student in London, 20, 37; in Kaunas Ghetto, 10–11, 228; escape, 24, 229; in hiding, 28; and family in Soviet camps, 49, 50, 77; as lecturer, 64, 80, 123

Abramovich, Gill, 176

Abramovich, Katia (Katerina), 172, 203

Abramovich, Dr Leo (Leon) *see* Brahm, Dr Leon

Abramovich, Max, 18, 29

Abramovich, Max, Anna, Boris and Rivochka (Mrs Riva Garell), 13, 17–18, 28, 29, 228–9

Abramovich, Miriam *see* Reich née Abramovich, Miriam

Abramovich, Natalia (Natasha), 172, 176

Abramovich, Dr Rebecca *see* Griliches, Dr Rebecca

Abramovich, Rivochka *see* Garell née Abramovich, Riva

Abramovich, Ruvim, Basia, Miriam and Boria, 13, 16–17, 228; died in Port Kunda camp Estonia, 17, 28

Abramovich, Shlomo-Itcik, 12, 29, 37, 38; death, 28, 229

Abramovich née Propp, Sira, 11, 28–9, 38; death, 28, 229

Abramovich, Dr Solomon, 49, 82, 105, 129, 172, 174, 176, 203

Abramovich, Dr Yakov (Jacob), as student in Montpellier, Paris, 14, 20, 38; military service, 9, 14–15; in Kaunas Ghetto, 13–14, 227–9; escape, 24, 229; testament, 25–6; in hiding, 28, 229; rescuing lost children, 40–2; and Rebelsky, 33, 41; helping relatives in Soviet camps, 48–9; as surgeon, 9, 50, 95, 129, 230; 94, 134, 139,170

Abramovich Sef, Ariela *see* Sef née Abramovich, Ariela, birth and Ghetto 10, 12, 13; and Great Action, 10–11; and in the orphanage, 21–2; and Julia Dautartiene, 23–7, 31; early life, 44, 48, 65, 67, 74, 78, 80, 91; at school, 54, 63; as student 68, 93, 97, 114, 117; and 'Novi' Cabaret, 111–13; in Paris, 100, 135, 164, 166, 117, 216; and family, 172, 174, 175, 176; memories of, 170, 186–7, 190–4; 195, 197, 200–3, 204–7, 208–12, 213, 214, 215–23, 224; death of 177, 185, 186, 203

Abrams (Abramovich), Aron, 29, 30, 38, 65, 103, 104–5, 115, 227

Agricultural College, Kaunas, 119, 120

Akhmatova, Anna, 119

Aleshnikova, 120, 123

Alexeyev, dean, 117

Alexotai, Kaunas, 119

Alpers, Galina, 148

Antibes, 134

Aragon, Louis, 149
Ardant, Fanny, 218
Ardashnikova, Sonya, 124
Ardstrup, Niels, 218
Arkhangelsk Region, 49, 71
Arrabal, Fernando, 217
Arp, Jean, 137, 140–1, 219
Aubervilliers, 217
Auschwitz, 17–18, 19, 29
Avenue Montaigne, 218

BAFTA (British Academy of Film and
    Television Arts), 192
Bakulev Heart Institute, 98,103
Balthus, (Balthasar Klossowski de Rola),
    142
Bardot, Brigitte, 111, 118
Barsky, 118
Baudlaire, Charles, 148,152
Baublys, Dr Petras, 21–2, 228
Bauer family, 136
BBC, 50
Bejart, Maurice, 204
Belskaya, Nelly see Cournot née
    Belskaya, Nelly
Beria, Lavrentiy, Head of NKVD, 148
Berlin, 37,38, 100
Bigard, Lydia (Lida), 143, 197
Bigard, Oxana, 197
Binkis, Kazys, 19
Bolshoi Theatre, 185, 197, 205, 222
Borodulina, Marfuta, 122–3
Bouffes du Nord, 217
Boulevard Saint-Germain-des-Près,
    137,145,165
Brahm (Abramovich), Dr Leon, 29,
    30, 38, 39, 105, 227; and Kisyuta,
    38
Brahms (Abramovich), Ben, 56, 78,
    82, 122, 126, 173–4, 176, 182–3,
    191–2, 203, 214
Brahms, Jacob, 174, 176
Brahms, Lena, 189
Brancusi, Constantin, 147
Braque, Georges, 141
Brest-Litovsk, 100, 115, 129-132
Breton, Andre, 141,142
Brook, Peter, 217
Brui, William and Silva, 152
Brun and Brun, Ida, 90
Burakovsky, Dr Vladimir, 98

Café Flore, 100
Calder, Alexander, 141
Camacho, Jorge, 140
Canada, 16, 17, 39,134
Cannes, 134
Cannes Festival, 143, 180, 192, 195
Caplan, Z., Goldie and Rebecca, 228
Cardenas, Agustin, 114, 136, 140
Cardenas-Malagodi, Elena, 114, 134–6,
    140–1, 153
Carrington, Leonora, 141
Carlton hotel, 180
Carrara, 115
Cartoucherie, 217
Cavaleau, Germaine, 101, 110
Cavaleau, Pierre, 93, 100, 102, 110,
    115–16
Cesaire, Aime, 142
Chagall, Mark, 139,141
Chekhonin, Sergei, 219
Chekhov Street, 124
'Children's Action', 230–1
De Chirico, Georgio, 142
Chukovsky, Kornei, 125
Ciurlionis, Mikalojus, 19
Closerie des Lilas, 215
Colomb, Denise, 114, 141–2
Comedie Francaise, 181
Cournot, Michel, 134–5, 199
Cournot née Belskaya, Nelly, 101,
    113–14, 116, 129, 134–5, 155,
    199; and Ivan, 136
Covent Garden, 175, 177
Cvirka, Petras, 67

Daninos, Pierre, 114
Daudet, Alfonse, 67
Dautartas (Dovtort), Juozapas, 23–4, 31
Dautartas, Juozas, 25
Dautartas, Leonas (Lyonka), 26–7
Dautartas, Vladas (Vladik), 26–7, 31
Dautartas, Zigmas, 21, 23–5
Dautartiene, Julia, 21, 23–4, 31
Delon, Alain, 111
Demidova, Alla, 170, 178, 185, 188
Denisov and Denisov, Aldona, 73, 75
Diner family and Yolanta, 43
Dmitrievich, Valentin and Alexey, 111
'Doctors' Plot', 89
Druskininkai (Druskeniki), 114
Dykhovichnyi, Ivan, 179

East Prussia, 2, 37–8
Ecole de Paris, 146–7, 175
Edwards, John, 183
Efros, Anatolii, 124
Ehrenburg, Ilya, 67, 150
Eisenmenger Syndrome, 50, 173
Elin (Elinaite), Esther (Esya), 20; and
    Elin, Meir, 20
Elin, Chaim, 19
Elkes, Dr Elkhanan, 18
Elyutina, Larisa and Elyutin, 120–2
Ernst, Max, 114, 137, 140–1, 142, 143

Fini, Leonor, 141
Fleming, Renée, 175
Fort VII in Kaunas, 9, 10
Fort IX in Kaunas, 227–8
Frid, Valery, 192

'Galère Pierre', 141
Galich, Alexandr, 124
Gallimard, Madame, 152
Gare du Nord, 100
Gary, Romain, 144, 152
Genis family, 73
Gertner, Yehuda and Sheinale, 54, 55
Giacometti, Alberto, 141,142
Ginkas, Kama, 20, 33, 169
Ginkas, Dr Miron, 19, 33
Giroux, Francois, 144
Gold, 40
Golden Globe, 193
Goldschmidt née Maizel, Dr Nadia, 37
Goncharova, Natalia, 143
Gorky Park, 209
Grand Opera, 184, 222
Gravlin family, 95
'Great Action', 1, 10, 228
'Green (or Forest) Brothers', 41, 73,
    145, 148
Griliches, Joseph and Dr Samuel, 28–9,
    229
Griliches née Abramovich, Dr Rebecca,
    38; in Kaunas Ghetto, 23, 229–30;
    died in Stutthof, 29
Grinberg, Lev Adolfovich, 138–9,
    216–17
Grodzenski, Sholem, 33
Grosman, Aba, 90
Gurvich, Noemi, 33
Gurvichiene (Gurvich), Dr Fruma, 42

Gusman, Yulii, 195
Gutman, Dr Yakov, 49

Hackelis, Elena, 54
Haifa, 36, 133
Hamlet, 181
Hammersmith Hospital, 93, 103, 105
Hampstead, 2
Heine, Heinrich, 20
Holman, Dr Arthur, 104, 177
Holocaust, 3, 46, 175, 230
Hotel Crillon, 165
Hotel du Danube, 135
Hotel Le Meridien Villon, Vilnius, 182–
    3
Hugo, Victor, 63, 117

Ignatenko, Vitalii and Svetlana, 224
Ionesco, Eugene, 217
Ioseliani, Dr David, 122
Isadora Duncan School, 109
Israel, 17, 38, 88

Jacob, Max, 147
Japanese Empress, 213
Jardin de Luxembourg, 200
Jewish Agency (Sokhnut), 132–3
Jewish Anti-fascist Committee, 139
Jewish Hospital in Kaunas Ghetto, 227
Jewish school and orphanage in Kaunas,
    41–2, 54–7
Jews from Bukhara, 131–3

Kadishaite Levy née Ratner, Dr Tamara,
    41
Kamber, Marcus and Ilana (Ash née
    Kamber), 18
Karaganda, 148, 149
Karnovski, Mika, 33
Kasimov family, Olka, Buska and Emka,
    72, 75
Kasrashvili, Makvala, 197
Kaunas, 32, 37, 41, 45, 173, 179
Kaunas Ghetto, 10–20, 28, 227–31
Kaunas Medical Institute, 68, 173
Kazenas family and Polina, 74–5, 90
Kazeyev, Edouard see Loeb, Edouard
Kemerovo (Siberia), 49
KGB, 90, 118, 147,149, 156, 199
Khandamov, Rustam, 179, 182
Khiva, 180

Khlebnikov, Velimir (Victor Vladimirovich), 119
Khmelnitskii, Boris, 179
Khrushchev, Nikita; and 'thaw', 3, 149, 199
Kikoin, Michele, 147
Kinotavr festival, 188
Kitrosser (Kitroskii), Berta (Berthe), see Lipchitz née Kitrosser, Berta
Kitty, dog, 127-8, 130-4
Klee, Paul, 141
'Kol Zion la Gola' ('Voice of Zion aimed at the Diaspora'), 50
Kolmanovskiy, Eduard and Tamara, 80, 92, 112, 122
Komsomol (Soviet youth organization), 96-7
Korotkov, Yuri, 192
Kozlovskaya, Anna, Galina and Kozlovskii, Ivan, 123
Krasnoyarsk, 149
Kremegne (Kremen), Pinchus, 147
Krishtaponiene, Mrs and Niele, 75-6
Krivosheinyi, Nikita, 123
Kronzon née Maizel, Liza, 37
Kruchenykh, Alexei,119
Kulautuva village and Kumpaitis family, 27, 229
Kumpaitis, Jurgis, 27
Kunda camp, Estonia, 17, 28
Kupritz (Kaplan), Anita, 51,
Kupritz, Madame, 51–3; and Mr Kaplan, 52

Lam, Wilfredo, 137, 142
Lausanne, 204
Lavrushenskii Lane, Moscow, 119, 204
Le Corbusier, 146, 162, 189
Leningrad, 92, 129
LenKom Theatre, 208
Les Halles, 112
Levinson, Hanna, 129
Lezhneva, Lydia Pavlovna and Lezhnev, 116, 118–19, 122
Lifshin, Dr and Celia, 90
Likhachova, Natasha and Likhachov,I.A., 117
Limonov, Eduard, 144, 165
Lipp Brasserie, 134, 144, 165, 217
Lipchitz née Kitrosser (Kitrosky), Berta and Andrei, 147, 150; and Michail

Shimkevich, 146–8; and Modigliani, 147, 162
Lipchitz, Jacques, 4,146; and Ecole de Paris, 146–7; and Berta, 147–8, 150; and Andrei, 148, 162
Lipchitz, Yulla, 162-3
Lithuanian 16th Division (Soviet), 18, 129
Loeb, Edouard, 114, 116, 135, 137–8, 140, 142-3; and Françoise, 140; and Joan Miro, 140; and family, 141, 143–4; and Surrealist circle, 142; and gallery, 143
Loeb, Pierre, 140, 143; and Joan Miro, 140; and André Breton, 141; and Surrealist circle, 141
Lost in Siberia (film), 191
Lubyanka prison, 149,155, 202
Luksakaimis farm, 27; and Kumpaitis family, 27
Lunacharsky, Anatolii, 148

Maar, Dora, 140,141
Magadan, 149
Maizel, Anya also see Sigal née Maizel (Abramovich), Anya
Maizel née Bogriansky, Berta (Bluma), 36–7, 48
Maizel, Isaac Arie, 36
Maizel née Fain, Lily, 46–7, 49, 84-5, 87
Maizel, Liza see Kronzon, Liza
Maizel, Dr Nadia see Goldschmidt, Dr Nadia
Maizel, Naum, 37, 46, 48, 86, 88; and NKVD arrest, 47
Malaya Bronnaya Theatre, 208
Malkin, 49
Mallarmé, Stephane, 117
Manchester, 103
Mandelshtam, Acad, family, 124
Manielli, Albert, 142—3
Man Ray (Emmanuel Radnitzky), 141
Mansurov (Mansuroff), Paul, 153
Mariona (nanny), 34
Marshak, Samuil, 42
Masson, André, 142, 218
Matisse, Henri, 142
Matta, Roberto, 137
Maurice Thorez Institute of Foreign Languages, Moscow, 68, 81, 93, 96, 117–18
Medical Institute, Kaunas, 173

Melrose, Dr Denis, 98, 101, 104
Mendes- France, Pierre, 144
Menier, Antoine, 112
'Metropole', 44
Michaux,Henry, 142
Mikhoels, Solomon and family, 139
Mintz, Beba and Veva, 16
Miro, Joan, 140,141
Mirvits, 77
Mishin, Professor, 124
Mitta, Alexander and Lilia, 187, 192
Mitterrand, Francois,144
Mitterrand, Frederic, 153
Modigliani, Amedeo, 147, 162
Molotov-Ribbentrop Pact, 2, 3, 27, 36, 47
Montand, Yves, 111
Montmartre, 112
Montparnas
Montpellier, 38
Moore, Henry, 137
Mordovia Region, 3, 77
Morin, Dr Bernard, 106, 113, 115, 201
Moscow, 92–3, 117, 120, 124, 204, 206, 220
Moscow Conservatoire, 124, 204
Moscow Hospital No. 24, 96, 103
Moscow House of Fashion, 120–1
Moscow State Jewish Theatre, 139
Moscowicz, Colonel, 154
Mosfilm Studios, 192
Muratov, Pavel, 216, 222
Muratova, Asya (Xenya), 139, 215
Muravyova, Liza, 117
Museum of Fine Arts, Moscow, 222
Museum of Modern Art, Paris, 175
My Fair Lady, 125

Nantes, 101, 110
Nanterre, 217
Narkevich (Narkevichiute), 118
Nashchokin Gallery, 205
National Gallery, 174
Nekroshius, Eimuntas, 205
Nevskii Prospekt, 92
Nikolaevich, Sergei, 204
Nikolsky, Alyosha, 65
NKVD (Soviet secret police), 47, 50, 73, 149
'Non-conformist' artists, 123
'Novi' Cabaret, 109–11

Novikov, Lev, 205
Novsky and Novskaya, 110–1, 113

Obrazcova, Elena, 185
October Revolution Holiday, 112
Odinov, Professor David, 89; and 'Doctors' Plot', 89
Okudzhava, Bulat, 112, 201
Onute (nanny), 60, 79–83,
Opera Bastille, 180, 222
Orlov, Prince, 112

Pact of Mutual Soviet-Lithuanian Assistance, 2
Palais de Chaillot, 217
Palanga, 78-83, 91, 159
Paleckis, Justas,PM, 67
Palestine, 36–7, 78–83
Paris, 30, 37–8, 99, 175, 179, 181
Park de Monceau, 136
Passover, 9, 89
Pavlovitch, Dr Jana, 137
Pechalin family, 81
Pechora,149
Peipert, Shmuel, 41
Per family, 33
Peredvizhniki (Wanderers), 206
Peshkov, Alexey (Maxim Gorky), 150
Petrauskas family, Algis and Danguole, 76
Picasso, Pablo, 137, 141
Piccolo Company, 217
Pierre Cardin Fashion House, 165
Pitoeff, Sacha, 217
Pitsunda, 190
Plisetskaya, Maya, 172
Plombières-les-Bains, 30
Polyakov, Serge, 109
Polyakov, Volodya (Vladimir), 109, 111, 112
Ponomaryova, Liusya, 208
Portofino, 175
Potma, 71
Pozdneyeva, Professor, 123
Pozner, Vladimir, 118
Progress Publishers, 123, 149
Prokofiev family, 122
Pushkin Museum of Fine Arts, 147

Rabinovitch, Jacob, 15
Rachkauskas, Vairas, 66

Rachkovskaya, Nina, 66–8
Raudondvaris (Raudondvare), 229
Rauka, Helmut, 10
Rebelski, Colonel, Dr Ioseph, 33, 40, 41
Red Army, 228, 230
Raguchio Street, 12,14
Reich née Abramovich, Miriam, 17, 29
Remeris, Z., 32
Reznikov, Colonel Dr Pyotr, and Tatyana, 89
Riga, 180
Rina, 52
Riopelle, Jean-Paul 142
Rome, 134
Ronconi, Luca, 218
Royal Academy, 174
Royal Opera House, 176
Rozdennaya v Getto (Born in the Ghetto), 2
Rozenblum, Professor Anatolii, 90
Rozenblum, Moisei, 33
Rue des Cannettes, 145
Rue de Grenelle, 220
Rue Jacob, 135
Russian Revolution, 2, 66, 119, 147
Rybinsk (White Sea Canal), 49 ,71
Rykiel, Sonia, 184, 204, 219–20

Sables d'Olonnes, 110
Safronova, Lidia, 117
Saint Geneviève House, 165
Saint Louis Hospital, Paris, 14
Salomon (Salomon), Boris, 113
Samarkand, 180
Samizdat (books), 124
Schimkewitsch (Shimkevich), Andrei (Andre), 4,145, 147, 152, 158, 166, 203; and Roman Sef,124, 148, 151; and Soviet camps, 148; and Wallenberg, 150, 155–7; and J. Lipchitz, 148, 162
Schonau Castle, 132
Sef née Abramovich, Ariela see Abramovich Sef, Ariela
Sef, Roman, 124–5, 131, 145, 148, 150–1, 166, 174, 176, 203
De Segur, Mme, La Countesse, nee Countess Sofiya Rostopchina, 65
Seyrig, Delphine, 217
Shakhnazarov, Karen, 192, 214

Shanciai (Sanchiai) Kaunas concentration camp, 229, 231
Shauliai (Sauliai, Schawel) Ghetto, 228, 230
Shaw, Bernard, 125, 181
Shchapova-de-Carli, Lena, 144
Shilialis village (near Raudondvaris) and Dautartas family, 24, 229
Shimkevich, Michail, 147–8
Shimkevich, Professor Vladimir, 147
Shneider, Romy, 111
Shubzda, Irene, 197
Shved, Sonya (Sofia), 134
Sidorov, Rector, 117
Sigal née Maizel (Abramovich), Anya, 47–9, 62, 70–1, 77, 137
Signoret, Simone 111
Slepyshev, Anatoliy, 179
Slobodka see Vilijampole (Kaunas Ghetto)
Snechkus, Antanas, 67
Soblis family, 172
Sochi, 116, 121, 122, 126, 211
Sokhnut see Jewish Agency
Sooster, Yulo, 124
Sorbonne, 43, 106, 113
South Africa, 38
Soutine, Chaim, 147
Soviet camps, 49–50, 71, 77, 86, 148–9
'Sovietisation' programme, 2, 51, 64
Sovieyskaya Hotel, 143
SPEC Group, 183
De Stael, Nicolas, 141
Stalingrad Front, 210–11
Stanislavsky Centre, 205
Strassburg, Marusia, 17
Streller, Frank, 218
Stupel, Iosif and Klavdia, 89
Stutthof, 29
Steinberg, Edik (Eduard), 135
Sukhumi, 121
Svetlanov, Yevgenii, 211

Taft, Dr Yakov, 33
Taganka Theatre, Moscow, 170, 179
Tashkent, 180
Tate Modern, 174
Tauber, Sophie, 141
Taurage town, 19, 37–8; and Abramovich family, 37–8
Tbilisi, 149

Tedik, 40
Tel Aviv, 134
Tel Ha-Shomer Hospital, 134
Tereschenko, 113
Thatcher, Margaret, 183–4
Theatre Odeon, 217
The Assassin of the Tsar, 214
The Cherry Orchard, 205–6
The Millionaires, 181
Timofeyeva, Lidia, 117
Tishkevich, Count (stately home), 82, 83,222
Tretyakov Gallery, 204
Triolet, Elsa, 149
Tsitses, Larisa and Madame Tsitses, 52
Turkey, 148,149

University College Hospital, 104
USA, 25, 39

Varchenko, Alla, 67
Vasileva, Maria, (Vassilieff, Marie), 147
Vendée, 110
Venice, 134
Viera da Silva, Maria,142

'Versailles', 44
Victory Day, 9, 185, 209–11
Vienna, 132
Vikentievna, Yadviga, 57, 65–6, 68
Vilijampole Ghetto (Slobodka) *see* Kaunas Ghetto
Villon Le Meridien, Vilnius, 182–3, 206
Vilnius, 47, 181–2
Vilnius Ghetto, 228
Virkietiene née Dautartaite, Maria, 225
Vitez, Antoine, 217
'Voice of America', 50
Wallenberg, Raoul, 4, 150, 155–7
Wols (Alfred Otto Wolfgang Schulze), 143

Yakhontov, Andrey, 213
Yakovleva, Olga, 124, 208
Yalta, 65, 202
Yellow Prison, Kaunas, 9, 227
Yudilevich family and Dalia, 33

Zadkine, Ossip, 147
Zakharin, Dr Benjamin, 18–19
Zilberg, Dr Abraham, 19